A WEEK ON THE CONCORD AND
MERRIMACK RIVERS

Henry David Thoreau

A WEEK
ON THE CONCORD
AND MERRIMACK
RIVERS

SENTRY EDITION

HOUGHTON MIFFLIN COMPANY BOSTON

FOURTH PRINTING, SENTRY EDITION   C

PRINTED IN THE U.S.A.

CONTENTS

CONTENTS

PUBLISHER'S NOTE

This edition is reprinted from the plates of Volume I of the Walden Edition (1906) of *The Writings of Henry David Thoreau,* the standard edition of Thoreau's works.

BIOGRAPHICAL SKETCH

BY R. W. EMERSON

HENRY DAVID THOREAU was the last male descend-
ant of a French ancestor who came to this country
from the Isle of Guernsey. His character exhibited
occasional traits drawn from this blood in singular
combination with a very strong Saxon genius.

He was born in Concord, Massachusetts, on the
12th of July, 1817. He was graduated at Harvard College in 1837, but without any literary distinction. An
iconoclast in literature, he seldom thanked colleges for
their service to him, holding them in small esteem, whilst
yet his debt to them was important. After leaving the
University, he joined his brother in teaching a private
school, which he soon renounced. His father was a
manufacturer of lead-pencils, and Henry applied himself for a time to this craft, believing he could make
a better pencil than was then in use. After completing
his experiments, he exhibited his work to chemists and
artists in Boston, and having obtained their certificates
to its excellence and to its equality with the best London
manufacture, he returned home contented. His friends
congratulated him that he had now opened his way to
fortune. But he replied that he should never make
another pencil. "Why should I? I would not do again
what I have done once." He resumed his endless walks

and miscellaneous studies, making every day some new acquaintance with Nature, though as yet never speaking of zoölogy or botany, since, though very studious of natural facts, he was incurious of technical and textual science.

At this time, a strong, healthy youth, fresh from college, whilst all his companions were choosing their profession, or eager to begin some lucrative employment, it was inevitable that his thoughts should be exercised on the same question, and it required rare decision to refuse all the accustomed paths, and keep his solitary freedom at the cost of disappointing the natural expectations of his family and friends: all the more difficult that he had a perfect probity, was exact in securing his own independence, and in holding every man to the like duty. But Thoreau never faltered. He was a born protestant. He declined to give up his large ambition of knowledge and action for any narrow craft or profession, aiming at a much more comprehensive calling, the art of living well. If he slighted and defied the opinions of others, it was only that he was more intent to reconcile his practice with his own belief. Never idle or self-indulgent, he preferred, when he wanted money, earning it by some piece of manual labor agreeable to him, as building a boat or a fence, planting, grafting, surveying, or other short work, to any long engagements. With his hardy habits and few wants, his skill in wood-craft, and his powerful arithmetic, he was very competent to live in any part of the world. It would cost him less time to supply his wants than another. He was therefore secure of his leisure.

A natural skill for mensuration, growing out of his mathematical knowledge and his habit of ascertaining the measures and distances of objects which interested him, the size of trees, the depth and extent of ponds and rivers, the height of mountains, and the air-line distance of his favorite summits, — this, and his intimate knowledge of the territory about Concord, made him drift into the profession of land-surveyor. It had the advantage for him that it led him continually into new and secluded grounds, and helped his studies of Nature. His accuracy and skill in this work were readily appreciated, and he found all the employment he wanted.

He could easily solve the problems of the surveyor, but he was daily beset with graver questions, which he manfully confronted. He interrogated every custom, and wished to settle all his practice on an ideal foundation. He was a protestant à *outrance*, and few lives contain so many renunciations. He was bred to no profession; he never married; he lived alone; he never went to church; he never voted; he refused to pay a tax to the State; he ate no flesh, he drank no wine, he never knew the use of tobacco; and, though a naturalist, he used neither trap nor gun. He chose, wisely, no doubt, for himself, to be the bachelor of thought and Nature. He had no talent for wealth, and knew how to be poor without the least hint of squalor or inelegance. Perhaps he fell into his way of living without forecasting it much, but approved it with later wisdom. "I am often reminded," he wrote in his journal, "that, if I had bestowed on me the wealth of Crœsus, my aims must be still the same, and my means essentially the same." He had no temptations

to fight against, — no appetites, no passions, no taste for
elegant trifles. A fine house, dress, the manners and talk
of highly cultivated people were all thrown away on him.
He much preferred a good Indian, and considered these
refinements as impediments to conversation, wishing to
meet his companion on the simplest terms. He declined
invitations to dinner-parties, because there each was in
every one's way, and he could not meet the individuals
to any purpose. "They make their pride," he said,
"in making their dinner cost much; I make my pride
in making my dinner cost little." When asked at table
what dish he preferred, he answered, "The nearest."
He did not like the taste of wine, and never had a vice
in his life. He said, "I have a faint recollection of
pleasure derived from smoking dried lily-stems, before
I was a man. I had commonly a supply of these. I have
never smoked anything more noxious."

He chose to be rich by making his wants few, and
supplying them himself. In his travels, he used the railroad only to get over so much country as was unimportant to the present purpose, walking hundreds of miles,
avoiding taverns, buying a lodging in farmers' and
fishermen's houses, as cheaper, and more agreeable to
him, and because there he could better find the men and
the information he wanted.

There was somewhat military in his nature not to be
subdued, always manly and able, but rarely tender, as if
he did not feel himself except in opposition. He wanted
a fallacy to expose, a blunder to pillory, I may say
required a little sense of victory, a roll of the drum, to
call his powers into full exercise. It cost him nothing to

say No; indeed, he found it much easier than to say Yes. It seemed as if his first instinct on hearing a proposition was to controvert it, so impatient was he of the limitations of our daily thought. This habit, of course, is a little chilling to the social affections; and though the companion would in the end acquit him of any malice or untruth, yet it mars conversation. Hence, no equal companion stood in affectionate relations with one so pure and guileless. "I love Henry," said one of his friends, "but I cannot like him; and as for taking his arm, I should as soon think of taking the arm of an elm tree."

Yet, hermit and stoic as he was, he was really fond of sympathy, and threw himself heartily and childlike into the company of young people whom he loved, and whom he delighted to entertain, as he only could, with the varied and endless anecdotes of his experiences by field and river. And he was always ready to lead a huckleberry party or a search for chestnuts or grapes. Talking, one day, of a public discourse, Henry remarked, that whatever succeeded with the audience was bad. I said, "Who would not like to write something which all can read, like 'Robinson Crusoe'? and who does not see with regret that his page is not solid with a right materialistic treatment, which delights everybody?" Henry objected, of course, and vaunted the better lectures which reached only a few persons. But, at supper, a young girl, understanding that he was to lecture at the Lyceum, sharply asked him, "whether his lecture would be a nice, interesting story, such as she wished to hear, or whether it was one of those old philosophical things that she did not care about." Henry turned to her, and be-

thought himself, and, I saw, was trying to believe that
he had matter that might fit her and her brother, who
were to sit up and go to the lecture, if it was a good one
for them.

He was a speaker and actor of the truth, — born
such, — and was ever running into dramatic situations
from this cause. In any circumstance, it interested all
bystanders to know what part Henry would take, and
what he would say; and he did not disappoint expecta-
tion, but used an original judgment on each emergency.
In 1845 he built himself a small framed house on the
shores of Walden Pond, and lived there two years alone,
a life of labor and study. This action was quite native
and fit for him. No one who knew him would tax him
with affectation. He was more unlike his neighbors in
his thought than in his action. As soon as he had exhausted the advantages of that solitude, he abandoned
it. In 1847, not approving some uses to which the public
expenditure was applied, he refused to pay his town tax.
and was put in jail. A friend paid the tax for him, and
he was released. The like annoyance was threatened the
next year. But, as his friends paid the tax, notwithstanding his protest, I believe he ceased to resist. No
opposition or ridicule had any weight with him. He
coldly and fully stated his opinion without affecting to
believe that it was the opinion of the company. It was of
no consequence if every one present held the opposite
opinion. On one occasion he went to the University
Library to procure some books. The librarian refused
to lend them. Mr. Thoreau repaired to the President.
who stated to him the rules and usages, which permitted

the loan of books to resident graduates, to clergymen who were alumni, and to some others resident within a circle of ten miles' radius from the College. Mr. Thoreau explained to the President that the railroad had destroyed the old scale of distances, — that the library was useless, yes, and President and College useless, on the terms of his rules, — that the one benefit he owed to the College was its library, — that, at this moment, not only his want of books was imperative, but he wanted a large number of books, and assured him that he, Thoreau, and not the librarian, was the proper custodian of these. In short, the President found the petitioner so formidable, and the rules getting to look so ridiculous, that he ended by giving him a privilege which in his hands proved unlimited thereafter.

No truer American existed than Thoreau. His preference of his country and condition was genuine, and his aversation from English and European manners and tastes almost reached contempt. He listened impatiently to news or *bonmots* gleaned from London circles; and though he tried to be civil, these anecdotes fatigued him. The men were all imitating each other, and on a small mould. Why can they not live as far apart as possible, and each be a man by himself ? What he sought was the most energetic nature; and he wished to go to Oregon, not to London. "In every part of Great Britain," he wrote in his diary, "are discovered traces of the Romans, their funereal urns, their camps, their roads, their dwellings. But New England, at least, is not based on any Roman ruins. We have not to lay the foundations of our houses on the ashes of a former civilization."

But, idealist as he was, standing for abolition of
slavery, abolition of tariffs, almost for abolition of government, it is needless to say he found himself not only
unrepresented in actual politics, but almost equally
opposed to every class of reformers. Yet he paid the
tribute of his uniform respect to the Anti-Slavery party.
One man, whose personal acquaintance he had formed,
he honored with exceptional regard. Before the first
friendly word had been spoken for Captain John Brown,
after the arrest, he sent notices to most houses in Concord, that he would speak in a public hall on the condition and character of John Brown, on Sunday evening,
and invited all people to come. The Republican Committee, the Abolitionist Committee, sent him word that
it was premature and not advisable. He replied, "I
did not send to you for advice, but to announce that I
am to speak." The hall was filled at an early hour by
people of all parties, and his earnest eulogy of the hero
was heard by all respectfully, by many with a sympathy
that surprised themselves.

It was said of Plotinus that he was ashamed of his
body, and 't is very likely he had good reason for it, —
that his body was a bad servant, and he had not skill
in dealing with the material world, as happens often to
men of abstract intellect. But Mr. Thoreau was equipped
with a most adapted and serviceable body. He was of
short stature, firmly built, of light complexion, with
strong, serious blue eyes, and a grave aspect, — his
face covered in the late years with a becoming beard.
His senses were acute, his frame well-knit and hardy,
his hands strong and skillful in the use of tools. And

there was a wonderful fitness of body and mind. He could pace sixteen rods more accurately than another man could measure them with rod and chain. He could find his path in the woods at night, he said, better by his feet than his eyes. He could estimate the measure of a tree very well by his eyes; he could estimate the weight of a calf or a pig, like a dealer. From a box containing a bushel or more of loose pencils, he could take up with his hands fast enough just a dozen pencils at every grasp. He was a good swimmer, runner, skater, boatman, and would probably outwalk most countrymen in a day's journey. And the relation of body to mind was still finer than we have indicated. He said he wanted every stride his legs made. The length of his walk uniformly made the length of his writing. If shut up in the house, he did not write at all.

He had a strong common sense, like that which Rose Flammock, the weaver's daughter, in Scott's romance, commends in her father, as resembling a yardstick which, whilst it measures dowlas and diaper, can equally well measure tapestry and cloth of gold. He had always a new resource. When I was planting forest-trees, and had procured half a peck of acorns, he said that only a small portion of them would be sound, and proceeded to examine them, and select the sound ones. But finding this took time, he said, "I think, if you put them all into water, the good ones will sink;" which experiment we tried with success. He could plan a garden, or a house, or a barn; would have been competent to lead a "Pacific Exploring Expedition;" could give judicious counsel in the gravest private or public affairs.

He lived for the day, not cumbered and mortified by his memory. If he brought you yesterday a new proposition, he would bring you to-day another not less revolutionary. A very industrious man, and setting, like all highly organized men, a high value on his time, he seemed the only man of leisure in town, always ready for any excursion that promised well, or for conversation prolonged into late hours. His trenchant sense was never stopped by his rules of daily prudence, but was always up to the new occasion. He liked and used the simplest food, yet, when some one urged a vegetable diet, Thoreau thought all diets a very small matter, saying that "the man who shoots the buffalo lives better than the man who boards at the Graham House." He said: "You can sleep near the railroad, and never be disturbed: Nature knows very well what sounds are worth attending to, and has made up her mind not to hear the railroad-whistle. But things respect the devout mind, and a mental ecstasy was never interrupted." He noted what repeatedly befell him, that, after receiving from a distance a rare plant, he would presently find the same in his own haunts. And those pieces of luck which happen only to good players happened to him. One day, walking with a stranger, who inquired where Indian arrowheads could be found, he replied, "Everywhere," and, stooping forward, picked one on the instant from the ground. At Mount Washington, in Tuckerman's Ravine, Thoreau had a bad fall, and sprained his foot. As he was in the act of getting up from his fall, he saw for the first time the leaves of the *Arnica mollis*.

His robust common sense, armed with stout hands,
keen perceptions, and strong will, cannot yet account
for the superiority which shone in his simple and hidden life. I must add the cardinal fact, that there was
an excellent wisdom in him, proper to a rare class of
men, which showed him the material world as a means
and symbol. This discovery, which sometimes yields
to poets a certain casual and interrupted light, serving
for the ornament of their writing, was in him an un-
sleeping insight; and whatever faults or obstructions
of temperament might cloud it, he was not disobedient
to the heavenly vision. In his youth, he said, one day,
"The other world is all my art: my pencils will draw
no other; my jack-knife will cut nothing else; I do not
use it as a means." This was the muse and genius that
ruled his opinions, conversation, studies, work, and
course of life. This made him a searching judge of men.
At first glance he measured his companion, and, though
insensible to some fine traits of culture, could very well
report his weight and calibre. And this made the impression of genius which his conversation often gave.

He understood the matter in hand at a glance, and
saw the limitations and poverty of those he talked with,
so that nothing seemed concealed from such terrible
eyes. I have repeatedly known young men of sen-
sibility converted in a moment to the belief that this
was the man they were in search of, the man of men,
who could tell them all they should do. His own
dealing with them was never affectionate, but superior,
didactic, — scorning their petty ways, — very slowly
conceding, or not conceding at all, the promise of his

society at their houses, or even at his own. "Would he
not walk with them?" "He did not know. There was
nothing so important to him as his walk; he had no
walks to throw away on company." Visits were offered
him from respectful parties, but he declined them.
Admiring friends offered to carry him at their own
cost to the Yellowstone River, — to the West Indies,
— to South America. But though nothing could be
more grave or considered than his refusals, they remind one in quite new relations of that fop Brummel's
reply to the gentleman who offered him his carriage
in a shower, "But where will *you* ride, then?" — and
what accusing silences, and what searching and irresistible speeches, battering down all defenses, his companions can remember!

Mr. Thoreau dedicated his genius with such entire
love to the fields, hills, and waters of his native town,
that he made them known and interesting to all reading Americans, and to people over the sea. The river
on whose banks he was born and died he knew from
its springs to its confluence with the Merrimack. He
had made summer and winter observations on it for
many years, and at every hour of the day and the night.
The result of the recent survey of the Water Commis-
sioners appointed by the State of Massachusetts he
had reached, by his private experiments, several years
earlier. Every fact which occurs in the bed, on the
banks, or in the air over it; the fishes, and their spawning and nests, their manners, their food; the shad-flies
which fill the air on a certain evening once a year, and
which are snapped at by the fishes so ravenously that

many of these die of repletion; the conical heaps of
small stones on the river-shallows, the huge nests of
small fishes, one of which will sometimes overfill a
cart; the birds which frequent the stream, heron, duck,
sheldrake, loon, osprey; the snake, muskrat, otter, woodchuck, and fox, on the banks; the turtle, frog, hyla,
and cricket, which make the banks vocal, — were all
known to him, and, as it were, townsmen and fellow
creatures; so that he felt an absurdity or violence in
any narrative of one of these by itself apart, and still
more of its dimensions on an inch-rule, or in the exhi-
bition of its skeleton, or the specimen of a squirrel or a
bird in brandy. He liked to speak of the manners of the
river, as itself a lawful creature, yet with exactness, and
always to an observed fact. As he knew the river, so
the ponds in this region.

One of the weapons he used, more important than
microscope or alcohol-receiver to other investigators,
was a whim which grew on him by indulgence, yet
appeared in gravest statement, namely, of extolling his
own town and neighborhood as the most favored centre for natural observation. He remarked that the
Flora of Massachusetts embraced almost all the important plants of America, — most of the oaks, most
of the willows, the best pines, the ash, the maple, the
beech, the nuts. He returned Kane's "Arctic Voyage"
to a friend of whom he had borrowed it, with the remark, that "most of the phenomena noted might be
observed in Concord." He seemed a little envious of
the Pole, for the coincident sunrise and sunset, or five
minutes' day after six months: a splendid fact, which

Annursnuc had never afforded him. He found red snow in one of his walks, and told me that he expected to find yet the *Victoria regia* in Concord. He was the attorney of the indigenous plants, and owned to a preference of the weeds to the imported plants, as of the Indian to the civilized man, — and noticed, with pleasure, that the willow bean-poles of his neighbor had grown more than his beans. "See these weeds," he said, "which have been hoed at by a million farmers all spring and summer, and yet have prevailed, and just now come out triumphant over all lanes, pastures, fields, and gardens, such is their vigor. We have insulted them with low names, too, — as Pigweed, Wormwood, Chickweed, Shad-Blossom." He says, "They have brave names, too, — Ambrosia, Stellaria, Amelanchier, Amaranth, etc."

I think his fancy for referring everything to the meridian of Concord did not grow out of any ignorance or depreciation of other longitudes or latitudes, but was rather a playful expression of his conviction of the indifference of all places, and that the best place for each is where he stands. He expressed it once in this wise: "I think nothing is to be hoped from you, if this bit of mould under your feet is not sweeter to you to eat than any other in this world, or in any world."

The other weapon with which he conquered all obstacles in science was patience. He knew how to sit immovable, a part of the rock he rested on, until the bird, the reptile, the fish, which had retired from him, should come back, and resume its habits, nay, moved by curiosity, should come to him and watch him.

It was a pleasure and a privilege to walk with him.
He knew the country like a fox or a bird, and passed
through it as freely by paths of his own. He knew every
track in the snow or on the ground, and what creature
had taken this path before him. One must submit ab-
jectly to such a guide, and the reward was great. Under
his arm he carried an old music-book to press plants;
in his pocket, his diary and pencil, a spy-glass for birds,
microscope, jack-knife, and twine. He wore straw hat,
stout shoes, strong gray trousers to brave shrub oaks
and smilax, and to climb a tree for a hawk's or a squirrel's nest. He waded into the pool for the water-plants,
and his strong legs were no insignificant part of his
armor. On the day I speak of he looked for the meny-
anthes, detected it across the wide pool, and, on exam-
ination of the florets, decided that it had been in flower
five days. He drew out of his breast-pocket his diary,
and read the names of all the plants that should bloom
on this day, whereof he kept account as a banker when
his notes fall due. The cypripedium not due till to-
morrow. He thought, that, if waked up from a trance,
in this swamp, he could tell by the plants what time of
the year it was within two days. The redstart was flying
about, and presently the fine grosbeaks, whose brilliant scarlet makes the rash gazer wipe his eye, and
whose fine clear note Thoreau compared to that of a
tanager which has got rid of its hoarseness. Presently
he heard a note which he called that of the night-warbler,
a bird he had never identified, had been in search of
twelve years, which always, when he saw it, was in the
act of diving down into a tree or bush, and which it

was vain to seek; the only bird that sings indifferently
by night and by day. I told him he must beware of
finding and booking it, lest life should have nothing
more to show him. He said, "What you seek in vain
for, half your life, one day you come full upon, all the
family at dinner. You seek it like a dream, and as
soon as you find it you become its prey."

His interest in the flower or the bird lay very deep in
his mind, was connected with Nature, — and the meaning of Nature was never attempted to be defined by
him. He would not offer a memoir of his observations
to the Natural History Society. "Why should I? To
detach the description from its connections in my mind
would make it no longer true or valuable to me; and
they do not wish what belongs to it." His power of observation seemed to indicate additional senses. He saw
as with microscope, heard as with ear-trumpet, and his
memory was a photographic register of all he saw and
heard. And yet none knew better than he that it is not
the fact that imports, but the impression or effect of
the fact on your mind. Every fact lay in glory in his
mind, a type of the order and beauty of the whole.

His determination on Natural History was organic.
He confessed that he sometimes felt like a hound or a
panther, and, if born among Indians, would have been
a fell hunter. But, restrained by his Massachusetts
culture, he played out the game in this mild form of
botany and ichthyology. His intimacy with animals
suggested what Thomas Fuller records of Butler the
apiologist, that "either he had told the bees things or
the bees had told him." Snakes coiled round his leg,

the fishes swam into his hand, and he took them out of the water; he pulled the woodchuck out of its hole by the tail, and took the foxes under his protection from the hunters. Our naturalist had perfect magnanimity; he had no secrets: he would carry you to the heron's haunt, or even to his most prized botanical swamp, — possibly knowing that you could never find it again, yet willing to take his risks.

No college ever offered him a diploma, or a professor's chair; no academy made him its corresponding secretary, its discoverer, or even its member. Perhaps these learned bodies feared the satire of his presence. Yet so much knowledge of Nature's secret and genius few others possessed, none in a more large and religious synthesis. For not a particle of respect had he to the opinions of any man or body of men, but homage solely to the truth itself; and as he discovered everywhere among doctors some leaning of courtesy, it discredited them. He grew to be revered and admired by his townsmen, who had at first known him only as an oddity. The farmers who employed him as a surveyor soon discovered his rare accuracy and skill, his knowledge of their lands, of trees, of birds, of Indian remains, and the like, which enabled him to tell every farmer more than he knew before of his own farm; so that he began to feel as if Mr. Thoreau had better rights in his land than he. They felt, too, the superiority of character which addressed all men with a native authority.

Indian relics abound in Concord, — arrowheads, stone chisels, pestles, and fragments of pottery; and on the river-bank, large heaps of clamshells and ashes

mark spots which the savages frequented. These, and
every circumstance touching the Indian, were important in his eyes. His visits to Maine were chiefly for
love of the Indian. He had the satisfaction of seeing
the manufacture of the bark canoe, as well as of trying
his hand in its management on the rapids. He was
inquisitive about the making of the stone arrowhead,
and in his last days charged a youth setting out for the
Rocky Mountains to find an Indian who could tell him
that: "It was well worth a visit to California to learn
it." Occasionally, a small party of Penobscot Indians
would visit Concord, and pitch their tents for a few
weeks in summer on the river-bank. He failed not to
make acquaintance with the best of them; though he
well knew that asking questions of Indians is like cate-
chising beavers and rabbits. In his last visit to Maine
he had great satisfaction from Joseph Polis, an intelligent Indian of Oldtown, who was his guide for some
weeks.

He was equally interested in every natural fact. The
depth of his perception found likeness of law throughout Nature, and I know not any genius who so swiftly
inferred universal law from the single fact. He was no
pedant of a department. His eye was open to beauty,
and his ear to music. He found these, not in rare conditions, but wheresoever he went. He thought the best
of music was in single strains; and he found poetic
suggestion in the humming of the telegraph-wire.

His poetry might be bad or good; he no doubt wanted
a lyric facility and technical skill; but he had the source
of poetry in his spiritual perception. He was a good

reader and critic, and his judgment on poetry was to the ground of it. He could not be deceived as to the presence or absence of the poetic element in any composition, and his thirst for this made him negligent and perhaps scornful of superficial graces. He would pass by many delicate rhythms, but he would have detected every live stanza or line in a volume, and knew very well where to find an equal poetic charm in prose. He was so enamored of the spiritual beauty that he held all actual written poems in very light esteem in the comparison. He admired Æschylus and Pindar; but, when some one was commending them, he said that "Æschylus and the Greeks, in describing Apollo and Orpheus, had given no song, or no good one. They ought not to have moved trees, but to have chanted to the gods such a hymn as would have sung all their old ideas out of their heads, and new ones in." His own verses are often rude and defective. The gold does not yet run pure, is drossy and crude. The thyme and marjoram are not yet honey. But if he want lyric fineness and technical merits, if he have not the poetic temperament, he never lacks the causal thought, showing that his genius was better than his talent. He knew the worth of the Imagination for the uplifting and consolation of human life, and liked to throw every thought into a symbol. The fact you tell is of no value, but only the impression. For this reason his presence was poetic, always piqued the curiosity to know more deeply the secrets of his mind. He had many reserves, an unwillingness to exhibit to profane eyes what was still sacred in his own, and knew well how to throw a poetic veil over his experience. All readers of "Walden" will remember his mythical record of his disappointments: —

"I long ago lost a hound, a bay horse, and a turtle-dove, and am still on their trail. Many are the travelers I have spoken concerning them, describing their tracks and what calls they answered to. I have met one or two who had heard the hound, and the tramp of the horse, and even seen the dove disappear behind a cloud; and they seemed as anxious to recover them as if they had lost them themselves." [1]

His riddles were worth the reading, and I confide, that, if at any time I do not understand the expression, it is yet just. Such was the wealth of his truth that it was not worth his while to use words in vain. His poem entitled "Sympathy" reveals the tenderness under that triple steel of stoicism, and the intellectual subtilty it could animate. His classic poem on "Smoke" suggests Simonides, but is better than any poem of Simonides. His biography is in his verses. His habitual thought makes all his poetry a hymn to the Cause of causes, the Spirit which vivifies and controls his own.

> "I hearing get, who had but ears,
>   And sight, who had but eyes before;
> I moments live, who lived but years,
>   And truth discern, who knew but learning's lore."

And still more in these religious lines: —

> "Now chiefly in my natal hour,
>   And only now my prime of life;
> I will not doubt the love untold,
>   Which not my worth or want hath bought,
>   Which wooed me young, and wooes me old,
> And to this evening hath me brought."

[1] *Walden*, p. 18.

Whilst he used in his writings a certain petulance of remark in reference to churches or churchmen, he was a person of a rare, tender, and absolute religion, a person incapable of any profanation, by act or by thought. Of course, the same isolation which belonged to his original thinking and living detached him from the social religious forms. This is neither to be censured nor regretted. Aristotle long ago explained it, when he said, "One who surpasses his fellow-citizens in virtue is no longer a part of the city. Their law is not for him, since he is a law to himself."

Thoreau was sincerity itself, and might fortify the convictions of prophets in the ethical laws by his holy living. It was an affirmative experience which refused to be set aside. A truth-speaker he, capable of the most deep and strict conversation; a physician to the wounds of any soul; a friend, knowing not only the secret of friendship, but almost worshiped by those few persons who resorted to him as their confessor and prophet, and knew the deep value of his mind and great heart. He thought that without religion or devotion of some kind nothing great was ever accomplished; and he thought that the bigoted sectarian had better bear this in mind.

His virtues, of course, sometimes ran into extremes. It was easy to trace to the inexorable demand on all for exact truth that austerity which made this willing hermit more solitary even than he wished. Himself of a perfect probity, he required not less of others. He had a disgust at crime, and no worldly success could cover it. He detected paltering as readily in dignified and prosperous persons as in beggars, and with equal scorn. Such dangerous frankness was in his dealing that his admirers called him "that terrible Thoreau," as if he spoke when silent, and was still present when he had departed. I think the severity of his ideal interfered to deprive him of a healthy sufficiency of human society.

The habit of a realist to find things the reverse of their appearance inclined him to put every statement in a paradox. A certain habit of antagonism defaced his earlier writings, — a trick of rhetoric not quite outgrown in his later, of substituting for the obvious word and thought its diametrical opposite. He praised wild mountains and winter forests for their domestic air, in snow and ice he would find sultriness, and commended the wilderness for resembling Rome and Paris. "It was so dry, that you might call it wet."

The tendency to magnify the moment, to read all the laws of Nature in the one object or one combination under your eye, is of course comic to those who do not share the philosopher's perception of identity. To him there was no such thing as size. The pond was a small ocean; the Atlantic, a large Walden Pond. He referred every minute fact to cosmical laws. Though he meant to be just, he seemed haunted by a certain chronic assumption that the science of the day pretended completeness, and he had just found out that the *savans* had neglected to discriminate a particular botanical variety, had failed to describe the seeds or count the sepals. "That is to say," we replied, "the blockheads were not born in Concord; but who said they were? It was their unspeakable misfortune to be born in London, or Paris, or Rome; but, poor fellows, they did what they could, considering that they never saw Bateman's Pond, or Nine-Acre Corner, or Becky Stow's Swamp. Besides, what were you sent into the world for, but to add this observation?"

Had his genius been only contemplative, he had been fitted to his life, but with his energy and practical ability he seemed born for great enterprise and for command; and I so much regret the loss of his rare powers of action, that I cannot help counting it a fault in him that he had no ambition. Wanting this, instead of engineering for all America, he was the captain of a huckleberry party. Pounding beans is good to the end of pounding empires one of these days; but if, at the end of years, it is still only beans!

But these foibles, real or apparent, were fast vanishing in the incessant growth of a spirit so robust and wise, and which effaced its defeats with new triumphs. His study of Nature was a perpetual ornament to him, and inspired his friends with curiosity to see the world through his eyes, and to hear his adventures. They possessed every kind of interest.

He had many elegances of his own, whilst he scoffed at conventional elegance. Thus, he could not bear to hear the sound of his own steps, the grit of gravel; and therefore never willingly walked in the road, but in the grass, on mountains and in woods. His senses were acute, and he remarked that by night every dwelling-house gives out bad air, like a slaughter-house. He liked the pure fragrance of melilot. He honored certain plants with special regard, and, over all, the pond-lily,

— then, the gentian, and the *Mikania scandens*, and "life-everlasting," and a bass tree which he visited every year when it bloomed, in the middle of July. He thought the scent a more oracular inquisition than the sight, — more oracular and trustworthy. The scent, of course, reveals what is concealed from the other senses. By it he detected earthiness. He delighted in echoes, and said they were almost the only kind of kindred voices that he heard. He loved Nature so well, was so happy in her solitude, that he became very jealous of cities, and the sad work which their refinements and artifices made with man and his dwelling. The axe was always destroying his forest. "Thank God," he said, "they cannot cut down the clouds!" "All kinds of figures are drawn on the blue ground with this fibrous white paint."

I subjoin a few sentences taken from his unpublished manuscripts, not only as records of his thought and feeling, but for their power of description and literary excellence.

"Some circumstantial evidence is very strong, as when you find a trout in the milk."

"The chub is a soft fish, and tastes like boiled brown paper salted."

"The youth gets together his materials to build a bridge to the moon, or, perchance, a palace or temple on the earth, and at length the middle-aged man concludes to build a wood-shed with them."

"The locust z-ing."

"Devil's-needles zigzagging along the Nut Meadow Brook."

"Sugar is not so sweet to the palate as sound to the healthy ear."

"I put on some hemlock boughs, and the rich salt crackling of their leaves was like mustard to the ear, the crackling of unaccountable regiments.   Dead trees love the fire."

"The bluebird carries the sky on his back."

"The tanager flies through the green foliage as if it would ignite the leaves."

"If I wish for a horse-hair for my compass sight, I must go to the stable; but the hair-bird, with her sharp eyes, goes to the road."

"Immortal water, alive even to the superficies."

"Fire is the most tolerable third party."

"Nature made ferns for pure leaves, to show what she could do in that line."

"No tree has so fair a bole and so handsome an in-step as the beech."

"How did these beautiful rainbow tints get into the shell of the fresh-water clam, buried in the mud at the bottom of our dark river?"

"Hard are the times when the infant's shoes are sec-ond-foot."

"We are strictly confined to our men to whom we give liberty."

"Nothing is so much to be feared as fear. Atheism may comparatively be popular with God himself."

"Of what significance the things you can forget? A little thought is sexton to all the world."

"How can we expect a harvest of thought who have not had a seed-time of character?"

"Only he can be trusted with gifts who can present a face of bronze to expectations."

"I ask to be melted. You can only ask of the metals that they be tender to the fire that melts them. To naught else can they be tender."

There is a flower known to botanists, one of the same genus with our summer plant called "life-everlasting," a *Gnaphalium* like that, which grows on the most inaccessible cliffs of the Tyrolese mountains, where the chamois dare hardly venture, and which the hunter, tempted by its beauty, and by his love (for it is immensely valued by the Swiss maidens), climbs the cliffs to gather, and is sometimes found dead at the foot, with the flower in his hand. It is called by botanists the *Gnaphalium Leontopodium*, but by the Swiss *Edelweiss*, which signifies *Noble Purity*. Thoreau seemed to me living in the hope to gather this plant, which belonged to him of right. The scale on which his studies proceeded was so large as to require longevity, and we were the less prepared for his sudden disappearance. The country knows not yet, or in the least part, how great a son it has lost. It seems an injury that he should leave in the midst his broken task, which none else can finish, — a kind of indignity to so noble a soul, that he should depart out of Nature before yet he has been really shown to his peers for what he is. But he, at least, is content. His soul was made for the noblest society; he had in a short life exhausted the capabilities of this world; wherever there is knowledge, wherever there is virtue, wherever there is beauty, he will find a home.

INTRODUCTORY NOTE

It was in August and September, 1839, as the chronicle notes, that the voyage recorded in these pages was made. Thoreau was just past his twenty-second birthday; he had been two years out of college, and though he had thus far printed nothing, he had already, four years before, begun that practice of noting his experience, observation, and reflection in a diary which he continued through life, so that not only did his journal furnish him with the first draft of what he published in his lifetime, but it formed a magazine from which, after his death, friendly editors drew successive volumes.

The "Week" is much more than a mere reproduction of his journal during the period under consideration. It was not published as a book until 1849, ten years after the excursion which it commemorated; but in its final form were inclosed many verses and some prose passages which had already appeared in the short-lived historic "Dial." It will be remembered that Thoreau was not only a contributor to that periodical from the beginning, but for a while had editorial charge of it; the editing, indeed, seemed to be handed about from one to another of the circle most concerned in its issue. Thus in the first number, July, 1840, appeared the excursus on Aulus Persius Flaccus, printed in the "Week," pp. 327–333. So, also, his poems on Friendship saw the light first in the second number of "The

Dial," and there also appeared the poems "The Inward Morning," "The Poet's Delay," "Rumors from
an Æolian Harp," and others, as well as the study of
Anacreon, with examples in translation. It is easy for
the reader to see that the "Week" is Thoreau's commonplace book as well as journal.

He was living in his hut on Walden Pond when he
edited his manuscripts for publication in book form,
and Alcott, visiting him one evening there, heard him
read some passages from the work. It is interesting to
observe how immediately this man of fine instincts
perceived the worth of what had as yet struck his ear
only, listening as a friend. "The book," he writes in
his diary, "is purely American, fragrant with the life
of New England woods and streams, and could have
been written nowhere else. Especially am I touched by
his sufficiency and soundness, his aboriginal vigor, —
as if a man had once more come into Nature who knew
what Nature meant him to do with her; Virgil and
White of Selborne and Izaak Walton and Yankee
settler all in one. I came home at midnight through
the snowy woodpaths, and slept with the pleasing dream
that presently the press would give me two books to
be proud of, — Emerson's 'Poems' and Thoreau's
'Week.'" [1]

This was written in March, 1847, and Thoreau was
probably just about to try the publishers, if his manuscript were not even now resting in his hut from one of
its journeys. For in a letter to Emerson, at that time

[1] *A. Bronson Alcott; his Life and Philosophy.* By F. B. Sanborn
and William T. Harris. p. 446.

in England, written November 14, 1847, Thoreau says, "I suppose you will like to hear of my book, though I have nothing worth writing about it. Indeed, for the last month or two I have forgotten it, but shall certainly remember it again. Wiley & Putnam, Munroe, the Harpers, and Crosby & Nichols have all declined printing it with the least risk to themselves; but Wiley & Putnam will print it in their series, and any of them anywhere, at *my* risk. If I liked the book well enough, I should not delay; but for the present I am indifferent. I believe this is, after all, the course you advised, — to let it lie." [1]   Apparently he used the opportunity of having it by him to touch it up now and then, for in a letter to Mr. J. Elliot Cabot, written in March, 1848, he says: "My book, fortunately, did not find a publisher ready to undertake it, and you can imagine the effect of delay on an author's estimate of his own work. However, I like it well enough to mend it, and shall look at it again directly when I have dispatched some other things." [2]   The essay on Friendship which precedes the poem "Friends, Romans, Countrymen, and Lovers," already referred to, appears to have been written at this time, for Mr. Alcott in his diary, under date of January 13, 1848, notes: "Henry Thoreau came in after my hours with the children, and we had a good deal of talk on the modes of popular influence. He read me a manuscript essay of his on Friendship, which he had just written, and which I thought superior to anything I had heard." [3]

[1] *Familiar Letters.*   [2] *Ibid.*

[3] *Henry D. Thoreau.* By F. B. Sanborn [American Men of Letters] p. 304.

Apparently Thoreau was convinced of the impossibility of persuading any publisher to take the book at his own risk, and was sufficiently confident of the worth of the volume to bear the expense of publication himself, although to do this he was obliged to borrow money, and, since the book did not meet its expenses, afterward to take up the occupation of surveying in order to cancel his obligation. The book was published by James Munroe & Co., Boston and Cambridge, apparently in the summer of 1849. Mr. George Ripley wrote a kindly notice of it in "The Tribune," and James Russell Lowell reviewed it in a dozen pages in the "Massachusetts Quarterly Review" for December of the same year. With his own cunning in literary art he quickly divined the interior structure of the "Week." "The great charm," he says, "of Mr. Thoreau's book seems to be that its being a book at all is a happy fortuity. The door of the portfolio cage has been left open, and the thoughts have flown out of themselves. The paper and types are only accidents. The page is confidential like a diary. . . . He begins honestly enough as the Boswell of Musketaquid and Merrimack. . . . As long as he continues an honest Boswell, his book is delightful, but sometimes he serves his two rivers as Hazlitt did Northcote, and makes them run Thoreau or Emerson or indeed anything but their own transparent element. . . . We have digressions on Boodh, on Anacreon (with translations hardly so good as Cowley), on Persius, on Friendship, and we know not what. We come upon them like snags, jolting us headforemost out of our places as we are rowing placidly up

stream, or drifting down. Mr. Thoreau becomes so
absorbed in these discussions that he seems as it were
to catch a crab and disappears uncomfortably from
his seat at the bow oar. We could forgive them all, especially that on Books and that on Friendship (which
is worthy of one who has so long communed with Nature and with Emerson), we could welcome them all
were they put by themselves at the end of the book.
But, as it is, they are out of proportion and out of place
and mar our Merrimacking dreadfully. We were bid
to a river-party, — not to be preached at." After dis-
tributing praise and blame over the poetical interludes,
Lowell closes his review with the words: "Since we
have found fault with what we may be allowed to call
worsification, we should say that the prose work is done
conscientiously and neatly. The style is compact, and
the language has an antique purity like wine grown
colorless with age."

In spite of the generous reception which the book
had thus at the hands of men like Alcott, Ripley, and
Lowell, the public was indifferent enough. Thoreau
recounts the issue of the venture with grim humor in
an entry in his diary, October 28, 1853, after the book
had been in the bookstores for four years. "For a year
or two past my *publisher*, falsely so called, has been
writing from time to time to ask what disposition should
be made of the copies of 'A Week on the Concord and
Merrimack Rivers' still on hand, and at last suggest-
ing that he had use for the room they occupied in his
cellar. So I had them all sent to me here, and they have
arrived to-day by express, filling the man's wagon, —

706 copies out of an edition of 1000 which I bought of
Munroe four years ago and have been ever since paying
for, and have not quite paid for yet. The wares are sent
to me at last, and I have an opportunity to examine
my purchase. They are something more substantial
than fame, as my back knows, which has borne them
up two flights of stairs to a place similar to that to
which they trace their origin. Of the remaining two
hundred and ninety and odd, seventy-five were given
away, the rest sold. I have now a library of nearly
nine hundred volumes, over seven hundred of which I
wrote myself. Is it not well that the author should
behold the fruits of his labor? My works are piled up
on one side of my chamber half as high as my head, my
opera omnia. This is authorship; these are the work of
my brain. There was just one piece of good luck in the
venture. The unbound were tied up by the printer four
years ago in stout paper wrappers, and inscribed, —

H. D. Thoreau's

Concord River

50 cops.

So Munroe had only to cross out 'River' and write
'Mass.,' and deliver them to the expressman at once.
I can see now what I write for, the result of my labors.
Nevertheless, in spite of this result, sitting beside the
inert mass of my works, I take up my pen to-night to
record what thought or experience I may have had,
with as much satisfaction as ever. Indeed, I believe
that this result is more inspiring and better for me than
if a thousand had bought my wares. It affects my privacy less and leaves me freer."

We have quoted from the judgments of Alcott and
Lowell on the book because one is curious to know how
the contemporaries of Thoreau regarded his work; later
critics have the advantage and disadvantage of seeing
such writing through an atmosphere charged with many
men's breathing of criticism and appreciation. Lowell
himself, when he returned to Thoreau sixteen years
later, had in a measure re-formed his appreciation. But
after all, no judgment of an author is quite so interesting as that which the author himself passes, even
though one has to correct this estimate by other observations on the author and his work. At any rate, Thoreau shall be the last here to comment on this book: —

"I thought that one peculiarity of my 'Week' was
its *hypæthral* character, to use an epithet applied to
those Egyptian temples which are open to the heavens
above, *under the ether*. I thought that it had little of
the atmosphere of the house about it, but might wholly
have been written, as in fact it was to a considerable
extent, out-of-doors. It was only at a late period in writing it, as it happened, that I used any phrases implying
that I lived in a house or led a *domestic* life. I trust it
does not smell [so much] of the study and library, even
of the poet's attic, as of the fields and woods; that it is
a hypæthral or unroofed book, lying open under the
ether and permeated by it, open to all weathers, not
easy to be kept on a shelf."

   ᵗ *Journal,* June 29, 1851.

A WEEK ON THE CONCORD AND
MERRIMACK RIVERS

Where'er thou sail'st who sailed with me,
Though now thou climbest loftier mounts,
And fairer rivers dost ascend,
Be thou my Muse, my Brother —.

I am bound, I am bound, for a distant shore.
By a lonely isle, by a far Azore,
There it is, there it is, the treasure I seek,
On the barren sands of a desolate creek.

I sailed up a river with a pleasant wind,
New lands, new people, and new thoughts to find;
Many fair reaches and headlands appeared,
And many dangers were there to be feared;
But when I remember where I have been,
And the fair landscapes that I have seen,
THOU seemest the only permanent shore,
The cape never rounded, nor wandered o'er.

Fluminaque obliquis cinxit declivia ripis;
Quæ, diversa locis, partim sorbentur ab ipsa;
In mare perveniunt partim, campoque recepta
Liberioris aquæ pro ripis litora pulsant.

He confined the rivers within their sloping banks,
Which in different places are part absorbed by the earth,
Part reach the sea, and being received within the plain
Of its freer waters, beat the shore for banks.

OVID, *Met.* I. 39.

CONCORD RIVER

Beneath low hills, in the broad interval
Through which at will our Indian rivulet
Winds mindful still of sannup and of squaw,
Whose pipe and arrow oft the plough unburies,
Here in pine houses built of new-fallen trees,
Supplanters of the tribe, the farmers dwell.

EMERSON.

THE Musketaquid, or Grass-ground River, though probably as old as the Nile or Euphrates, did not begin to have a place in civilized history until the fame of its grassy meadows and its fish attracted settlers out of England in 1635, when it received the other but kindred name of CONCORD from the first plantation on its banks, which appears to have been commenced in a spirit of peace and harmony. It will be Grass-ground River as long as grass grows and water runs here; it will be Concord River only while men lead peaceable lives on its banks. To an extinct race it was grass-ground, where they hunted and fished; and it is still perennial grass-ground to Concord farmers, who own the Great Meadows, and get the hay from year to year. "One branch of it," according to the historian of Concord, for I love to quote so good authority, "rises in the south part of Hopkinton, and another from a pond and a large cedar-swamp in Westborough," and flowing between Hopkinton and Southborough, through Framingham, and between Sudbury and Wayland, where it is some-

times called Sudbury River, it enters Concord at the
south part of the town, and after receiving the North or
Assabet River, which has its source a little farther to
the north and west, goes out at the northeast angle,
and, flowing between Bedford and Carlisle, and through
Billerica, empties into the Merrimack at Lowell. In
Concord, it is in summer from four to fifteen feet deep,
and from one hundred to three hundred feet wide, but
in the spring freshets, when it overflows its banks, it
is in some places nearly a mile wide. Between Sudbury and Wayland the meadows acquire their greatest
breadth, and when covered with water, they form a
handsome chain of shallow vernal lakes, resorted to
by numerous gulls and ducks.   Just above Sherman's
Bridge, between these towns, is the largest expanse; and
when the wind blows freshly in a raw March day, heaving up the surface into dark and sober billows or regular
swells, skirted as it is in the distance with alder swamps
and smoke-like maples, it looks like a smaller Lake
Huron, and is very pleasant and exciting for a landsman
to row or sail over. The farmhouses along the Sudbury
shore, which rises gently to a considerable height, command fine water prospects at this season. The shore is
more flat on the Wayland side, and this town is the
greatest loser by the flood. Its farmers tell me that thousands of acres are flooded now, since the dams have been
erected, where they remember to have seen the white
honeysuckle or clover growing once, and they could go
dry with shoes only in summer. Now there is nothing
but blue-joint and sedge and cut-grass there, standing in
water all the year round. For a long time, they made the

most of the driest season to get their hay, working sometimes till nine o'clock at night, sedulously paring with
their scythes in the twilight round the hummocks left
by the ice; but now it is not worth the getting when they
can come at it, and they look sadly round to their wood-
lots and upland as a last resource.

It is worth the while to make a voyage up this stream,
if you go no farther than Sudbury, only to see how
much country there is in the rear of us: great hills,
and a hundred brooks, and farmhouses, and barns, and
haystacks, you never saw before, and men everywhere;
Sudbury, that is *Southborough* men, and Wayland, and
Nine-Acre-Corner men, and Bound Rock, where four
towns bound on a rock in the river, Lincoln, Wayland,
Sudbury, Concord. Many waves are there agitated by
the wind, keeping nature fresh, the spray blowing in
your face, reeds and rushes waving; ducks by the
hundred, all uneasy in the surf, in the raw wind, just
ready to rise, and now going off with a clatter and
a whistling like riggers straight for Labrador, flying
against the stiff gale with reefed wings, or else circling
round first, with all their paddles briskly moving, just
over the surf, to reconnoitre you before they leave these
parts; gulls wheeling overhead, muskrats swimming
for dear life, wet and cold, with no fire to warm them
by that you know of, their labored homes rising here and
there like haystacks; and countless mice and moles and
winged titmice along the sunny, windy shore; cranberries tossed on the waves and heaving up on the beach,
their little red skiffs beating about among the alders; —
such healthy natural tumult as proves the last day is not

yet at hand. And there stand all around the alders, and birches, and oaks, and maples, full of glee and sap, holding in their buds until the waters subside. You shall perhaps run aground on Cranberry Island, only some spires of last year's pipe-grass above water to show where the danger is, and get as good a freezing there as anywhere on the Northwest Coast. I never voyaged so far in all my life. You shall see men you never heard of before, whose names you don't know, going away down through the meadows with long ducking guns, with water-tight boots wading through the fowl-meadow grass, on bleak, wintry, distant shores, with guns at half-cock; and they shall see teal, — blue-winged, green-winged, — sheldrakes, whistlers, black ducks, ospreys, and many other wild and noble sights before night, such as they who sit in parlors never dream of. You shall see rude and sturdy, experienced and wise men, keeping their castles, or teaming up their summer's wood, or chopping alone in the woods; men fuller of talk and rare adventure in the sun and wind and rain, than a chestnut is of meat, who were out not only in '75 and 1812, but have been out every day of their lives; greater men than Homer, or Chaucer, or Shakespeare, only they never got time to say so; they never took to the way of writing. Look at their fields, and imagine what they might write, if ever they should put pen to paper. Or what have they not written on the face of the earth already, clearing, and burning, and scratching, and harrowing, and plowing, and subsoiling, in and in, and out and out, and over and over, again and again, erasing what they had already written for want of parchment.

As yesterday and the historical ages are past, as the work of to-day is present, so some flitting perspectives and demi-experiences of the life that is in nature are in time veritably future, or rather outside to time, perennial, young, divine, in the wind and rain which never die.

> The respectable folks, —
> Where dwell they?
> They whisper in the oaks,
> And they sigh in the hay;
> Summer and winter, night and day,
> Out on the meadow, there dwell they.
> They never die,
> Nor snivel nor cry,
> Nor ask our pity
> With a wet eye.
> A sound estate they ever mend,
> To every asker readily lend;
> To the ocean wealth,
> To the meadow health,
> To Time his length,
> To the rocks strength,
> To the stars light,
> To the weary night,
> To the busy day,
> To the idle play;
> And so their good cheer never ends,
> For all are their debtors, and all their friends.

Concord River is remarkable for the gentleness of its current, which is scarcely perceptible, and some have referred to its influence the proverbial moderation of the inhabitants of Concord, as exhibited in the Revolution, and on later occasions. It has been proposed that the town should adopt for its coat of arms a field verdant, with the Concord circling nine times round. I have read

that a descent of an eighth of an inch in a mile is sufficient to produce a flow. Our river has, probably, very
near the smallest allowance. The story is current, at
any rate, though I believe that strict history will not
bear it out, that the only bridge ever carried away on
the main branch, within the limits of the town, was
driven up-stream by the wind. But wherever it makes a
sudden bend it is shallower and swifter, and asserts its
title to be called a river. Compared with the other tributaries of the Merrimack, it appears to have been properly
named Musketaquid, or Meadow River, by the Indians.
For the most part, it creeps through broad meadows,
adorned with scattered oaks, where the cranberry is
found in abundance, covering the ground like a moss-
bed. A row of sunken dwarf willows borders the stream
on one or both sides, while at a greater distance the
meadow is skirted with maples, alders, and other
fluviatile trees, overrun with the grape-vine, which bears
fruit in its season, purple, red, white, and other grapes.
Still farther from the stream, on the edge of the firm
land, are seen the gray and white dwellings of the inhabitants. According to the valuation of 1831, there were
in Concord two thousand one hundred and eleven acres,
or about one seventh of the whole territory, in meadow;
this standing next in the list after pasturage and unimproved lands; and, judging from the returns of previous
years, the meadow is not reclaimed so fast as the woods
are cleared.

Let us here read what old Johnson says of these
meadows in his "Wonder-Working Providence," which
gives the account of New England from 1628 to 1652.

and see how matters looked to him. He says of the
Twelfth Church of Christ gathered at Concord: "This
town is seated upon a fair fresh river, whose rivulets
are filled with fresh marsh, and her streams with fish,
it being a branch of that large river of Merrimack.
Allwifes and shad in their season come up to this town,
but salmon and dace cannot come up, by reason of the
rocky falls, which causeth their meadows to lie much
covered with water, the which these people, together
with their neighbor town, have several times essayed to
cut through but cannot, yet it may be turned another
way with an hundred pound charge as it appeared."
As to their farming he says: "Having laid out their
estate upon cattle at 5 to 20 pound a cow, when they
came to winter them with inland hay, and feed upon
such wild fother as was never cut before, they could not
hold out the winter, but, ordinarily the first or second
year after their coming up to a new plantation, many of
their cattle died." And this from the same author: "Of
the Planting of the 19th Church in the Mattachusets'
Government, called Sudbury:" "This year [does he
mean 1654?] the town and church of Christ at Sudbury
began to have the first foundation stones laid, taking
up her station in the inland country, as her elder sister
Concord had formerly done, lying further up the same
river, being furnished with great plenty of fresh marsh,
but, it lying very low is much indamaged with land
floods, insomuch that when the summer proves wet they
lose part of their hay; yet are they so sufficiently provided that they take in cattle of other towns to winter."

The sluggish artery of the Concord meadows steals

thus unobserved through the town, without a murmur
or a pulse-beat, its general course from southwest to
northeast, and its length about fifty miles; a huge volume of matter, ceaselessly rolling through the plains
and valleys of the substantial earth with the moccasined
tread of an Indian warrior, making haste from the high
places of the earth to its ancient reservoir. The murmurs of many a famous river on the other side of the
globe reach even to us here, as to more distant dwellers
on its banks; many a poet's stream, floating the helms
and shields of heroes on its bosom. The Xanthus or
Scamander is not a mere dry channel and bed of a
mountain torrent, but fed by the ever-flowing springs
of fame: —

> " And thou Simois, that as an arrowe, clere
>   Through Troy rennest, aie downward to the sea;" —

and I trust that I may be allowed to associate our muddy
but much abused Concord River with the most famous
in history.

> " Sure there are poets which did never dream
>   Upon Parnassus, nor did taste the stream
>   Of Helicon; we therefore may suppose
>   Those made not poets, but the poets those."

The Mississippi, the Ganges, and the Nile, those
journeying atoms from the Rocky Mountains, the Himmaleh, and Mountains of the Moon, have a kind of
personal importance in the annals of the world. The
heavens are not yet drained over their sources, but the
Mountains of the Moon still send their annual tribute
to the Pasha without fail, as they did to the Pharaohs,

though he must collect the rest of his revenue at the
point of the sword. Rivers must have been the guides
which conducted the footsteps of the first travelers.
They are the constant lure, when they flow by our doors,
to distant enterprise and adventure; and, by a natural impulse, the dwellers on their banks will at length
accompany their currents to the lowlands of the globe,
or explore at their invitation the interior of continents.
They are the natural highways of all nations, not only
leveling the ground and removing obstacles from the
path of the traveler, quenching his thirst and bearing
him on their bosoms, but conducting him through the
most interesting scenery, the most populous portions of
the globe, and where the animal and vegetable kingdoms
attain their greatest perfection.

I had often stood on the banks of the Concord, watching the lapse of the current, an emblem of all progress,
following the same law with the system, with time, and
all that is made; the weeds at the bottom gently bending down the stream, shaken by the watery wind, still
planted where their seeds had sunk, but ere long to die
and go down likewise; the shining pebbles, not yet
anxious to better their condition, the chips and weeds,
and occasional logs and stems of trees that floated past,
fulfilling their fate, were objects of singular interest to
me, and at last I resolved to launch myself on its bosom
and float whither it would bear me.

SATURDAY

Come, come, my lovely fair, and let us try
Those rural delicacies.
                    QUARLES, *Christ's Invitation to the Soul.*

AT length, on Saturday, the last day of August, 1839, we two, brothers, and natives of Concord, weighed anchor in this river port; for Concord, too, lies under the sun, a port of entry and departure for the bodies as well as the souls of men; one shore at least exempted from all duties but such as an honest man will gladly discharge. A warm, drizzling rain had obscured the morning, and threatened to delay our voyage, but at length the leaves and grass were dried, and it came out a mild afternoon, as serene and fresh as if Nature were maturing some greater scheme of her own. After this long dripping and oozing from every pore, she began to respire again more healthily than ever. So with a vigorous shove we launched our boat from the bank, while the flags and bulrushes courtesied a God-speed, and dropped silently down the stream.

Our boat, which had cost us a week's labor in the spring, was in form like a fisherman's dory, fifteen feet long by three and a half in breadth at the widest part, painted green below, with a border of blue, with reference to the two elements in which it was to spend its existence. It had been loaded the evening before at our door, half a mile from the river, with potatoes and melons, from a patch which we had cultivated, and a few utensils; and was provided with wheels in order to be rolled around falls, as well as with two sets of oars, and several slender poles for shoving in shallow places, and also two masts, one of which served for a tent-pole at night; for a buffalo-skin was to be our bed, and a tent of cotton cloth our roof. It was strongly built, but heavy, and hardly of better model than usual. If rightly made, a boat would be a sort of amphibious animal, a creature of two elements, related by one half its structure to some swift and shapely fish, and by the other to some strong-winged and graceful bird. The fish shows where there should be the greatest breadth of beam and depth in the hold; its fins direct where to set the oars, and the tail gives some hint for the form and position of the rudder. The bird shows how to rig and trim the sails, and what form to give to the prow, that it may balance the boat and divide the air and water best. These hints we had but partially obeyed. But the eyes, though they are no sailors, will never be satisfied with any model, however fashionable, which does not answer all the requisitions of art. However, as art is all of a ship but the wood, and yet the wood alone will rudely serve the purpose of a ship, so our boat, being of wood, gladly availed itself of the old law that the heavier shall float the lighter, and though a dull water-fowl, proved a sufficient buoy for our purpose.

> "Were it the will of Heaven, an osier bough
> Were vessel safe enough the seas to plough."

Some village friends stood upon a promontory lower down the stream to wave us a last farewell; but we,

having already performed these shore rites, with excus-
able reserve, as befits those who are embarked on unusual enterprises, who behold but speak not, silently
glided past the firm lands of Concord, both peopled
cape and lonely summer meadow, with steady sweeps.
And yet we did unbend so far as to let our guns speak
for us, when at length we had swept out of sight, and
thus left the woods to ring again with their echoes; and
it may be many russet-clad children, lurking in those
broad meadows, with the bittern and the woodcock and
the rail, though wholly concealed by brakes and hard-
hack and meadow-sweet, heard our salute that afternoon.

We were soon floating past the first regular battle-
ground of the Revolution, resting on our oars between
the still visible abutments of that " North Bridge " over
which in April, 1775, rolled the first faint tide of that
war which ceased not till, as we read on the stone on
our right, it " gave peace to these United States." As
Concord poet has sung: —

> "By the rude bridge that arched the flood,
>   Their flag to April's breeze unfurled,
>   Here once the embattled farmers stood
>   And fired the shot heard round the world.
>
> "The foe long since in silence slept;
>   Alike the conqueror silent sleeps;
>   And Time the ruined bridge has swept
>   Down the dark stream which seaward creeps."

Our reflections had already acquired a historical
remoteness from the scenes we had left, and we ourselves
essayed to sing: —

Ah, 't is in vain the peaceful din
   That wakes the ignoble town,
Not thus did braver spirits win
   A patriot's renown.

There is one field beside this stream
   Wherein no foot does fall,
But yet it beareth in my dream
   A richer crop than all.

Let me believe a dream so dear,
   Some heart beat high that day,
Above the petty Province here,
   And Britain far away;

Some hero of the ancient mould,
   Some arm of knightly worth,
Of strength unbought, and faith unsold,
   Honored this spot of earth;

Who sought the prize his heart described,
   And did not ask release,
Whose free-born valor was not bribed
   By prospect of a peace.

The men who stood on yonder height
   That day are long since gone;
Not the same hand directs the fight
   And monumental stone.

Ye were the Grecian cities then,
   The Romes of modern birth,
Where the New England husbandmen
   Have shown a Roman worth.

In vain I search a foreign land
   To find our Bunker Hill,
And Lexington and Concord stand
   By no Laconian rill.

With such thoughts we swept gently by this now peaceful pasture-ground, on waves of Concord, in which was long since drowned the din of war.

> But since we sailed
> Some things have failed,
> And many a dream
> Gone down the stream.

> Here then an aged shepherd dwelt,
> Who to his flock his substance dealt,
> And ruled them with a vigorous crook,
> By precept of the sacred Book;
> But he the pierless bridge passed o'er,
> And solitary left the shore.

> Anon a youthful pastor came,
> Whose crook was not unknown to fame,
> His lambs he viewed with gentle glance,
> Spread o'er the country's wide expanse,
> And fed with "Mosses from the Manse."
> Here was our Hawthorne in the dale,
> And here the shepherd told his tale.

That slight shaft had now sunk behind the hills, and we had floated round the neighboring bend, and under the new North Bridge between Ponkawtasset and the Poplar Hill, into the Great Meadows, which, like a broad moccasin-print, have leveled a fertile and juicy place in nature.

> On Ponkawtasset, since we took our way
> Down this still stream to far Billericay,
> A poet wise has settled, whose fine ray
> Doth often shine on Concord's twilight day.

> Like those first stars, whose silver beams on high,
> Shining more brightly as the day goes by,

Most travelers cannot at first descry,
But eyes that wont to range the evening sky,

And know celestial lights, do plainly see,
And gladly hail them, numbering two or three;
For lore that's deep must deeply studied be,
As from deep wells men read star-poetry.

These stars are never paled, though out of sight,
But like the sun they shine forever bright;
Ay, *they* are suns, though earth must in its flight
Put out its eyes that it may see their light.

Who would neglect the least celestial sound,
Or faintest light that falls on earthly ground,
If he could know it one day would be found
That star in Cygnus whither we are bound,
And pale our sun with heavenly radiance round?

Gradually the village murmur subsided, and we
seemed to be embarked on the placid current of our
dreams, floating from past to future as silently as one
awakes to fresh morning or evening thoughts. We
glided noiselessly down the stream, occasionally driving
a pickerel or a bream from the covert of the pads, and
the smaller bittern now and then sailed away on sluggish
wings from some recess in the shore, or the larger lifted
itself out of the long grass at our approach, and carried its precious legs away to deposit them in a place of
safety. The tortoises also rapidly dropped into the
water, as our boat ruffled the surface amid the willows,
breaking the reflections of the trees. The banks had
passed the height of their beauty, and some of the
brighter flowers showed by their faded tints that the
season was verging towards the afternoon of the year;

but this sombre tinge enhanced their sincerity, and in the still unabated heats they seemed like the mossy brink of some cool well. The narrow-leaved willow (*Salix Purshiana*) lay along the surface of the water in masses of light green foliage, interspersed with the large balls of the button-bush. The small rose-colored polygonum raised its head proudly above the water on either hand, and flowering at this season and in these localities, in front of dense fields of the white species which skirted the sides of the stream, its little streak of red looked very rare and precious. The pure white blossoms of the arrowhead stood in the shallower parts, and a few cardinals on the margin still proudly surveyed themselves reflected in the water, though the latter, as well as the pickerel-weed, was now nearly out of blossom. The snake-head (*Chelone glabra*) grew close to the shore, while a kind of coreopsis, turning its brazen face to the sun, full and rank, and a tall dull-red flower (*Eupatorium purpureum*, or trumpet-weed) formed the rear rank of the fluvial array. The bright-blue flowers of the soapwort gentian were sprinkled here and there in the adjacent meadows, like flowers which Proserpine had dropped, and still farther in the fields or higher on the bank were seen the purple gerardia, the Virginian rhexia, and drooping neottia or ladies'-tresses; while from the more distant waysides which we occasionally passed, and banks where the sun had lodged, was reflected still a dull-yellow beam from the ranks of tansy, now past its prime. In short, Nature seemed to have adorned herself for our departure with a profusion of fringes and curls, mingled with the bright tints of flowers,

reflected in the water. But we missed the white water-
lily, which is the queen of river flowers, its reign being
over for this season. He makes his voyage too late, perhaps, by a true water clock who delays so long. Many
of this species inhabit our Concord water. I have passed
down the river before sunrise on a summer morning,
between fields of lilies still shut in sleep; and when, at
length, the flakes of sunlight from over the bank fell on
the surface of the water, whole fields of white blossoms
seemed to flash open before me, as I floated along, like
the unfolding of a banner, so sensible is this flower
to the influence of the sun's rays.

As we were floating through the last of these familiar
meadows, we observed the large and conspicuous flowers
of the hibiscus, covering the dwarf willows and mingled
with the leaves of the grape, and wished that we could
inform one of our friends behind of the locality of this
somewhat rare and inaccessible flower before it was too
late to pluck it; but we were just gliding out of sight
of the village spire before it occurred to us that the
farmer in the adjacent meadow would go to church on
the morrow, and would carry this news for us; and so
by the Monday, while we should be floating on the
Merrimack, our friend would be reaching to pluck this
blossom on the bank of the Concord.

After a pause at Ball's Hill, the St. Anne's of Concord
voyageurs, not to say any prayer for the success of our
voyage, but to gather the few berries which were still
left on the hills, hanging by very slender threads, we
weighed anchor again, and were soon out of sight of our
native village. The land seemed to grow fairer as we

withdrew from it. Far away to the southwest lay the quiet village, left alone under its elms and buttonwoods in mid-afternoon; and the hills, notwithstanding their blue, ethereal faces, seemed to cast a saddened eye on their old playfellows; but, turning short to the north, we bade adieu to their familiar outlines, and addressed ourselves to new scenes and adventures. Naught was familiar but the heavens, from under whose roof the voyageur never passes; but with their countenance, and the acquaintance we had with river and wood, we trusted to fare well under any circumstances.

From this point the river runs perfectly straight for a mile or more to Carlisle Bridge, which consists of twenty wooden piers, and when we looked back over it, its surface was reduced to a line's breadth, and appeared like a cobweb gleaming in the sun. Here and there might be seen a pole sticking up, to mark the place where some fisherman had enjoyed unusual luck, and in return had consecrated his rod to the deities who preside over these shallows. It was full twice as broad as before, deep and tranquil, with a muddy bottom, and bordered with willows, beyond which spread broad lagoons covered with pads, bulrushes, and flags.

Late in the afternoon we passed a man on the shore fishing with a long birch pole, its silvery bark left on, and a dog at his side, rowing so near as to agitate his cork with our oars, and drive away luck for a season; and when we had rowed a mile as straight as an arrow, with our faces turned towards him, and the bubbles in our wake still visible on the tranquil surface, there stood the fisher still with his dog, like statues under the other

side of the heavens, the only objects to relieve the eye
in the extended meadow; and there would he stand
abiding his luck, till he took his way home through the
fields at evening with his fish. Thus, by one bait or
another, Nature allures inhabitants into all her recesses.
This man was the last of our townsmen whom we saw,
and we silently through him bade adieu to our friends.

The characteristics and pursuits of various ages and
races of men are always existing in epitome in every
neighborhood. The pleasures of my earliest youth have
become the inheritance of other men. This man is still
a fisher, and belongs to an era in which I myself have
lived. Perchance he is not confounded by many know-
ledges, and has not sought out many inventions; but
how to take many fishes before the sun sets, with his
slender birchen pole and flaxen line, that is invention
enough for him. It is good even to be a fisherman in
summer and in winter. Some men are judges, these
August days, sitting on benches, even till the court rises;
they sit judging there honorably, between the seasons
and between meals, leading a civil, politic life, arbitrating in the case of Spaulding *versus* Cummings, it
may be, from highest noon till the red vesper sinks into
the west. The fisherman, meanwhile, stands in three
feet of water, under the same summer's sun, arbitrating
in other cases between muck-worm and shiner, amid
the fragrance of water-lilies, mint, and pontederia, leading his life many rods from the dry land, within a pole's
length of where the larger fishes swim. Human life is
to him very much like a river, —

" renning aie downward to the sea."

This was his observation. His honor made a great discovery in bailments.

I can just remember an old brown-coated man who
was the Walton of this stream, who had come over
from Newcastle, England, with his son, — the latter a
stout and hearty man who had lifted an anchor in his
day. A straight old man he was, who took his way in
silence through the meadows, having passed the period
of communication with his fellows; his old experienced
coat, hanging long and straight and brown as the yellow
pine bark, glittering with so much smothered sunlight,
if you stood near enough, no work of art but naturalized
at length. I often discovered him unexpectedly amid
the pads and the gray willows when he moved, fishing in some old country method, — for youth and age
then went a-fishing together, — full of incommunicable
thoughts, perchance about his own Tyne and Northum-
berland. He was always to be seen in serene afternoons
haunting the river, and almost rustling with the sedge;
so many sunny hours in an old man's life, entrapping
silly fish; almost grown to be the sun's familiar; what
need had he of hat or raiment any, having served out
his time, and seen through such thin disguises? I have
seen how his coeval fates rewarded him with the yellow
perch, and yet I thought his luck was not in proportion
to his years; and I have seen when, with slow steps and
weighed down with aged thoughts, he disappeared with
his fish under his low-roofed house on the skirts of the
village. I think nobody else saw him; nobody else
remembers him now, for he soon after died, and mi-
grated to new Tyne streams. His fishing was not a sport,

nor solely a means of subsistence, but a sort of solemn
sacrament and withdrawal from the world, just as the
aged read their Bibles.

Whether we live by the seaside, or by the lakes and
rivers, or on the prairie, it concerns us to attend to the
nature of fishes, since they are not phenomena confined
to certain localities only, but forms and phases of the life
in nature universally dispersed. The countless shoals
which annually coast the shores of Europe and America
are not so interesting to the student of nature as the more
fertile law itself, which deposits their spawn on the tops
of mountains and on the interior plains; the fish principle in nature, from which it results that they may be
found in water in so many places, in greater or less
numbers. The natural historian is not a fisherman who
prays for cloudy days and good luck merely; but as
fishing has been styled "a contemplative man's recreation," introducing him profitably to woods and water,
so the fruit of the naturalist's observations is not in new
genera or species, but in new contemplations still, and
science is only a more contemplative man's recreation.
The seeds of the life of fishes are everywhere dissemi-
nated, whether the winds waft them, or the waters float
them, or the deep earth holds them; wherever a pond is
dug, straightway it is stocked with this vivacious race.
They have a lease of nature, and it is not yet out. The
Chinese are bribed to carry their ova from province to
province in jars or in hollow reeds, or the water-birds to
transport them to the mountain tarns and interior lakes.
There are fishes wherever there is a fluid medium, and

even in clouds and in melted metals we detect their semblance. Think how in winter you can sink a line down straight in a pasture through snow and through ice, and pull up a bright, slippery, dumb, subterranean silver or golden fish! It is curious, also, to reflect how they make one family, from the largest to the smallest. The least minnow that lies on the ice as bait for pickerel looks like a huge sea-fish cast up on the shore. In the waters of this town there are about a dozen distinct species, though the inexperienced would expect many more.

It enhances our sense of the grand security and serenity of nature to observe the still undisturbed economy and content of the fishes of this century, their happiness a regular fruit of the summer. The fresh-water sun-fish, bream, or ruff (*Pomotis vulgaris*), as it were without ancestry, without posterity, still represents the fresh-water sun-fish in nature. It is the most common of all, and seen on every urchin's string; a simple and inoffensive fish, whose nests are visible all along the shore, hollowed in the sand, over which it is steadily poised through the summer hours on waving fin. Sometimes there are twenty or thirty nests in the space of a few rods, two feet wide by half a foot in depth, and made with no little labor, the weeds being removed, and the sand shoved up on the sides, like a bowl. Here it may be seen early in summer assiduously brooding, and driving away minnows and larger fishes, even its own species, which would disturb its ova, pursuing them a few feet, and circling round swiftly to its nest again; the minnows, like young sharks, instantly entering the empty nests, meanwhile, and swallowing the spawn, which is attached to the weeds and to the bottom, on the sunny side. The spawn is exposed to so many dangers that a very small proportion can ever become fishes, for beside being the constant prey of birds and fishes, a great many nests are made so near the shore, in shallow water, that they are left dry in a few days, as the river goes down. These and the lamprey's are the only fishes' nests that I have observed, though the ova of some species may be seen floating on the surface. The breams are so careful of their charge that you may stand close by in the water and examine them at your leisure. I have thus stood over them half an hour at a time, and stroked them familiarly without frightening them, suffering them to nibble my fingers harmlessly, and seen them erect their dorsal fins in anger when my hand approached their ova, and have even taken them gently out of the water with my hand; though this cannot be accomplished by a sudden movement, however dexterous, for instant warning is conveyed to them through their denser element, but only by letting the fingers gradually close about them as they are poised over the palm, and with the utmost gentleness raising them slowly to the surface. Though stationary, they kept up a constant sculling or waving motion with their fins, which is exceedingly graceful, and expressive of their humble happiness; for unlike ours, the element in which they live is a stream which must be constantly resisted. From time to time they nibble the weeds at the bottom or overhanging their nests, or dart after a fly or a worm. The dorsal fin, besides answering the purpose of a keel, with the anal, serves to keep the fish upright, for in shallow water, where this is not covered, they fall on their sides. As you stand thus stooping over the bream in its nest, the edges of the dorsal and caudal fins have a singular dusty golden reflection, and its eyes, which stand out from the head, are transparent and colorless. Seen in its native element, it is a very beautiful and compact fish, perfect in all its parts, and looks like a brilliant coin fresh from the mint. It is a perfect jewel of the river, the green, red, coppery, and golden reflections of its mottled sides being the concentration of such rays as struggle through the floating pads and flowers to the sandy bottom, and in harmony with the sunlit brown and yellow pebbles. Behind its watery shield it dwells far from many accidents inevitable to human life.

There is also another species of bream found in our river, without the red spot on the operculum, which, according to M. Agassiz, is undescribed.

The common perch (*Perca flavescens*, which name describes well the gleaming, golden reflections of its scales as it is drawn out of the water, its red gills standing out in vain in the thin element) is one of the handsomest and most regularly formed of our fishes, and at such a moment as this reminds us of the fish in the picture which wished to be restored to its native element until it had grown larger; and indeed most of this species that are caught are not half grown. In the ponds there is a light-colored and slender kind, which swim in shoals of many hundreds in the sunny water, in company with the shiner, averaging not more than six or seven inches in length, while only a few larger specimens are

found in the deepest water, which prey upon their weaker
brethren. I have often attracted these small perch to the
shore at evening, by rippling the water with my fingers,
and they may sometimes be caught while attempting
to pass inside your hands. It is a tough and heedless
fish, biting from impulse, without nibbling, and from
impulse refraining to bite, and sculling indifferently
past. It rather prefers the clear water and sandy bottoms, though here it has not much choice. It is a true
fish, such as the angler loves to put into his basket or
hang at the top of his willow twig, in shady afternoons
along the banks of the stream. So many unquestionable
fishes he counts, and so many shiners, which he counts
and then throws away. Old Josselyn in his " New England's Rarities," published in 1672, mentions the Perch
or River Partridge.

The chivin, dace, roach, cousin trout, or whatever
else it is called (*Leuciscus pulchellus*), white and red, is
always an unexpected prize, which, however, any angler
is glad to hook for its rarity; — a name that reminds us
of many an unsuccessful ramble by swift streams, when
the wind rose to disappoint the fisher. It is commonly a
silvery soft-scaled fish, of graceful, scholarlike, and classical look, like many a picture in an English book. It
loves a swift current and a sandy bottom, and bites inad-
vertently, yet not without appetite for the bait. The
minnows are used as bait for pickerel in the winter. The
red chivin, according to some, is still the same fish, only
older, or with its tints deepened as they think by the
darker water it inhabits, as the red clouds swim in the
twilight atmosphere. He who has not hooked the red

chivin is not yet a complete angler. Other fishes, methinks, are slightly amphibious, but this is a denizen of
the water wholly. The cork goes dancing down the swift-
rushing stream, amid the weeds and sands, when suddenly, by a coincidence never to be remembered, emerges
this fabulous inhabitant of another element, a thing
heard of but not seen, as if it were the instant creation
of an eddy, a true product of the running stream. And
this bright cupreous dolphin was spawned and has
passed its life beneath the level of your feet in your native
fields. Fishes, too, as well as birds and clouds, derive
their armor from the mine. I have heard of mackerel
visiting the copper banks at a particular season; this
fish, perchance, has its habitat in the Coppermine River.
I have caught white chivin of great size in the Aboljack-
nagesic, where it empties into the Penobscot, at the base
of Mount Ktaadn, but no red ones there. The latter
variety seems not to have been sufficiently observed.

The dace (*Leuciscus argenteus*) is a slight silvery
minnow, found generally in the middle of the stream
where the current is most rapid, and frequently confounded with the last named.

The shiner (*Leuciscus chrysoleucus*) is a soft-scaled
and tender fish, the victim of its stronger neighbors,
found in all places, deep and shallow, clear and turbid;
generally the first nibbler at the bait, but, with its small
mouth and nibbling propensities, not easily caught. It is
a gold or silver bit that passes current in the river, its
limber tail dimpling the surface in sport or flight. I have
seen the fry, when frightened by something thrown into
the water, leap out by dozens, together with the dace,

and wreck themselves upon a floating plank. It is
the little light-infant of the river, with body armor of
gold or silver spangles, slipping, gliding its life through
with a quirk of the tail, half in the water, half in the
air, upward and ever upward with flitting fin to more
crystalline tides, yet still abreast of us dwellers on the
bank. It is almost dissolved by the summer heats. A
slighter and lighter-colored shiner is found in one of
our ponds.

The pickerel (*Esox reticulatus*), the swiftest, wariest,
and most ravenous of fishes, which Josselyn calls the
Fresh-Water or River Wolf, is very common in the
shallow and weedy lagoons along the sides of the stream.
It is a solemn, stately, ruminant fish, lurking under the
shadow of a pad at noon, with still, circumspect, vora-
cious eye, motionless as a jewel set in water, or moving
slowly along to take up its position, darting from time
to time at such unlucky fish or frog or insect as comes
within its range, and swallowing it at a gulp. I have
caught one which had swallowed a brother pickerel half
as large as itself, with the tail still visible in its mouth,
while the head was already digested in its stomach.
Sometimes a striped snake, bound to greener meadows
across the stream, ends its undulatory progress in the
same receptacle. They are so greedy and impetuous
that they are frequently caught by being entangled in
the line the moment it is cast. Fishermen also distinguish the brook pickerel, a shorter and thicker fish than
the former.

The horned pout (*Pimelodus nebulosus*), sometimes
called Minister, from the peculiar squeaking noise it

makes when drawn out of the water, is a dull and blun-
dering fellow, and, like the eel, vespertinal in his habits
and fond of the mud. It bites deliberately, as if about its
business. They are taken at night with a mass of worms
strung on a thread, which catches in their teeth, sometimes three or four, with an eel, at one pull. They are
extremely tenacious of life, opening and shutting their
mouths for half an hour after their heads have been cut
off; a bloodthirsty and bullying race of rangers, inhabit-
ing the fertile river bottoms, with ever a lance in rest,
and ready to do battle with their nearest neighbor. I
have observed them in summer, when every other one
had a long and bloody scar upon his back, where the
skin was gone, the mark, perhaps, of some fierce encounter. Sometimes the fry, not an inch long, are seen
darkening the shore with their myriads.

The suckers (*Catostomi Bostonienses* and *tuberculati*),
common and horned, perhaps on an average the largest
of our fishes, may be seen in shoals of a hundred or
more, stemming the current in the sun, on their mysterious migrations, and sometimes sucking in the bait which
the fisherman suffers to float toward them. The former,
which sometimes grow to a large size, are frequently
caught by the hand in the brooks, or like the red chivin
are jerked out by a hook fastened firmly to the end of a
stick, and placed under their jaws. They are hardly
known to the mere angler, however, not often biting at
his baits, though the spearer carries home many a mess
in the spring. To our village eyes, these shoals have a
foreign and imposing aspect, realizing the fertility of the
seas.

The common eel, too (*Murœna Bostoniensis*), the only
species of eel known in the State, a slimy, squirming
creature, informed of mud, still squirming in the pan, is
speared and hooked up with various success. Methinks
it too occurs in picture, left after the deluge, in many a
meadow high and dry.

In the shallow parts of the river, where the current is
rapid and the bottom pebbly, you may sometimes see
the curious circular nests of the lamprey eel (*Petromy-
zon Americanus*), the American stone-sucker, as large
as a cart-wheel, a foot or two in height, and sometimes
rising half a foot above the surface of the water. They
collect these stones, of the size of a hen's egg, with their
mouths, as their name implies, and are said to fashion
them into circles with their tails. They ascend falls by
clinging to the stones, which may sometimes be raised
by lifting the fish by the tail. As they are not seen on
their way down the streams, it is thought by fishermen
that they never return, but waste away and die, clinging
to rocks and stumps of trees for an indefinite period; a
tragic feature in the scenery of the river bottoms worthy
to be remembered with Shakespeare's description of the
sea-floor. They are rarely seen in our waters at present,
on account of the dams, though they are taken in great
quantities at the mouth of the river in Lowell. Their
nests, which are very conspicuous, look more like art
than anything in the river.

If we had leisure this afternoon, we might turn our
prow up the brooks in quest of the classical trout and the
minnows. Of the last alone, according to M. Agassiz,
several of the species found in this town are yet unde-

scribed. These would, perhaps, complete the list of our finny contemporaries in the Concord waters.

Salmon, shad, and alewives were formerly abundant here, and taken in weirs by the Indians, who taught this method to the whites, by whom they were used as food and as manure, until the dam and afterward the canal at Billerica, and the factories at Lowell, put an end to their migrations hitherward; though it is thought that a few more enterprising shad may still occasionally be seen in this part of the river. It is said, to account for the destruction of the fishery, that those who at that time represented the interests of the fishermen and the fishes, remembering between what dates they were accustomed to take the grown shad, stipulated that the dams should be left open for that season only, and the fry, which go down a month later, were consequently stopped and destroyed by myriads. Others say that the fish-ways were not properly constructed. Perchance, after a few thousands of years, if the fishes will be patient, and pass their summers elsewhere meanwhile, nature will have leveled the Billerica dam, and the Lowell factories, and the Grass-ground River run clear again, to be explored by new migratory shoals, even as far as the Hopkinton pond and Westborough swamp.

One would like to know more of that race, now extinct, whose seines lie rotting in the garrets of their children, who openly professed the trade of fishermen, and even fed their townsmen creditably, not skulking through the meadows to a rainy afternoon sport. Dim visions we still get of miraculous draughts of fishes, and heaps uncountable by the riverside, from the tales of

our seniors sent on horseback in their childhood from
the neighboring towns, perched on saddle-bags, with
instructions to get the one bag filled with shad, the other
with alewives. At least one memento of those days may
still exist in the memory of this generation, in the
familiar appellation of a celebrated train-band of this
town, whose untrained ancestors stood creditably at
Concord North Bridge. Their captain, a man of pisca-
tory tastes, having duly warned his company to turn out
on a certain day, they, like obedient soldiers, appeared
promptly on parade at the appointed time, but, unfortunately, they went undrilled, except in the manœuvres
of a soldier's wit and unlicensed jesting, that May day;
for their captain, forgetting his own appointment, and
warned only by the favorable aspect of the heavens, as
he had often done before, went a-fishing that afternoon,
and his company thenceforth was known to old and
young, grave and gay, as "The Shad," and by the youths
of this vicinity this was long regarded as the proper
name of all the irregular militia in Christendom. But,
alas! no record of these fishers' lives remains that we
know, unless it be one brief page of hard but unquestionable history, which occurs in Day Book No. 4, of an
old trader of this town, long since dead, which shows
pretty plainly what constituted a fisherman's stock in
trade in those days. It purports to be a Fisherman's
Account Current, probably for the fishing season of the
year 1805, during which months he purchased daily rum
and sugar, sugar and rum, N. E. and W. I., "one cod
line," "one brown mug," and "a line for the seine;"
rum and sugar, sugar and rum, "good loaf sugar," and

"good brown," W. I. and N. E., in short and uniform
entries to the bottom of the page, all carried out in
pounds, shillings, and pence, from March 25 to June 5,
and promptly settled by receiving "cash in full" at the
last date. But perhaps not so settled altogether. These
were the necessaries of life in those days; with salmon,
shad, and alewives, fresh and pickled, he was thereafter
independent on the groceries. Rather a preponderance
of the fluid elements; but such is the fisherman's nature.
I can faintly remember to have seen this same fisher in
my earliest youth, still as near the river as he could get,
with uncertain, undulatory step, after so many things
had gone down-stream, swinging a scythe in the meadow, his bottle like a serpent hid in the grass; himself
as yet not cut down by the Great Mower.

Surely the fates are forever kind, though Nature's
laws are more immutable than any despot's, yet to man's
daily life they rarely seem rigid, but permit him to relax
with license in summer weather. He is not harshly
reminded of the things he may not do. She is very kind
and liberal to all men of vicious habits, and certainly
does not deny them quarter; they do not die without
priest. Still they maintain life along the way, keeping
this side the Styx, still hearty, still resolute, "never better in their lives;" and again, after a dozen years have
elapsed, they start up from behind a hedge, asking for
work and wages for able-bodied men. Who has not met
such

> "a beggar on the way,
> Who sturdily could gang? . . .
> Who cared neither for wind nor wet,
> In lands where'er he past?"

"That bold adopts each house he views, his own;
Makes every purse his checquer, and, at pleasure,
Walks forth, and taxes all the world, like Cæsar;" —

as if consistency were the secret of health, while the poor
inconsistent aspirant man, seeking to live a pure life,
feeding on air, divided against himself, cannot stand,
but pines and dies after a life of sickness, on beds of
down.

The unwise are accustomed to speak as if some were
not sick; but methinks the difference between men in
respect to health is not great enough to lay much stress
upon. Some are reputed sick and some are not. It
often happens that the sicker man is the nurse to the
sounder.

Shad are still taken in the basin of Concord River,
at Lowell, where they are said to be a month earlier
than the Merrimack shad, on account of the warmth of
the water. Still patiently, almost pathetically, with
instinct not to be discouraged, not to be *reasoned* with,
revisiting their old haunts, as if their stern fates would
relent, and still met by the Corporation with its dam.
Poor shad! where is thy redress? When Nature gave
thee instinct, gave she thee the heart to bear thy fate?
Still wandering the sea in thy scaly armor to inquire
humbly at the mouths of rivers if man has perchance left
them free for thee to enter. By countless shoals loitering
uncertain meanwhile, merely stemming the tide there, in
danger from sea foes in spite of thy bright armor, await-
ing new instructions, until the sands, until the water
itself, tell thee if it be so or not. Thus by whole migrating nations, full of instinct, which is thy faith, in this

backward spring, turned adrift, and perchance knowest
not where men do *not* dwell, where there are *not* factories,
in these days. Armed with no sword, no electric shock,
but mere shad, armed only with innocence and a just
cause, with tender dumb mouth only forward, and scales
easy to be detached. I for one am with thee, and who
knows what may avail a crowbar against that Billerica
dam ? — Not despairing when whole myriads have gone
to feed those sea monsters during thy suspense, but still
brave, indifferent, on easy fin there, like shad reserved
for higher destinies. Willing to be decimated for man's
behoof after the spawning season. Away with the superficial and selfish phil-*anthropy* of men, — who knows
what admirable virtue of fishes may be below low-water-
mark, bearing up against a hard destiny, not admired
by that fellow-creature who alone can appreciate it!
Who hears the fishes when they cry ? It will not be forgotten by some memory that we were contemporaries.
Thou shalt ere long have thy way up the rivers, up all
the rivers of the globe, if I am not mistaken. Yea, even
thy dull watery dream shall be more than realized. If
it were not so, but thou wert to be overlooked at first
and at last, then would not I take their heaven. Yes, I
say so, who think I know better than thou canst. Keep
a stiff fin, then, and stem all the tides thou mayst
meet.

At length it would seem that the interests, not of the
fishes only, but of the men of Wayland, of Sudbury, of
Concord, demand the leveling of that dam. Innumerable acres of meadow are waiting to be made dry land,
wild native grass to give place to English. The farmers

stand with scythes whet, waiting the subsiding of the
waters, by gravitation, by evaporation, or otherwise,
but sometimes their eyes do not rest, their wheels do not
roll, on the quaking meadow ground during the haying
season at all. So many sources of wealth inaccessible.
They rate the loss hereby incurred in the single town of
Wayland alone as equal to the expense of keeping a
hundred yoke of oxen the year round. One year, as I
learn, not long ago, the farmers standing ready to drive
their teams afield as usual, the water gave no signs of
falling; without new attraction in the heavens, without
freshet or visible cause, still standing stagnant at an
unprecedented height. All hydrometers were at fault;
some trembled for their English, even. But speedy emissaries revealed the unnatural secret, in the new float-
board, wholly a foot in width, added to their already too
high privileges by the dam proprietors. The hundred
yoke of oxen, meanwhile, standing patient, gazing wish-
fully meadowward, at that inaccessible waving native
grass, uncut but by the great mower Time, who cuts so
broad a swath, without so much as a wisp to wind about
their horns.

That was a long pull from Ball's Hill to Carlisle
Bridge, sitting with our faces to the south, a slight breeze
rising from the north; but nevertheless water still runs
and grass grows, for now, having passed the bridge between Carlisle and Bedford, we see men haying far off
in the meadow, their heads waving like the grass which
they cut. In the distance the wind seemed to bend all
alike. As the night stole over, such a freshness was

wafted across the meadow that every blade of cut grass
seemed to teem with life. Faint purple clouds began
to be reflected in the water, and the cow-bells tinkled
louder along the banks, while, like sly water-rats, we
stole along nearer the shore, looking for a place to pitch
our camp.

At length, when we had made about seven miles, as
far as Billerica, we moored our boat on the west side of a
little rising ground which in the spring forms an island
in the river. Here we found huckleberries still hanging
upon the bushes, where they seemed to have slowly
ripened for our especial use. Bread and sugar, and cocoa
boiled in river water, made our repast, and as we had
drank in the fluvial prospect all day, so now we took a
draft of the water with our evening meal to propitiate
the river gods, and whet our vision for the sights it was
to behold. The sun was setting on the one hand, while
our eminence was contributing its shadow to the night
on the other. It seemed insensibly to grow lighter as the
night shut in, and a distant and solitary farmhouse was
revealed, which before lurked in the shadows of the
noon. There was no other house in sight, nor any cultivated field. To the right and left, as far as the horizon,
were straggling pine woods with their plumes against the
sky, and across the river were rugged hills, covered with
shrub oaks, tangled with grape-vines and ivy, with here
and there a gray rock jutting out from the maze. The
sides of these cliffs, though a quarter of a mile distant,
were almost heard to rustle while we looked at them, it
was such a leafy wilderness; a place for fauns and
satyrs, and where bats hung all day to the rocks, and at

SATURDAY

their light under the grass and leaves against the night.
When we had pitched our tent on the hillside, a few rods
from the shore, we sat looking through its triangular
door in the twilight at our lonely mast on the shore just
seen above the alders, and hardly yet come to a stand-
still from the swaying of the stream; the first encroach-
ment of commerce on this land. There was our port, our
Ostia. That straight, geometrical line against the water
and the sky stood for the last refinements of civilized
life, and what of sublimity there is in history was there
symbolized.

For the most part, there was no recognition of human
life in the night; no human breathing was heard, only
the breathing of the wind. As we sat up, kept awake
by the novelty of our situation, we heard at intervals
foxes stepping about over the dead leaves, and brushing
the dewy grass close to our tent, and once a musquash
fumbling among the potatoes and melons in our boat;
but when we hastened to the shore we could detect only
a ripple in the water ruffling the disk of a star. At intervals we were serenaded by the song of a dreaming sparrow or the throttled cry of an owl; but after each sound
which near at hand broke the stillness of the night, each
crackling of the twigs, or rustling among the leaves,
there was a sudden pause, and deeper and more conscious silence, as if the intruder were aware that no life
was rightfully abroad at that hour. There was a fire in
Lowell, as we judged, this night, and we saw the horizon
blazing, and heard the distant alarm-bells, as it were a
faint tinkling music borne to these woods. But the most

constant and memorable sound of a summer's night,
which we did not fail to hear every night afterward,
though at no time so incessantly and so favorably as
now, was the barking of the house-dogs, from the loudest
and hoarsest bark to the faintest aerial palpitation under
the eaves of heaven, from the patient but anxious mastiff
to the timid and wakeful terrier, at first loud and rapid,
then faint and slow, to be imitated only in a whisper;
wow-wow-wow-wow — wo — wo — w — w. Even in
a retired and uninhabited district like this, it was a
sufficiency of sound for the ear of night, and more impressive than any music. I have heard the voice of a
hound, just before daylight, while the stars were shining,
from over the woods and river, far in the horizon, when
it sounded as sweet and melodious as an instrument.
The hounding of a dog pursuing a fox or other animal
in the horizon may have first suggested the notes of the
hunting-horn to alternate with and relieve the lungs of
the dog. This natural bugle long resounded in the woods
of the ancient world before the horn was invented. The
very dogs that sullenly bay the moon from farm-yards
in these nights excite more heroism in our breasts than
all the civil exhortations or war sermons of the age. "I
would rather be a dog, and bay the moon," than many
a Roman that I know. The night is equally indebted
to the clarion of the cock, with wakeful hope, from the
very setting of the sun, prematurely ushering in the
dawn. All these sounds, the crowing of cocks, the baying
of dogs, and the hum of insects at noon, are the evidence
of nature's health or *sound* state. Such is the never-
failing beauty and accuracy of language, the most per-

fect art in the world; the chisel of a thousand years
retouches it.

At length the antepenultimate and drowsy hours drew
on, and all sounds were denied entrance to our ears.

> Who sleeps by day and walks by night,
> Will meet no spirit, but some sprite.

SUNDAY

The river calmly flows,
Through shining banks, through lonely glen,
Where the owl shrieks, though ne'er the cheer of men
Has stirred its mute repose,
Still if you should walk there, you would go there again.

CHANNING.

The Indians tell us of a beautiful river lying far to the south, which they call Merrimack. — SIEUR DE MONTS, *Relations of the Jesuits*, 1604.

IN the morning the river and adjacent country were covered with a dense fog, through which the smoke of our fire curled up like a still subtiler mist; but before we had rowed many rods, the sun arose and the fog rapidly dispersed, leaving a slight steam only to curl along the surface of the water. It was a quiet Sunday morning, with more of the auroral rosy and white than of the yellow light in it, as if it dated from earlier than the fall of man, and still preserved a heathenish integrity: —

An early unconverted Saint,
Free from noontide or evening taint,
Heathen without reproach,
That did upon the civil day encroach,
And ever since its birth
Had trod the outskirts of the earth.

But the impressions which the morning makes vanish with its dews, and not even the most "persevering mortal" can preserve the memory of its freshness to midday.

As we passed the various islands, or what were islands in the spring, rowing with our backs down-stream, we gave names to them. The one on which we had camped we called Fox Island, and one fine densely wooded island surrounded by deep water and overrun by grape-vines, which looked like a mass of verdure and of flowers cast upon the waves, we named Grape Island. From Ball's Hill to Billerica meeting-house, the river was still twice as broad as in Concord, a deep, dark, and dead stream, flowing between gentle hills and sometimes cliffs, and well wooded all the way. It was a long woodland lake bordered with willows. For long reaches we could see neither house nor cultivated field, nor any sign of the vicinity of man. Now we coasted along some shallow shore by the edge of a dense palisade of bulrushes, which straightly bounded the water as if clipped by art, reminding us of the reed forts of the East-Indians of which we had read; and now the bank, slightly raised, was overhung with graceful grasses and various species of brake, whose downy stems stood closely grouped and naked as in a vase, while their heads spread several feet on either side. The dead limbs of the willow were rounded and adorned by the climbing mikania (*Mikania scandens*), which filled every crevice in the leafy bank, contrasting agreeably with the gray bark of its supporter and the balls of the button-bush. The water willow (*Salix Purshiana*), when it is of large size and entire, is the most graceful and ethereal of our trees. Its masses of light-green foliage, piled one upon another to the height of twenty or thirty feet, seemed to float on the surface of the water, while the slight gray stems and the shore were hardly visible between them. No tree is so wedded to the water, and harmonizes so well with still streams. It is even more graceful than the weeping willow, or any pendulous trees which dip their branches in the stream instead of being buoyed up by it. Its limbs curved outward over the surface as if attracted by it. It had not a New England but an Oriental character, reminding us of trim Persian gardens, of Haroun Alraschid, and the artificial lakes of the East.

As we thus dipped our way along between fresh masses of foliage overrun with the grape and smaller flowering vines, the surface was so calm, and both air and water so transparent, that the flight of a kingfisher or robin over the river was as distinctly seen reflected in the water below as in the air above. The birds seemed to flit through submerged groves, alighting on the yielding sprays, and their clear notes to come up from below. We were uncertain whether the water floated the land, or the land held the water in its bosom. It was such a season, in short, as that in which one of our Concord poets sailed on its stream, and sung its quiet glories.

> "There is an inward voice, that in the stream
> Sends forth its spirit to the listening ear,
> And in a calm content it floweth on,
> Like wisdom, welcome with its own respect.
> Clear in its breast lie all these beauteous thoughts,
> It doth receive the green and graceful trees,
> And the gray rocks smile in its peaceful arms."

And more he sung, but too serious for our page. For every oak and birch, too, growing on the hilltop, as well as for these elms and willows, we knew that there was a graceful ethereal and ideal tree making down from the roots, and sometimes Nature in high tides brings her mirror to its foot and makes it visible. The stillness was intense and almost conscious, as if it were a natural Sabbath, and we fancied that the morning was the evening of a celestial day. The air was so elastic and crystalline that it had the same effect on the landscape that a glass has on a picture, to give it an ideal remoteness and perfection. The landscape was clothed in a mild and quiet light, in which the woods and fences checkered and partitioned it with new regularity, and rough and uneven fields stretched away with lawn-like smoothness to the horizon, and the clouds, finely distinct and picturesque, seemed a fit drapery to hang over fairyland. The world seemed decked for some holiday or prouder pageantry, with silken streamers flying, and the course of our lives to wind on before us like a green lane into a country maze, at the season when fruit-trees are in blossom.

Why should not our whole life and its scenery be actually thus fair and distinct? All our lives want a suitable background. They should at least, like the life of the anchorite, be as impressive to behold as objects in the desert, a broken shaft or crumbling mound against a limitless horizon. Character always secures for itself this advantage, and is thus distinct and unrelated to near or trivial objects, whether things or persons. On this same stream a maiden once sailed in my boat, thus unattended but by invisible guardians, and as she sat in the prow there was nothing but herself between the steersman and the sky. I could then say with the poet, —

"Sweet falls the summer air
Over her frame who sails with me;
Her way like that is beautifully free,
Her nature far more rare,
And is her constant heart of virgin purity."

At evening, still the very stars seem but this maiden's emissaries and reporters of her progress.

Low in the eastern sky
Is set thy glancing eye;
And though its gracious light
Ne'er riseth to my sight,
Yet every star that climbs
Above the gnarled limbs
    Of yonder hill,
Conveys thy gentle will.

Believe I knew thy thought,
And that the zephyrs brought
Thy kindest wishes through,
As mine they bear to you,
That some attentive cloud
Did pause amid the crowd
    Over my head,
While gentle things were said.

Believe the thrushes sung,
And that the flower-bells rung,
That herbs exhaled their scent,
And beasts knew what was meant,
The trees a welcome waved,
And lakes their margins laved,
    When thy free mind
To my retreat did wind.

It was a summer eve,
The air did gently heave

While yet a low-hung cloud
Thy eastern skies did shroud ;
The lightning's silent gleam,
Startling my drowsy dream,
    Seemed like the flash
Under thy dark eyelash.

Still will I strive to be
As if thou wert with me ;
Whatever path I take,
It shall be for thy sake,
Of gentle slope and wide,
As thou wert by my side,
    Without a root
To trip thy gentle foot.

I 'll walk with gentle pace,
And choose the smoothest place,
And careful dip the oar,
And shun the winding shore,
And gently steer my boat
Where water-lilies float,
    And cardinal-flowers
Stand in their sylvan bowers.

It required some rudeness to disturb with our boat the mirror-like surface of the water, in which every twig and blade of grass was so faithfully reflected; too faithfully indeed for art to imitate, for only Nature may exaggerate herself. The shallowest still water is unfathomable. Wherever the trees and skies are reflected, there is more than Atlantic depth, and no danger of fancy running aground. We notice that it required a separate intention of the eye, a more free and abstracted vision, to see the reflected trees and the sky, than to see the river bottom merely; and so are there manifold

visions in the direction of every object, and even the most
opaque reflect the heavens from their surface. Some
men have their eyes naturally intended to the one and
some to the other object.

> "A man that looks on glass,
>   On it may stay his eye,
>   Or, if he pleaseth, through it pass,
>   And the heavens espy."

Two men in a skiff, whom we passed hereabouts,
floating buoyantly amid the reflections of the trees, like
a feather in mid-air, or a leaf which is wafted gently from
its twig to the water without turning over, seemed still in
their element, and to have very delicately availed themselves of the natural laws. Their floating there was a
beautiful and successful experiment in natural philosophy, and it served to ennoble in our eyes the art of navigation; for as birds fly and fishes swim, so these men
sailed. It reminded us how much fairer and nobler all
the actions of man might be, and that our life in its
whole economy might be as beautiful as the fairest works
of art or nature.

The sun lodged on the old gray cliffs, and glanced
from every pad; the bulrushes and flags seemed to rejoice in the delicious light and air; the meadows were
a-drinking at their leisure; the frogs sat meditating, all
Sabbath thoughts, summing up their week, with one eye
out on the golden sun, and one toe upon a reed, eying
the wondrous universe in which they act their part; the
fishes swam more staid and soberly, as maidens go to
church; shoals of golden and silver minnows rose to the
surface to behold the heavens, and then sheered off into

more sombre aisles; they swept by as if moved by one
mind, continually gliding past each other, and yet preserving the form of their battalion unchanged, as if they
were still embraced by the transparent membrane which
held the spawn; a young band of brethren and sisters
trying their new fins; now they wheeled, now shot
ahead, and when we drove them to the shore and cut
them off, they dexterously tacked and passed under-
neath the boat. Over the old wooden bridges no traveler
crossed, and neither the river nor the fishes avoided to
glide between the abutments.

Here was a village not far off behind the woods,
Billerica, settled not long ago, and the children still
bear the names of the first settlers in this late "howling
wilderness;" yet to all intents and purposes it is as old
as Fernay or as Mantua, an old gray town where men
grow old and sleep already under moss-grown monuments, — outgrow their usefulness. This is ancient Billerica (Villarica?), now in its dotage, named from the
English Billericay, and whose Indian name was Shaw-
shine. I never heard that it was young. See, is not
nature here gone to decay, farms all run out, meeting-
house grown gray and racked with age? If you would
know of its early youth, ask those old gray rocks in the
pasture. It has a bell that sounds sometimes as far as
Concord woods; I have heard that, — ay, hear it now.
No wonder that such a sound startled the dreaming
Indian, and frightened his game, when the first bells
were swung on trees, and sounded through the forest
beyond the plantations of the white man; but to-day I
like best the echo amid these cliffs and woods. It is no

feeble imitation, but rather its original, or as if some rural Orpheus played over the strain again to show how it should sound.

> Dong, sounds the brass in the east,
> As if to a funeral feast,
> But I like that sound the best
> Out of the fluttering west.
>
> The steeple ringeth a knell,
> But the fairies' silvery bell
> Is the voice of that gentle folk,
> Or else the horizon that spoke.
>
> Its metal is not of brass,
> But air, and water, and glass,
> And under a cloud it is swung,
> And by the wind it is rung.
>
> When the steeple tolleth the noon,
> It soundeth not so soon,
> Yet it rings a far earlier hour,
> And the sun has not reached its tower.

On the other hand, the road runs up to Carlisle, city of the woods, which, if it is less civil, is the more natural. It does well hold the earth together. It gets laughed at because it is a small town, I know, but nevertheless it is a place where great men may be born any day, for fair winds and foul blow right on over it without distinction. It has a meeting-house and horse-sheds, a tavern and a blacksmith's shop, for centre, and a good deal of wood to cut and cord yet. And

> "Bedford, most noble Bedford,
> I shall not thee forget."

History has remembered thee; especially that meek and

humble petition of thy old planters, like the wailing of the
Lord's own people, "To the gentlemen, the selectmen"
of Concord, praying to be erected into a separate parish.
We can hardly credit that so plaintive a psalm resounded
but little more than a century ago along these Baby-
lonish waters. "In the extreme difficult seasons of heat
and cold," said they, "we were ready to say of the Sabbath, Behold what a weariness is it." "Gentlemen, if
our seeking to draw off proceed from any disaffection
to our present Reverend Pastor, or the Christian Society
with whom we have taken such sweet counsel together,
and walked unto the house of God in company, then hear
us not this day; but we greatly desire, if God please,
to be eased of our burden on the Sabbath, the travel and
fatigue thereof, that the word of God may be nigh to us,
near to our houses and in our hearts, that we and our
little ones may serve the Lord. We hope that God, who
stirred up the spirit of Cyrus to set forward temple work,
has stirred us up to ask, and will stir you up to grant, the
prayer of our petition; so shall your humble petitioners
ever pray, as in duty bound" — And so the temple
work went forward here to a happy conclusion. Yonder
in Carlisle the building of the temple was many wearisome years delayed, not that there was wanting of Shit-
tim wood, or the gold of Ophir, but a site therefor convenient to all the worshipers; whether on "Buttrick's
Plain," or rather on "Poplar Hill." It was a tedious
question.

In this Billerica solid men must have lived, select from
year to year; a series of town clerks, at least; and there
are old records that you may search. Some spring the

white man came, built him a house, and made a clearing here, letting in the sun, dried up a farm, piled up the old gray stones in fences, cut down the pines around his dwelling, planted orchard seeds brought from the old country, and persuaded the civil apple-tree to blossom next to the wild pine and the juniper, shedding its perfume in the wilderness. Their old stocks still remain. He culled the graceful elm from out the woods and from the riverside, and so refined and smoothed his village plot. He rudely bridged the stream, and drove his team afield into the river meadows, cut the wild grass, and laid bare the homes of beaver, otter, muskrat, and with the whetting of his scythe scared off the deer and bear. He set up a mill, and fields of English grain sprang in the virgin soil. And with his grain he scattered the seeds of the dandelion and the wild trefoil over the meadows, mingling his English flowers with the wild native ones. The bristling burdock, the sweet-scented catnip, and the humble yarrow planted themselves along his woodland road, they, too, seeking "freedom to worship God" in their way. And thus he plants a town. The white man's mullein soon reigned in Indian corn-fields, and sweet-scented English grasses clothed the new soil. Where, then, could the red man set his foot? The honey-bee hummed through the Massachusetts woods, and sipped the wild-flowers round the Indian's wigwam, perchance unnoticed, when, with prophetic warning, it stung the red child's hand, forerunner of that industrious tribe that was to come and pluck the wild-flower of his race up by the root.

The white man comes, pale as the dawn, with a load

of thought, with a slumbering intelligence as a fire raked
up, knowing well what he knows, not guessing but cal-
culating; strong in community, yielding obedience to
authority; of experienced race; of wonderful, wonderful common sense; dull but capable, slow but persevering, severe but just, of little humor but genuine; a laboring man, despising game and sport; building a house
that endures, a framed house. He buys the Indian's
moccasins and baskets, then buys his hunting-grounds,
and at length forgets where he is buried and plows up
his bones. And here town records, old, tattered, time-
worn, weather-stained chronicles, contain the Indian
sachem's mark perchance, an arrow or a beaver, and the
few fatal words by which he deeded his hunting-grounds
away. He comes with a list of ancient Saxon, Norman,
and Celtic names, and strews them up and down this
river, — Framingham, Sudbury, Bedford, Carlisle, Billerica, Chelmsford, — and this is New Angle-land, and
these are the New West Saxons, whom the red men
call, not Angle-ish or English, but Yengeese, and so at
last they are known for Yankees.

When we were opposite to the middle of Billerica, the
fields on either hand had a soft and cultivated English
aspect, the village spire being seen over the copses which
skirt the river, and sometimes an orchard straggled
down to the water-side, though, generally, our course
this forenoon was the wildest part of our voyage. It
seemed that men led a quiet and very civil life there.
The inhabitants were plainly cultivators of the earth,
and lived under an organized political government.
The schoolhouse stood with a meek aspect, entreating a

long truce to war and savage life. Every one finds by
his own experience, as well as in history, that the era in
which men cultivate the apple, and the amenities of the
garden, is essentially different from that of the hunter
and forest life, and neither can displace the other without
loss. We have all had our day-dreams, as well as more
prophetic nocturnal vision; but as for farming, I am
convinced that my genius dates from an older era than
the agricultural. I would at least strike my spade into
the earth with such careless freedom but accuracy as the
woodpecker his bill into a tree. There is in my nature,
methinks, a singular yearning toward all wildness. I
know of no redeeming qualities in myself but a sincere
love for some things, and when I am reproved I fall back
on to this ground. What have I to do with plows? I
cut another furrow than you see. Where the off ox
treads, there is it not, it is farther off; where the nigh ox
walks, it will not be, it is nigher still. If corn fails, my
crop fails not, and what are drought and rain to me?
The rude Saxon pioneer will sometimes pine for that
refinement and artificial beauty which are English, and
love to hear the sound of such sweet and classical names
as the Pentland and Malvern Hills, the Cliffs of Dover
and the Trosachs, Richmond, Derwent, and Winander-
mere, which are to him now instead of the Acropolis and
Parthenon, of Baiæ, and Athens, with its sea-walls, and
Arcadia and Tempe.

> Greece, who am I that should remember thee,
> Thy Marathon and thy Thermopylæ?
> Is my life vulgar, my fate mean,
> Which on these golden memories can lean?

We are apt enough to be pleased with such books as
Evelyn's Sylva, Actearium, and Kalendarium Hortense,
but they imply a relaxed nerve in the reader. Gardening
is civil and social, but it wants the vigor and freedom of
the forest and the outlaw. There may be an excess of
cultivation as well as of anything else, until civilization
becomes pathetic. A highly cultivated man, — all whose
bones can be bent! whose heaven-born virtues are but
good manners! The young pines springing up in the
corn-fields from year to year are to me a refreshing fact.
We talk of civilizing the Indian, but that is not the name
for his improvement. By the wary independence and
aloofness of his dim forest life he preserves his intercourse with his native gods, and is admitted from time
to time to a rare and peculiar society with Nature. He
has glances of starry recognition to which our saloons
are strangers. The steady illumination of his genius,
dim only because distant, is like the faint but satisfying
light of the stars compared with the dazzling but ineffectual and short-lived blaze of candles. The Society-
Islanders had their day-born gods, but they were not
supposed to be "of equal antiquity with the *atua fauau
po*, or night-born gods." It is true, there are the innocent
pleasures of country life, and it is sometimes pleasant to
make the earth yield her increase, and gather the fruits
in their season; but the heroic spirit will not fail to
dream of remoter retirements and more rugged paths.
It will have its garden-plots and its *parterres* elsewhere
than on the earth, and gather nuts and berries by the
way for its subsistence, or orchard fruits with such
heedlessness as berries. We would not always be sooth-

ing and taming nature, breaking the horse and the ox,
but sometimes ride the horse wild and chase the buffalo.
The Indian's intercourse with Nature is at least such as
admits of the greatest independence of each. If he is
somewhat of a stranger in her midst, the gardener is too
much of a familiar. There is something vulgar and foul
in the latter's closeness to his mistress, something noble
and cleanly in the former's distance. In civilization, as
in a southern latitude, man degenerates at length, and
yields to the incursion of more northern tribes, —

> "Some nation yet shut in
> With hills of ice."

There are other, savager and more primeval aspects of
nature than our poets have sung. It is only white man's
poetry. Homer and Ossian even can never revive in
London or Boston. And yet, behold how these cities are
refreshed by the mere tradition, or the imperfectly transmitted fragrance and flavor of these wild fruits. If we
could listen but for an instant to the chant of the Indian
muse, we should understand why he will not exchange
his savageness for civilization. Nations are not whimsical. Steel and blankets are strong temptations; but the
Indian does well to continue Indian.

After sitting in my chamber many days, reading the
poets, I have been out early on a foggy morning and
heard the cry of an owl in a neighboring wood as from
a nature behind the common, unexplored by science or
by literature. None of the feathered race has yet realized
my youthful conceptions of the woodland depths. I had
seen the red Election-birds brought from their recesses
on my comrades' string, and fancied that their plumage

would assume stranger and more dazzling colors, like the tints of evening, in proportion as I advanced farther into the darkness and solitude of the forest. Still less have I seen such strong and wilderness tints on any poet's string.

These modern ingenious sciences and arts do not affect me as those more venerable arts of hunting and fishing, and even of husbandry in its primitive and simple form; as ancient and honorable trades as the sun and moon and winds pursue, coeval with the faculties of man, and invented when these were invented. We do not know their John Gutenberg, or Richard Arkwright, though the poets would fain make them to have been gradually learned and taught. According to Gower, —

> " And Iadahel, as saith the boke,
>   Firste made nette, fishes toke.
> Of huntyng eke he fond the chace,
> Whiche nowe is knowe in many place ;
> A tent of clothe, with corde and stake,
> He sette up first, and did it make."

Also, Lydgate says: —

> "Jason first sayled, in story it is tolde,
> Toward Colchos, to wynne the flees of golde,
> Ceres the Goddess fond first the tilthe of londe ;
> . . . .
> Also, Aristeus fonde first the usage
> Of mylke, and cruddis, and of honey swote ;
> Peryodes, for grete avauntage,
> From flyntes smote fuyre, daryng in the roote."

We read that Aristeus "obtained of Jupiter and Neptune, that the pestilential heat of the dog-days, wherein was great mortality, should be mitigated with

wind." This is one of those dateless benefits conferred
on man which have no record in our vulgar day, though
we still find some similitude to them in our dreams, in
which we have a more liberal and juster apprehension
of things, unconstrained by habit, which is then in some
measure put off, and divested of memory, which we call
history.

According to fable, when the island of Ægina was
depopulated by sickness, at the instance of Æacus, Jupiter turned the ants into men, that is, as some think,
he made men of the inhabitants who lived meanly like
ants. This is perhaps the fullest history of those early
days extant.

The fable, which is naturally and truly composed, so
as to satisfy the imagination, ere it addresses the understanding, beautiful though strange as a wild-flower, is to
the wise man an apothegm, and admits of his most generous interpretation. When we read that Bacchus made
the Tyrrhenian mariners mad, so that they leaped into
the sea, mistaking it for a meadow full of flowers, and
so became dolphins, we are not concerned about the historical truth of this, but rather a higher poetical truth.
We seem to hear the music of a thought, and care not
if the understanding be not gratified. For their beauty,
consider the fables of Narcissus, of Endymion, of Memnon son of Morning, the representative of all promising
youths who have died a premature death, and whose
memory is melodiously prolonged to the latest morning;
the beautiful stories of Phaethon, and of the Sirens whose
isle shone afar off white with the bones of unburied men;

and the pregnant ones of Pan, Prometheus, and the
Sphinx; and that long list of names which have already
become part of the universal language of civilized men,
and from proper are becoming common names or nouns,
— the Sibyls, the Eumenides, the Parcæ, the Graces,
the Muses, Nemesis, etc.

It is interesting to observe with what singular unanim-
ity the farthest sundered nations and generations consent
to give completeness and roundness to an ancient fable,
of which they indistinctly appreciate the beauty or the
truth. By a faint and dream-like effort, though it be
only by the vote of a scientific body, the dullest posterity
slowly add some trait to the mythus. As when astronomers call the lately discovered planet Neptune; or the
asteroid Astræa, that the Virgin who was driven from
earth to heaven at the end of the golden age may have
her local habitation in the heavens more distinctly
assigned her, — for the slightest recognition of poetic
worth is significant. By such slow aggregation has
mythology grown from the first. The very nursery tales
of this generation were the nursery tales of primeval
races. They migrate from east to west, and again from
west to east; now expanded into the "tale divine" of
bards, now shrunk into a popular rhyme. This is an
approach to that universal language which men have
sought in vain. This fond reiteration of the oldest expressions of truth by the latest posterity, content with
slightly and religiously retouching the old material, is the
most impressive proof of a common humanity.

All nations love the same jests and tales, Jews, Christians, and Mahometans, and the same translated suffice

for all. All men are children, and of one family. The same tale sends them all to bed, and wakes them in the morning. Joseph Wolff, the missionary, distributed copies of Robinson Crusoe, translated into Arabic, among the Arabs, and they made a great sensation. "Robinson Crusoe's adventures and wisdom," says he, "were read by Mahometans in the market-places of Sanaa, Hodyeda, and Loheya, and admired and believed!" On reading the book, the Arabians exclaimed, "Oh, that Robinson Crusoe must have been a great prophet!"

To some extent, mythology is only the most ancient history and biography. So far from being false or fabulous in the common sense, it contains only enduring and essential truth, the I and you, the here and there, the now and then, being omitted. Either time or rare wisdom writes it. Before printing was discovered, a century was equal to a thousand years. The poet is he who can write some pure mythology to-day without the aid of posterity. In how few words, for instance, the Greeks would have told the story of Abelard and Heloise, making but a sentence for our classical dictionary, — and then, perchance, have stuck up their names to shine in some corner of the firmament. We moderns, on the other hand, collect only the raw materials of biography and history, "memoirs to serve for a history," which itself is but materials to serve for a mythology. How many volumes folio would the Life and Labors of Prometheus have filled, if perchance it had fallen, as perchance it did first, in days of cheap printing! Who knows what shape the fable of Columbus will at length assume, to be confounded with that of Jason and the

expedition of the Argonauts. And Franklin, — there
may be a line for him in the future classical dictionary,
recording what that demigod did, and referring him to
some new genealogy. "Son of —— and ——. He aided
the Americans to gain their independence, instructed
mankind in economy, and drew down lightning from the
clouds."

The hidden significance of these fables which is sometimes thought to have been detected, the ethics running
parallel to the poetry and history, are not so remarkable
as the readiness with which they may be made to express
a variety of truths. As if they were the skeletons of still
older and more universal truths than any whose flesh
and blood they are for the time made to wear. It is like
striving to make the sun, or the wind, or the sea symbols
to signify exclusively the particular thoughts of our day.
But what signifies it? In the mythus a superhuman intelligence uses the unconscious thoughts and dreams of
men as its hieroglyphics to address men unborn. In the
history of the human mind, these glowing and ruddy
fables precede the noonday thoughts of men, as Aurora
the sun's rays. The matutine intellect of the poet, keeping in advance of the glare of philosophy, always dwells
in this auroral atmosphere.

As we said before, the Concord is a dead stream, but
its scenery is the more suggestive to the contemplative
voyager, and this day its water was fuller of reflections
than our pages even. Just before it reaches the falls in
Billerica, it is contracted, and becomes swifter and shallower, with a yellow pebbly bottom, hardly passable for a

canal-boat, leaving the broader and more stagnant portion above like a lake among the hills. All through the
Concord, Bedford, and Billerica meadows we had heard
no murmur from its stream, except where some tributary
runnel tumbled in, —

> Some tumultuous little rill,
>   Purling round its storied pebble,
> Tinkling to the selfsame tune,
> From September until June,
>   Which no drought doth e'er enfeeble.
>
> Silent flows the parent stream,
>   And if rocks do lie below,
> Smothers with her waves the din,
> As it were a youthful sin,
>   Just as still, and just as slow.

But now at length we heard this staid and primitive
river rushing to her fall, like any rill. We here left its
channel, just above the Billerica Falls, and entered the
canal, which runs, or rather is conducted, six miles
through the woods to the Merrimack, at Middlesex; and
as we did not care to loiter in this part of our voyage,
while one ran along the tow-path drawing the boat by a
cord, the other kept it off the shore with a pole, so that
we accomplished the whole distance in little more than
an hour. This canal, which is the oldest in the country,
and has even an antique look beside the more modern
railroads, is fed by the Concord, so that we were still
floating on its familiar waters. It is so much water which
the river *lets* for the advantage of commerce. There
appeared some want of harmony in its scenery, since it
was not of equal date with the woods and meadows
through which it is led, and we missed the conciliatory

influence of time on land and water; but in the lapse
of ages, Nature will recover and indemnify herself, and
gradually plant fit shrubs and flowers along its borders.
Already the kingfisher sat upon a pine over the water,
and the bream and pickerel swam below. Thus all works
pass directly out of the hands of the architect into the
hands of Nature, to be perfected.

It was a retired and pleasant route, without houses
or travelers, except some young men who were lounging
upon a bridge in Chelmsford, who leaned impudently
over the rails to pry into our concerns, but we caught the
eye of the most forward, and looked at him till he was
visibly discomfited. Not that there was any peculiar
efficacy in our look, but rather a sense of shame left in
him which disarmed him.

It is a very true and expressive phrase, "He looked
daggers at me," for the first pattern and prototype of all
daggers must have been a glance of the eye. First, there
was the glance of Jove's eye, then his fiery bolt; then,
the material gradually hardening, tridents, spears,
javelins; and finally, for the convenience of private
men, daggers, krisses, and so forth, were invented. It is
wonderful how we get about the streets without being
wounded by these delicate and glancing weapons, a man
can so nimbly whip out his rapier, or without being
noticed carry it unsheathed. Yet it is rare that one gets
'eriously looked at.

As we passed under the last bridge over the canal,
just before reaching the Merrimack, the people coming
out of church paused to look at us from above, and
apparently, so strong is custom, indulged in some

heathenish comparisons; but we were the truest observers of this sunny day. According to Hesiod, —

> "The seventh is a holy day,
> For then Latona brought forth golden-rayed Apollo,"

and by our reckoning this was the seventh day of the
week, and not the first. I find among the papers of an
old Justice of the Peace and Deacon of the town of
Concord, this singular memorandum, which is worth
preserving as a relic of an ancient custom. After reform-
ing the spelling and grammar, it runs as follows: "Men
that traveled with teams on the Sabbath, December 18,
1803, were Jeremiah Richardson and Jonas Parker,
both of Shirley. They had teams with rigging such as is
used to carry barrels, and they were traveling westward.
Richardson was questioned by the Hon. Ephraim Wood,
Esq., and he said that Jonas Parker was his fellow-
traveler, and he further said that a Mr. Longley was his
employer, who promised to bear him out." We were the
men that were gliding northward, this September 1,
1839, with still team, and rigging not the most convenient to carry barrels, unquestioned by any squire or
church deacon, and ready to bear ourselves out if need
were. In the latter part of the seventeenth century,
according to the historian of Dunstable, "Towns were
directed to erect ' *a cage* ' near the meeting-house, and
in this all offenders against the sanctity of the Sabbath
were confined." Society has relaxed a little from its
strictness, one would say, but I presume that there is
not less *religion* than formerly. If the *ligature* is found
to be loosened in one part, it is only drawn the tighter in
another.

You can hardly convince a man of an error in a lifetime, but must content yourself with the reflection that
the progress of science is slow. If he is not convinced,
his grandchildren may be. The geologists tell us that it
took one hundred years to prove that fossils are organic,
and one hundred and fifty more to prove that they are
not to be referred to the Noachian deluge. I am not sure
but I should betake myself in extremities to the liberal
divinities of Greece, rather than to my country's God.
Jehovah, though with us he has acquired new attributes,
is more absolute and unapproachable, but hardly more
divine, than Jove. He is not so much of a gentleman, not
so gracious and catholic, he does not exert so intimate
and genial an influence on nature, as many a god of the
Greeks. I should fear the infinite power and inflexible
justice of the almighty mortal hardly as yet apotheosized,
so wholly masculine, with no sister Juno, no Apollo, no
Venus, nor Minerva, to intercede for me, θυμῷ φιλέουσά
τε, κηδομένη τε. The Grecian are youthful and erring
and fallen gods, with the vices of men, but in many
important respects essentially of the divine race. In my
Pantheon, Pan still reigns in his pristine glory, with his
ruddy face, his flowing beard, and his shaggy body, his
pipe and his crook, his nymph Echo, and his chosen
daughter Iambe; for the great god Pan is not dead, as
was rumored. No god ever dies. Perhaps of all the gods
of New England and of ancient Greece, I am most constant at his shrine.

It seems to me that the god that is commonly worshiped in civilized countries is not at all divine, though
he bears a divine name, but is the overwhelming author-

ity and respectability of mankind combined. Men
reverence one another, not yet God. If I thought that I
could speak with discrimination and impartiality of the
nations of Christendom, I should praise them, but it
tasks me too much. They seem to be the most civil and
humane, but I may be mistaken. Every people have
gods to suit their circumstances; the Society Islanders
had a god called Toahitu, "in shape like a dog; he saved
such as were in danger of falling from rocks and trees."
I think that we can do without him, as we have not much
climbing to do. Among them a man could make himself
a god out of a piece of wood in a few minutes, which
would frighten him out of his wits.

I fancy that some indefatigable spinster of the old
school, who had the supreme felicity to be born in "days
that tried men's souls," hearing this, may say with
Nestor, another of the old school, "But you are younger
than I. For time was when I conversed with greater men
than you. For not at any time have I seen such men,
nor shall see them, as Perithous, and Dryas, and ποιμένα
λαῶν," that is probably Washington, sole "Shepherd of
the People." And when Apollo has now six times rolled
westward, or seemed to roll, and now for the seventh
time shows his face in the east, eyes wellnigh glazed, long
glassed, which have fluctuated only between lamb's wool
and worsted, explore ceaselessly some good sermon
book. For six days shalt thou labor and do all thy knit-
ting, but on the seventh, forsooth, thy reading. Happy
we who can bask in this warm September sun, which
illumines all creatures, as well when they rest as when
they toil, not without a feeling of gratitude; whose life is

as blameless, how blameworthy soever it may be, on the Lord's Mona-day as on his Suna-day.

There are various, nay, incredible faiths; why should we be alarmed at any of them? What man believes, God believes. Long as I have lived, and many blasphemers as I have heard and seen, I have never yet heard or witnessed any direct and conscious blasphemy or irreverence; but of indirect and habitual, enough. Where is the man who is guilty of direct and personal insolence to Him that made him?

One memorable addition to the old mythology is due to this era, — the Christian fable. With what pains, and tears, and blood these centuries have woven this and added it to the mythology of mankind! The new Prometheus. With what miraculous consent, and patience, and persistency has this mythus been stamped on the memory of the race! It would seem as if it were in the progress of our mythology to dethrone Jehovah, and crown Christ in his stead.

If it is not a tragical life we live, then I know not what to call it. Such a story as that of Jesus Christ, — the history of Jerusalem, say, being a part of the Universal History. The naked, the embalmed, unburied death of Jerusalem amid its desolate hills, — think of it. In Tasso's poem I trust some things are sweetly buried. Consider the snappish tenacity with which they preach Christianity still. What are time and space to Christianity, eighteen hundred years, and a new world? — that the humble life of a Jewish peasant should have force to make a New York bishop so bigoted. Forty-four lamps, the gift of kings, now burning in a place called

the Holy Sepulchre; a church-bell ringing; some unaf-
fected tears shed by a pilgrim on Mount Calvary within
the week.

"Jerusalem, Jerusalem, when I forget thee, may my
right hand forget her cunning."

"By the waters of Babylon there we sat down, and
we wept when we remembered Zion."

I trust that some may be as near and dear to Buddha,
or Christ, or Swedenborg, who are without the pale of
their churches. It is necessary not to be Christian to
appreciate the beauty and significance of the life of
Christ. I know that some will have hard thoughts of me,
when they hear their Christ named beside my Buddha,
yet I am sure that I am willing they should love their
Christ more than my Buddha, for the love is the main
thing, and I like him too. "God is the letter Ku, as well
as Khu." Why need Christians be still intolerant and
superstitious? The simple-minded sailors were unwilling
to cast overboard Jonah at his own request.

> "Where is this love become in later age?
> Alas! 't is gone in endless pilgrimage
> From hence, and never to return, I doubt,
> Till revolution wheel those times about."

One man says, —

> "The worlde 's a popular disease, that reigns
> Within the froward heart and frantic brains
> Of poor distempered mortals."

Another, that

> "all the world 's a stage,
> And all the men and women merely players."

The world is a strange place for a playhouse to stand

within it. Old Drayton thought that a man that lived here, and would be a poet, for instance, should have in him certain "brave, translunary things," and a "fine madness" should possess his brain. Certainly it were as well, that he might be up to the occasion. That is a superfluous wonder, which Dr. Johnson expresses at the assertion of Sir Thomas Browne that "his life has been a miracle of thirty years, which to relate were not history but a piece of poetry, and would sound like a fable." The wonder is, rather, that all men do not assert as much. That would be a rare praise, if it were true, which was addressed to Francis Beaumont, — "Spectators sate part in your tragedies."

Think what a mean and wretched place this world is; that half the time we have to light a lamp that we may see to live in it. This is half our life. Who would undertake the enterprise if it were all? And, pray, what more has day to offer? A lamp that burns more clear, a purer oil, say winter-strained, that so we may pursue our idleness with less obstruction. Bribed with a little sunlight and a few prismatic tints, we bless our Maker, and stave off his wrath with hymns.

> I make ye an offer,
> Ye gods, hear the scoffer,
> The scheme will not hurt you,
> If ye will find goodness, I will find virtue
> Though I am your creature,
> And child of your nature,
> I have pride still unbended,
> And blood undescended,
> Some free independence,
> And my own descendants.

> I cannot toil blindly,
> Though ye behave kindly,
> And I swear by the rood,
> I'll be slave to no God.
> If ye will deal plainly,
> I will strive mainly,
> If ye will discover,
> Great plans to your lover,
> And give him a sphere
> Somewhat larger than here.

"Verily, my angels! I was abashed on account of my servant, who had no Providence but me; therefore did I pardon him." [1]

Most people with whom I talk, men and women even of some originality and genius, have their scheme of the universe all cut and dried, — very *dry*, I assure you, to hear, dry enough to burn, dry-rotted and powder-post, methinks, — which they set up between you and them in the shortest intercourse; an ancient and tottering frame with all its boards blown off. They do not walk without their bed. Some, to me, seemingly very unimportant and unsubstantial things and relations are for them everlastingly settled, — as Father, Son, and Holy Ghost, and the like. These are like the everlasting hills to them. But in all my wanderings I never came across the least vestige of authority for these things. They have not left so distinct a trace as the delicate flower of a remote geological period on the coal in my grate. The wisest man preaches no doctrines; he has no scheme; he sees no rafter, not even a cobweb, against the heavens.

[1] *The Gulistan* of Sadi.

It is clear sky. If I ever see more clearly at one time than
at another, the medium through which I see is clearer.
To see from earth to heaven, and see there standing,
still a fixture, that old Jewish scheme! What right have
you to hold up this obstacle to my understanding you,
to your understanding me! You did not invent it; it
was imposed on you. Examine your authority. Even
Christ, we fear, had his scheme, his conformity to tradition, which slightly vitiates his teaching. He had not
swallowed all formulas. He preached some mere doctrines. As for me, Abraham, Isaac, and Jacob are now
only the subtilest imaginable essences, which would not
stain the morning sky. Your scheme must be the framework of the universe; all other schemes will soon be
ruins. The perfect God in his revelations of himself has
never got to the length of one such proposition as you,
his prophets, state. Have you learned the alphabet of
heaven and can count three? Do you know the number
of God's family? Can you put mysteries into words?
Do you presume to fable of the ineffable? Pray, what
geographer are you, that speak of heaven's topography?
Whose friend are you, that speak of God's personality?
Do you, Miles Howard, think that he has made you
his confidant? Tell me of the height of the mountains
of the moon, or of the diameter of space, and I may
believe you, but of the secret history of the Almighty,
and I shall pronounce thee mad. Yet we have a sort of
family history of our God, — so have the Tahitians of
theirs, — and some old poet's grand imagination is imposed on us as adamantine everlasting truth, and God's
own word. Pythagoras says, truly enough, "A true as-

sertion respecting God is an assertion of God;" but we
may well doubt if there is any example of this in literature.

The New Testament is an invaluable book, though
I confess to having been slightly prejudiced against it in
my very early days by the church and the Sabbath-
school, so that it seemed, before I read it, to be the yel-
lowest book in the catalogue. Yet I early escaped from
their meshes. It was hard to get the commentaries out
of one's head and taste its true flavor. I think that Pilgrim's Progress is the best sermon which has been
preached from this text; almost all other sermons that
I have heard, or heard of, have been but poor imitations
of this. It would be a poor story to be prejudiced against
the Life of Christ because the book has been edited by
Christians. In fact, I love this book rarely, though it is
a sort of castle in the air to me, which I am permitted to
dream. Having come to it so recently and freshly, it has
the greater charm, so that I cannot find any to talk with
about it. I never read a novel, they have so little real
life and thought in them. The reading which I love best
is the scriptures of the several nations, though it happens
that I am better acquainted with those of the Hindoos,
the Chinese, and the Persians, than of the Hebrews,
which I have come to last. Give me one of these bibles,
and you have silenced me for a while. When I recover
the use of my tongue, I am wont to worry my neighbors
with the new sentences; but commonly they cannot see
that there is any wit in them. Such has been my experience with the New Testament. I have not yet got to the
crucifixion, I have read it over so many times. I should

love dearly to read it aloud to my friends, some of whom are seriously inclined; it is so good, and I am sure that they have never heard it, it fits their case exactly, and we should enjoy it so much together, — but I instinctively despair of getting their ears. They soon show, by signs not to be mistaken, that it is inexpressibly wearisome to them. I do not mean to imply that I am any better than my neighbors; for, alas! I know that I am only as good, though I love better books than they.

It is remarkable that, notwithstanding the universal favor with which the New Testament is outwardly received, and even the bigotry with which it is defended, there is no hospitality shown to, there is no appreciation of, the order of truth with which it deals. I know of no book that has so few readers. There is none so truly strange, and heretical, and unpopular. To Christians, no less than Greeks and Jews. it is foolishness and a stumbling-block. There are, indeed, severe things in it which no man should read aloud more than once. "Seek first the kingdom of heaven." "Lay not up for yourselves treasures on earth." "If thou wilt be perfect, go and sell that thou hast, and give to the poor, and thou shalt have treasure in heaven." "For what is a man profited, if he shall gain the whole world, and lose his own soul? Or what shall a man give in exchange for his soul?" Think of this, Yankees! "Verily, I say unto you, if ye have faith as a grain of mustard seed, ye shall say unto this mountain, Remove hence to yonder place, and it shall remove; and nothing shall be impossible unto you." Think of repeating these things to a New England audience! thirdly, fourthly, fifteenthly, till there are three barrels of sermons! who, without cant, can read them aloud? Who, without cant, can hear them, and not go out of the meeting-house? They never *were* read, they never *were* heard. Let but one of these sentences be rightly read, from any pulpit in the land, and there would not be left one stone of that meeting-house upon another.

Yet the New Testament treats of man and man's so-called spiritual affairs too exclusively, and is too constantly moral and personal, to alone content me, who am not interested solely in man's religious or moral nature, or in man even. I have not the most definite designs on the future. Absolutely speaking, Do unto others as you would that they should do unto you is by no means a golden rule, but the best of current silver. An honest man would have but little occasion for it. It is golden not to have any rule at all in such a case. The book has never been written which is to be accepted without any allowance. Christ was a sublime actor on the stage of the world. He knew what he was thinking of when he said, "Heaven and earth shall pass away, but my words shall not pass away." I draw near to him at such a time. Yet he taught mankind but imperfectly how to live; his thoughts were all directed toward another world. There is another kind of success than his. Even here we have a sort of living to get, and must buffet it somewhat longer. There are various tough problems yet to solve, and we must make shift to live, betwixt spirit and matter, such a human life as we can.

A healthy man, with steady employment, as wood-chopping at fifty cents a cord, and a camp in the woods, will not be a good subject for Christianity. The New Testament may be a choice book to him on some, but not on all or most of his days. He will rather go a-fishing in his leisure hours. The Apostles, though they were fishers too, were of the solemn race of sea-fishers, and never trolled for pickerel on inland streams.

Men have a singular desire to be good without being good for anything, because, perchance, they think vaguely that so it will be good for them in the end. The sort of morality which the priests inculcate is a very subtle policy, far finer than the politicians', and the world is very successfully ruled by them as the policemen. It is not worth the while to let our imperfections disturb us always. The conscience really does not, and ought not to monopolize the whole of our lives, any more than the heart or the head. It is as liable to disease as any other part. I have seen some whose consciences, owing undoubtedly to former indulgence, had grown to be as irritable as spoilt children, and at length gave them no peace. They did not know when to swallow their cud, and their lives of course yielded no milk.

> Conscience is instinct bred in the house;
> Feeling and Thinking propagate the sin
> By an unnatural breeding in and in.
> I say, Turn it outdoors,
> Into the moors.
> I love a life whose plot is simple,
> And does not thicken with every pimple,
> A soul so sound no sickly conscience binds it,
> That makes the universe no worse than 't finds it.
> I love an earnest soul,
> Whose mighty joy and sorrow

Are not drowned in a bowl,
And brought to life to-morrow;
That lives one tragedy,
And not seventy;
A conscience worth keeping,
Laughing not weeping;
A conscience wise and steady,
And forever ready ;
Not changing with events,
Dealing in compliments ;
A conscience exercised about
Large things, where one *may* doubt.
I love a soul not all of wood,
Predestinated to be good,
But true to the backbone
Unto itself alone,
And false to none ;
Born to its own affairs,
Its own joys and own cares ;
By whom the work which God begun
Is finished, and not undone;
Taken up where he left off,
Whether to worship or to scoff:
If not good, why then evil,
If not good god, good devil.
Goodness! — you hypocrite, come out of that,
Live your life, do your work, then take your hat.
I have no patience towards
Such conscientious cowards.
Give me simple laboring folk,
Who love their work,
Whose virtue is a song
To cheer God along.

I was once reproved by a minister who was driving
a poor beast to some meeting-house horse-sheds among
the hills of New Hampshire, because I was bending
my steps to a mountain-top on the Sabbath, instead of a

church, when I would have gone farther than he to hear
a true word spoken on that or any day. He declared
that I was "breaking the Lord's fourth command-
ment," and proceeded to enumerate, in a sepulchral
tone, the disasters which had befallen him whenever
he had done any ordinary work on the Sabbath. He
really thought that a god was on the watch to trip up
those men who followed any secular work on this day,
and did not see that it was the evil conscience of the
workers that did it. The country is full of this superstition, so that when one enters a village the church,
not only really but from association, is the ugliest looking building in it, because it is the one in which human
nature stoops the lowest and is most disgraced. Certainly, such temples as these shall ere long cease to
deform the landscape. There are few things more dis-
heartening and disgusting than when you are walking
the streets of a strange village on the Sabbath, to hear a
preacher shouting like a boatswain in a gale of wind, and
thus harshly profaning the quiet atmosphere of the day.
You fancy him to have taken off his coat, as when men
are about to do hot and dirty work.

If I should ask the minister of Middlesex to let me
speak in his pulpit on a Sunday, he would object because
I do not pray as he does, or because I am not ordained.
What under the sun are these things?

Really, there is no infidelity, nowadays, so great as
that which prays, and keeps the Sabbath, and rebuilds
the churches. The sealer of the South Pacific preaches
a truer doctrine. The church is a sort of hospital for
men's souls, and as full of quackery as the hospital for

their bodies. Those who are taken into it live like pensioners in their Retreat or Sailor's Snug Harbor, where you may see a row of religious cripples sitting outside in sunny weather. Let not the apprehension that he may one day have to occupy a ward therein discourage the cheerful labors of the able-souled man. While he remembers the sick in their extremities, let him not look thither as to his goal. One is sick at heart of this pagoda worship. It is like the beating of gongs in a Hindoo subterranean temple. In dark places and dungeons the preacher's words might perhaps strike root and grow, but not in broad daylight in any part of the world that I know. The sound of the Sabbath bell far away, now breaking on these shores, does not awaken pleasing associations, but melancholy and sombre ones rather. One involuntarily rests on his oar, to humor his unusually meditative mood. It is as the sound of many catechisms and religious books twanging a canting peal round the earth, seeming to issue from some Egyptian temple and echo along the shore of the Nile, right opposite to Pharaoh's palace and Moses in the bulrushes, startling a multitude of storks and alligators basking in the sun.

Everywhere "good men" sound a retreat, and the word has gone forth to fall back on innocence. Fall forward rather on to whatever there is there. Christianity only hopes. It has hung its harp on the willows, and cannot sing a song in a strange land. It has dreamed a sad dream, and does not yet welcome the morning with joy. The mother tells her falsehoods to her child, but, thank Heaven, the child does not grow up in its parent's shadow. Our mother's faith has not grown with her experience. Her experience has been too much for her. The lesson of life was too hard for her to learn.

It is remarkable that almost all speakers and writers feel it to be incumbent on them, sooner or later, to prove or to acknowledge the personality of God. Some Earl of Bridgewater, thinking it better late than never, has provided for it in his will. It is a sad mistake. In reading a work on agriculture, we have to skip the author's moral reflections, and the words "Providence" and "He" scattered along the page, to come at the profitable level of what he has to say. What he calls his religion is for the most part offensive to the nostrils. He should know better than expose himself, and keep his foul sores covered till they are quite healed. There is more religion in men's science than there is science in their religion. Let us make haste to the report of the committee on swine.

A man's real faith is never contained in his creed, nor is his creed an article of his faith. The last is never adopted. This it is that permits him to smile ever, and to live even as bravely as he does. And yet he clings anxiously to his creed, as to a straw, thinking that that does him good service because his sheet anchor does not drag.

In most men's religion, the ligature which should be its umbilical cord connecting them with divinity is rather like that thread which the accomplices of Cylon held in their hands when they went abroad from the temple of Minerva, the other end being attached to the statue of the goddess. But frequently, as in their case, the thread breaks, being stretched, and they are left without an asylum.

"A good and pious man reclined his head on the bosom of contemplation, and was absorbed in the ocean of a revery. At the instant when he awaked from his vision, one of his friends, by way of pleasantry, said, What rare gift have you brought us from that garden, where you have been recreating? He replied, I fancied to myself and said, when I can reach the rose-bower, I will fill my lap with the flowers, and bring them as a present to my friends; but when I got there, the fragrance of the roses so intoxicated me, that the skirt dropped from my hands. —— 'O bird of dawn! learn the warmth of affection from the moth; for that scorched creature gave up the ghost, and uttered not a groan: These vain pretenders are ignorant of him they seek after; for of him that knew him we never heard again:— O thou! who towerest above the flights of conjecture, opinion, and comprehension; whatever has been reported of thee we have heard and read; the congregation is dismissed, and life drawn to a close; and we still rest at our first encomium of thee!'" [1]

By noon we were let down into the Merrimack through the locks at Middlesex, just above Pawtucket Falls, by a serene and liberal-minded man, who came quietly from his book, though his duties, we supposed, did not require him to open the locks on Sundays. With him we had a just and equal encounter of the eyes, as between two honest men.

The movements of the eyes express the perpetual and unconscious courtesy of the parties. It is said that a

[1] Sadi.

rogue does not look you in the face, neither does an honest man look at you as if he had his reputation to establish. I have seen some who did not know when to turn aside their eyes in meeting yours. A truly confident and magnanimous spirit is wiser than to contend for the mastery in such encounters. Serpents alone conquer by the steadiness of their gaze. My friend looks me in the face and sees me, that is all.

The best relations were at once established between us and this man, and though few words were spoken, he could not conceal a visible interest in us and our excursion. He was a lover of the higher mathematics, as we found, and in the midst of some vast sunny problem, when we overtook him and whispered our conjectures. By this man we were presented with the freedom of the Merrimack. We now felt as if we were fairly launched on the ocean stream of our voyage, and were pleased to find that our boat would float on Merrimack water. We began again busily to put in practice those old arts of rowing, steering, and paddling. It seemed a strange phenomenon to us that the two rivers should mingle their waters so readily, since we had never associated them in our thoughts.

As we glided over the broad bosom of the Merrimack, between Chelmsford and Dracut, at noon, here a quarter of a mile wide, the rattling of our oars was echoed over the water to those villages, and their slight sounds to us. Their harbors lay as smooth and fairy-like as the Lida, or Syracuse, or Rhodes, in our imagination, while, like some strange roving craft, we flitted past what seemed the dwellings of noble home-staying men, seemingly as

conspicuous as if on an eminence, or floating upon a
tide which came up to those villagers' breasts. At a
third of a mile over the water we heard distinctly some
children repeating their catechism in a cottage near the
shore, while in the broad shallows between, a herd of
cows stood lashing their sides, and waging war with the
flies.

Two hundred years ago, other catechizing than this
was going on here; for here came the Sachem Wannalancet and his people, and sometimes Tahatawan, our
Concord Sachem, who afterwards had a church at home,
to catch fish at the falls; and here also came John Eliot,
with the Bible and Catechism, and Baxter's "Call to the
Unconverted," and other tracts, done into the Massachusetts tongue, and taught them Christianity meanwhile. "This place" says Gookin, referring to Wamesit, "being an ancient and capital seat of Indians, they
come to fish; and this good man takes this opportunity
to spread the net of the gospel, to fish for their souls."
"May 5, 1674," he continues, "according to our usual
custom, Mr. Eliot and myself took our journey to
Wamesit, or Pawtuckett; and arriving there that evening, Mr. Eliot preached to as many of them as could be
got together, out of Matt. xxii. 1–14, the parable of the
marriage of the king's son. We met at the wigwam of
one called Wannalancet, about two miles from the town,
near Pawtuckett falls, and bordering upon Merrimak
river. This person, Wannalancet, is the eldest son of
old Pasaconaway, the chiefest sachem of Pawtuckett.
He is a sober and grave person, and of years, between
_ty and sixty. He hath been always loving and friendly

to the English." As yet, however, they had not prevailed
on him to embrace the Christian religion. "But at this
time," says Gookin, "May 6, 1674," — "after some
deliberation and serious pause, he stood up, and made
a speech to this effect: 'I must acknowledge I have, all
my days, used to pass in an old canoe, [alluding to his
frequent custom to pass in a canoe upon the river,] and
now you exhort me to change and leave my old canoe,
and embark in a new canoe, to which I have hitherto
been unwilling; but now I yield up myself to your advice, and enter into a new canoe, and do engage to pray
to God hereafter.'" One "Mr. Richard Daniel, a gentleman that lived in Billerica," who with other "persons
of quality" was present, "desired brother Eliot to tell
the sachem from him, that it may be, while he went in
his old canoe, he passed in a quiet stream; but the end
thereof was death and destruction to soul and body. But
now he went into a new canoe, perhaps he would meet
with storms and trials, but yet he should be encouraged
to persevere, for the end of his voyage would be everlasting rest." "Since that time, I hear this sachem doth
persevere, and is a constant and diligent hearer of God's
word, and sanctifieth the Sabbath, though he doth travel
to Wamesit meeting every Sabbath, which is above two
miles; and though sundry of his people have deserted
him, since he subjected to the gospel, yet he continues
and persists." [1]

Already, as appears from the records, "At a General
Court held at Boston in New England, the 7th of the
first month, 1643–44," "Wassamequin, Nashoonon,

[1] Gookin's *Hist. Coll. of the Indians in New England*, 1674.

Kutchamaquin, Massaconomet, and Squaw Sachem, did voluntarily submit themselves " to the English; and among other things did " promise to be willing from time to time to be instructed in the knowledge of God." Being asked "not to do any unnecessary work on the Sabbath day, especially within the gates of Christian towns," they answered, " It is easy to them; they have not much to do on any day, and they can well take their rest on that day." "So," says Winthrop, in his Journal, " we causing them to understand the articles, and all the ten commandments of God, and they freely assenting to all, they were solemnly received, and then presented the Court with twenty-six fathom more of wampom; and the Court gave each of them a coat of two yards of cloth, and their dinner; and to them and their men, every of them, a cup of sack at their departure; so they took leave and went away."

What journeyings on foot and on horseback through the wilderness, to preach the gospel to these minks and muskrats! who first, no doubt, listened with their red ears out of a natural hospitality and courtesy, and afterward from curiosity or even interest, till at length there "were praying Indians," and, as the General Court wrote to Cromwell, the " work is brought to this perfection that some of the Indians themselves can pray and prophesy in a comfortable manner."

It was in fact an old battle and hunting ground through which we had been floating, the ancient dwelling-place of a race of hunters and warriors. Their weirs of stone, their arrowheads and hatchets, their pestles, and the mortars in which they pounded Indian corn

before the white man had tasted it, lay concealed in the
mud of the river bottom. Tradition still points out the
spots where they took fish in the greatest numbers,
by such arts as they possessed. It is a rapid story the
historian will have to put together. Miantonimo, —
Winthrop, — Webster. Soon he comes from Montaup
to Bunker Hill, from bear-skins, parched corn, bows
and arrows, to tiled roofs, wheat-fields, guns and swords.
Pawtucket and Wamesit, where the Indians resorted
in the fishing season, are now Lowell, the city of spindles
and Manchester of America, which sends its cotton
cloth round the globe. Even we youthful voyagers had
spent a part of our lives in the village of Chelmsford,
when the present city, whose bells we heard, was its
obscure north district only, and the giant weaver was not
yet fairly born. So old are we; so young is it.

We were thus entering the State of New Hampshire
on the bosom of the flood formed by the tribute of its
innumerable valleys. The river was the only key which
could unlock its maze, presenting its hills and valleys,
its lakes and streams, in their natural order and position.
The Merrimack, or Sturgeon River, is formed by the
confluence of the Pemigewasset, which rises near the
Notch of the White Mountains, and the Winnipiseogee,
which drains the lake of the same name, signifying " The
Smile of the Great Spirit." From their junction it runs
south seventy-eight miles to Massachusetts, and thence
east thirty-five miles to the sea. I have traced its stream
from where it bubbles out of the rocks of the White
Mountains above the clouds, to where it is lost amid the

salt billows of the ocean on Plum Island beach. At first it comes on murmuring to itself by the base of stately and retired mountains, through moist primitive woods whose juices it receives, where the bear still drinks it, and the cabins of settlers are far between, and there are few to cross its stream; enjoying in solitude its cascades still unknown to fame; by long ranges of mountains of Sandwich and of Squam, slumbering like tumuli of Titans, with the peaks of Moose-hillock, the Haystack, and Kearsarge reflected in its waters; where the maple and the raspberry, those lovers of the hills, flourish amid temperate dews; — flowing long and full of meaning, but untranslatable as its name Pemigewasset, by many a pastured Pelion and Ossa, where unnamed muses haunt, tended by Oreads, Dryads, Naiads, and receiving the tribute of many an untasted Hippocrene. There are earth, air, fire, and water, — very well, this is water and down it comes.

> Such water do the gods distill,
> And pour down every hill
>   For their New England men;
> A draught of this wild nectar bring,
> And I'll not taste the spring
>   Of Helicon again.

Falling all the way, and yet not discouraged by the lowest fall. By the law of its birth never to become stagnant, for it has come out of the clouds, and down the sides of precipices worn in the flood, through beaver-dams broke loose, not splitting but splicing and mending itself, until it found a breathing-place in this low land. There is no danger now that the sun will steal it back to heaven again before it reach the sea, for it has a warrant even to recover its own dews into its bosom again with interest at every eve.

It was already the water of Squam and Newfound Lake and Winnipiseogee, and White Mountain snow dissolved, on which we were floating, and Smith's and Baker's and Mad Rivers, and Nashua and Souhegan and Piscataquoag, and Suncook and Soucook and Contoocook, mingled in incalculable proportions, still fluid, yellowish, restless all, with an ancient, ineradicable inclination to the sea.

So it flows on down by Lowell and Haverhill, at which last place it first suffers a sea change, and a few masts betray the vicinity of the ocean. Between the towns of Amesbury and Newbury it is a broad, commercial river, from a third to half a mile in width, no longer skirted with yellow and crumbling banks, but backed by high green hills and pastures, with frequent white beaches on which the fishermen draw up their nets. I have passed down this portion of the river in a steamboat, and it was a pleasant sight to watch from its deck the fishermen dragging their seines on the distant shore, as in pictures of a foreign strand. At intervals you may meet with a schooner laden with lumber, standing up to Haverhill, or else lying at anchor or aground, waiting for wind or tide; until, at last, you glide under the famous Chain Bridge, and are landed at Newburyport. Thus she who at first was " poore of waters, naked of renowne," having received so many fair tributaries, as was said of the Forth, —

> "Doth grow the greater still, the further downe;
>   Till that abounding both in power and fame,
>   She long doth strive to give the sea her name;"

or if not her name, in this case, at least the impulse of her
stream.   From the steeples of Newburyport you may
review this river stretching far up into the country, with
many a white sail glancing over it like an inland sea, and
behold, as one wrote who was born on its head-waters,
"Down out at its mouth, the dark inky main blending
with the blue above. Plum Island, its sand ridges scol-
loping along the horizon like the sea-serpent, and the
distant outline broken by many a tall ship, leaning, *still*,
against the sky."

Rising at an equal height with the Connecticut, the
Merrimack reaches the sea by a course only half as
long, and hence has no leisure to form broad and fertile
meadows, like the former, but is hurried along rapids,
and down numerous falls, without long delay.   The
banks are generally steep and high, with a narrow interval reaching back to the hills, which is only rarely or partially overflown at present, and is much valued by the
farmers.   Between Chelmsford and Concord, in New
Hampshire, it varies from twenty to seventy-five rods in
width.   It is probably wider than it was formerly, in
many places, owing to the trees having been cut down,
and the consequent wasting away of its banks.   The
influence of the Pawtucket Dam is felt as far up as Cromwell's Falls, and many think that the banks are being
abraded and the river filled up again by this cause. Like
all our rivers, it is liable to freshets, and the Pemigewasset has been known to rise twenty-five feet in a few

hours. It is navigable for vessels of burden about twenty miles; for canal-boats, by means of locks, as far as Concord in New Hampshire, about seventy-five miles from its mouth; and for smaller boats to Plymouth, one hundred and thirteen miles. A small steamboat once plied between Lowell and Nashua, before the railroad was built, and one now runs from Newburyport to Haverhill.

Unfitted to some extent for the purposes of commerce by the sand-bar at its mouth, see how this river was devoted from the first to the service of manufactures. Issuing from the iron region of Franconia, and flowing through still uncut forests, by inexhaustible ledges of granite, with Squam, and Winnipiseogee, and Newfound, and Massabesic Lakes for its mill-ponds, it falls over a succession of natural dams, where it has been offering its *privileges* in vain for ages, until at last the Yankee race came to *improve* them. Standing at its mouth, look up its sparkling stream to its source, — a silver cascade which falls all the way from the White Mountains to the sea, — and behold a city on each successive plateau, a busy colony of human beaver around every fall. Not to mention Newburyport and Haverhill, see Lawrence, and Lowell, and Nashua, and Manchester, and Concord, gleaming one above the other. When at length it has escaped from under the last of the factories, it has a level and unmolested passage to the sea, a mere *waste water*, as it were, bearing little with it but its fame; its pleasant course revealed by the morning fog which hangs over it, and the sails of the few small vessels which transact the commerce of Haverhill and

Newburyport. But its real vessels are railroad cars, and
its true and main stream, flowing by an iron channel
farther south, may be traced by a long line of vapor
amid the hills, which no morning wind ever disperses, to
where it empties into the sea at Boston. This side is the
louder murmur now. Instead of the scream of a fish
hawk scaring the fishes, is heard the whistle of the steam-
engine, arousing a country to its progress.

This river too was at length discovered by the white
man, "trending up into the land," he knew not how far,
possibly an inlet to the South Sea. Its valley, as far as
the Winnipiseogee, was first surveyed in 1652. The first
settlers of Massachusetts supposed that the Connecticut,
in one part of its course, ran northwest, "so near the
great lake as the Indians do pass their canoes into it over
land." From which lake and the "hideous swamps"
about it, as they supposed, came all the beaver that was
traded between Virginia and Canada, — and the Poto-
mac was thought to come out of or from very near it.
Afterward the Connecticut came so near the course of
the Merrimack that, with a little pains, they expected to
divert the current of the trade into the latter river, and
its profits from their Dutch neighbors into their own
pockets.

Unlike the Concord, the Merrimack is not a dead but
a living stream, though it has less life within its waters
and on its banks. It has a swift current, and, in this part
of its course, a clayey bottom, almost no weeds, and comparatively few fishes. We looked down into its yellow
water with the more curiosity, who were accustomed

to the Nile-like blackness of the former river. Shad and alewives are taken here in their season, but salmon, though at one time more numerous than shad, are now more rare. Bass, also, are taken occasionally; but locks and dams have proved more or less destructive to the fisheries. The shad make their appearance early in May, at the same time with the blossoms of the pyrus, one of the most conspicuous early flowers, which is for this reason called the shad-blossom. An insect called the shad-fly also appears at the same time, covering the houses and fences. We are told that "their greatest run is when the apple-trees are in full blossom. The old shad return in August; the young, three or four inches long, in September. These are very fond of flies." A rather picturesque and luxurious mode of fishing was formerly practiced on the Connecticut, at Bellows Falls, where a large rock divides the stream. "On the steep sides of the island rock," says Belknap, "hang several arm-chairs, fastened to ladders, and secured by a counterpoise, in which fishermen sit to catch salmon and shad with dipping nets." The remains of Indian weirs, made of large stones, are still to be seen in the Winnipiseogee, one of the head-waters of this river.

It cannot but affect our philosophy favorably to be reminded of these shoals of migratory fishes, of salmon, shad, alewives, marsh-bankers, and others, which penetrate up the innumerable rivers of our coast in the spring, even to the interior lakes, their scales gleaming in the sun; and again, of the fry which in still greater numbers wend their way downward to the sea. "And is it not pretty sport," wrote Captain John Smith, who was

on this coast as early as 1614, " to pull up twopence, six-
pence, and twelvepence, as fast as you can haul and veer
a line ? " " And what sport doth yield a more pleasing
content, and less hurt or charge, than angling with a
hook, and crossing the sweet air from isle to isle, over the
silent streams of a calm sea ? "

On the sandy shore, opposite the Glass-house village
in Chelmsford, at the Great Bend, where we landed to
rest us and gather a few wild plums, we discovered the
Campanula rotundifolia, a new flower to us, the harebell
of the poets, which is common to both hemispheres,
growing close to the water. Here, in the shady branches
of an apple tree on the sand, we took our nooning, where
there was not a zephyr to disturb the repose of this
glorious Sabbath day, and we reflected serenely on the
long past and successful labors of Latona.

> "So silent is the cessile air,
>   That every cry and call,
> The hills, and dales, and forest fair
>   Again repeats them all.
>
> "The herds beneath some leafy trees,
>   Amidst the flowers they lie,
> The stable ships upon the seas
>   Tend up their sails to dry."

As we thus rested in the shade, or rowed leisurely
along, we had recourse, from time to time, to the Gazetteer, which was our Navigator, and from its bald natural
facts extracted the pleasure of poetry. Beaver River
comes in a little lower down, draining the meadows of
Pelham, Windham, and Londonderry. The Scotch-

Irish settlers of the latter town, according to this authority, were the first to introduce the potato into New
England, as well as the manufacture of linen cloth.

Everything that is printed and bound in a book contains some echo at least of the best that is in literature.
Indeed, the best books have a use, like sticks and stones,
which is above or beside their design, not anticipated
in the preface, not concluded in the appendix. Even
Virgil's poetry serves a very different use to me to-day
from what it did to his contemporaries. It has often an
acquired and accidental value merely, proving that man
is still man in the world. It is pleasant to meet with such
still lines as, —

"Jam laeto turgent in palmite gemmae;"
Now the buds swell on the joyful stem.

"Strata jacent passim sua quaeque sub arbore poma;"
The apples lie scattered everywhere, each under its tree.

In an ancient and dead language, any recognition of
living nature attracts us. These are such sentences as
were written while grass grew and water ran. It is no
small recommendation when a book will stand the test
of mere unobstructed sunshine and daylight.

What would we not give for some great poem to read
now, which would be in harmony with the scenery, —
for if men read aright, methinks they would never read
anything but poems. No history nor philosophy can
supply their place.

The wisest definition of poetry the poet will instantly
prove false by setting aside its requisitions. We can,
therefore, publish only our advertisement of it.

There is no doubt that the loftiest written wisdom is

either rhymed or in some way musically measured, — is, in form as well as substance, poetry; and a volume which should contain the condensed wisdom of mankind need not have one rhythmless line.

Yet poetry, though the last and finest result, is a natural fruit. As naturally as the oak bears an acorn, and the vine a gourd, man bears a poem, either spoken or done. It is the chief and most memorable success, for history is but a prose narrative of poetic deeds. What else have the Hindoos, the Persians, the Babylonians, the Egyptians done, that can be told ? It is the simplest relation of phenomena, and describes the commonest sensations with more truth than science does, and the latter at a distance slowly mimics its style and methods. The poet sings how the blood flows in his veins. He performs his functions, and is so well that he needs such stimulus to sing only as plants to put forth leaves and blossoms. He would strive in vain to modulate the remote and transient music which he sometimes hears, since his song is a vital function like breathing, and an integral result like weight. It is not the overflowing of life, but its subsidence rather, and is drawn from under the feet of the poet. It is enough if Homer but say the sun sets. He is as serene as nature, and we can hardly detect the enthusiasm of the bard. It is as if nature spoke. He presents to us the simplest pictures of human life, so the child itself can understand them, and the man must not think twice to appreciate his naturalness. Each reader discovers for himself that, with respect to the simpler features of nature, succeeding poets have done little else than copy his similes. His more memorable passages are

as naturally bright as gleams of sunshine in misty
weather. Nature furnishes him not only with words, but
with stereotyped lines and sentences from her mint.

"As from the clouds appears the full moon,
All shining, and then again it goes behind the shadowy clouds,
So Hector at one time appeared among the foremost,
And at another in the rear, commanding; and all with brass
He shone, like to the lightning of ægis-bearing Zeus."

He conveys the least information, even the hour of
the day, with such magnificence and vast expense of
natural imagery, as if it were a message from the gods.

"While it was dawn, and sacred day was advancing,
For that space the weapons of both flew fast, and the people fell;
But when now the woodcutter was preparing his morning meal,
In the recesses of the mountain, and had wearied his hands
With cutting lofty trees, and satiety came to his mind,
And the desire of sweet food took possession of his thoughts;
Then the Danaans, by their valor, broke the phalanxes,
Shouting to their companions from rank to rank."

When the army of the Trojans passed the night under
arms, keeping watch lest the enemy should reëmbark
under cover of the dark, —

"They, thinking great things, upon the neutral ground of war
Sat all the night; and many fires burned for them.
As when in the heavens the stars round the bright moon
Appear beautiful, and the air is without wind;
And all the heights, and the extreme summits,
And the wooded sides of the mountains appear; and from the heavens
    an infinite ether is diffused,
And all the stars are seen; and the shepherd rejoices in his heart;
So between the ships and the streams of Xanthus
Appeared the fires of the Trojans before Ilium.
A thousand fires burned on the plain; and by each
Sat fifty, in the light of the blazing fire;

And horses eating white barley and corn,
Standing by the chariots, awaited fair-throned Aurora."

The " white-armed goddess Juno," sent by the Father
of gods and men for Iris and Apollo, —

"Went down the Idæan mountains to far Olympus,
As when the mind of a man, who has come over much earth,
Sallies forth, and he reflects with rapid thoughts,
There was I, and there, and remembers many things;
So swiftly the august Juno hastening flew through the air,
And came to high Olympus."

His scenery is always true, and not invented. He does
not leap in imagination from Asia to Greece, through
mid-air, —

ἐπεὶ ἢ μάλα πολλὰ μεταξὺ
οὔρεά τε σκιόεντα, θάλασσά τε ἠχήεσσα.

For there are very many
Shady mountains and resounding seas between.

If his messengers repair but to the tent of Achilles, we
do not wonder how they got there, but accompany them
step by step along the shore of the resounding sea.
Nestor's account of the march of the Pylians against
the Epeians is extremely lifelike: —

"Then rose up at them sweet-worded Nestor, the shrill orator of the
    Pylians,
And words sweeter than honey flowed from his tongue."

This time, however, he addresses Patroclus alone: " A
certain river, Minyas by name, leaps seaward near to
Arene, where we Pylians wait the dawn, both horse and
foot. Thence with all haste we sped us on the morrow
ere 't was noonday, accoutred for the fight, even to
Alpheus's sacred source," etc. We fancy that we hear

the subdued murmuring of the Minyas discharging its
waters into the main the livelong night, and the hollow
sound of the waves breaking on the shore, — until at
length we are cheered at the close of a toilsome march by
the gurgling fountains of Alpheus.

There are few books which are fit to be remembered
in our wisest hours, but the Iliad is brightest in the
serenest days, and embodies still all the sunlight that fell
on Asia Minor. No modern joy or ecstasy of ours can
lower its height or dim its lustre, but there it lies in the
east of literature, as it were the earliest and latest production of the mind. The ruins of Egypt oppress and
stifle us with their dust, foulness preserved in cassia and
pitch, and swathed in linen; the death of that which
never lived. But the rays of Greek poetry struggle down
to us, and mingle with the sunbeams of the recent day.
The statue of Memnon is cast down, but the shaft of
the Iliad still meets the sun in his rising.

> "Homer is gone; and where is Jove? and where
> The rival cities seven? His song outlives
> Time, tower, and god, — all that then was, save Heaven.`

So, too, no doubt, Homer had his Homer, and
Orpheus his Orpheus, in the dim antiquity which preceded them. The mythological system of the ancients,
— and it is still the mythology of the moderns, the poem
of mankind, — interwoven so wonderfully with their astronomy, and matching in grandeur and harmony the
architecture of the heavens themselves, seems to point
to a time when a mightier genius inhabited the earth.
But, after all, man is the great poet, and not Homer nor
Shakespeare; and our language itself, and the common

arts of life, are his work. Poetry is so universally true
and independent of experience that it does not need any
particular biography to illustrate it, but we refer it sooner
or later to some Orpheus or Linus, and after ages to the
genius of humanity and the gods themselves.

It would be worth the while to select our reading,
for books are the society we keep; to read only the
serenely true; never statistics, nor fiction, nor news,
nor reports, nor periodicals, but only great poems, and
when they failed, read them again, or perchance write
more. Instead of other sacrifice, we might offer up our
perfect (τέλεια) thoughts to the gods daily, in hymns or
psalms. For we should be at the helm at least once a day.
The whole of the day should not be daytime; there
should be one hour, if no more, which the day did not
bring forth. Scholars are wont to sell their birthright for
a mess of learning. But is it necessary to know what the
speculator prints, or the thoughtless study, or the idle
read, the literature of the Russians and the Chinese, or
even French philosophy and much of German criticism?
Read the best books first, or you may not have a chance
to read them at all. "There are the worshipers with
offerings, and the worshipers with mortifications; and
again the worshipers with enthusiastic devotion; so
there are those the wisdom of whose reading is their
worship, men of subdued passions and severe manners.
— This world is not for him who doth not worship; and
where, O Arjoon, is there another?" Certainly, we do
not need to be soothed and entertained always like children. He who resorts to the easy novel, because he is

languid, does no better than if he took a nap. The front aspect of great thoughts can only be enjoyed by those who stand on the side whence they arrive. Books, not which afford us a cowering enjoyment, but in which each thought is of unusual daring; such as an idle man cannot read, and a timid one would not be entertained by, which even make us dangerous to existing institutions, — such call I good books.

All that are printed and bound are not books; they do not necessarily belong to letters, but are oftener to be ranked with the other luxuries and appendages of civilized life. Base wares are palmed off under a thousand disguises. "The way to trade," as a peddler once told me, "is to *put it right through*," no matter what it is, anything that is agreed on.

> "You grov'ling worldlings, you whose wisdom trades
> Where light ne'er shot his golden ray."

By dint of able writing and pen-craft, books are cunningly compiled, and have their run and success even among the learned, as if they were the result of a new man's thinking, and their birth were attended with some natural throes. But in a little while their covers fall off, for no binding will avail, and it appears that they are not Books or Bibles at all. There are new and patented inventions in this shape, purporting to be for the elevation of the race, which many a pure scholar and genius who has learned to read is for a moment deceived by, and finds himself reading a horse-rake, or spinning-jenny, or wooden nutmeg, or oak-leaf cigar, or steam-power press, or kitchen range, perchance, when he was seeking serene and biblical truths.

"Merchants, arise,
And mingle conscience with your merchandise."

Paper is cheap, and authors need not now erase one
book before they write another. Instead of cultivating
the earth for wheat and potatoes, they cultivate literature, and fill a place in the Republic of Letters. Or they
would fain write for fame merely, as others actually raise
crops of grain to be distilled into brandy. Books are for
the most part willfully and hastily written, as parts of a
system to supply a want real or imagined. Books of
natural history aim commonly to be hasty schedules,
or inventories of God's property, by some clerk. They
do not in the least teach the divine view of nature, but
the popular view, or rather the popular method of studying nature, and make haste to conduct the persevering
pupil only into that dilemma where the professors always
dwell.

"To Athens gowned he goes, and from that school
Returns unsped, a more instructed fool."

They teach the elements really of ignorance, not of
knowledge; for, to speak deliberately and in view of
the highest truths, it is not easy to distinguish elementary
knowledge. There is a chasm between knowledge and
ignorance which the arches of science can never span.
A book should contain pure discoveries, glimpses of
terra firma, though by shipwrecked mariners, and not
the art of navigation by those who have never been out
of sight of land. *They* must not yield wheat and potatoes, but must themselves be the unconstrained and
natural harvest of their author's lives.

"What I have learned is mine; I've had my thought,
    And me the Muses noble truths have taught."

We do not learn much from learned books, but from true, sincere, human books, from frank and honest biographies. The life of a good man will hardly improve us more than the life of a freebooter, for the inevitable laws appear as plainly in the infringement as in the observance, and our lives are sustained by a nearly equal expense of virtue of some kind. The decaying tree, while yet it lives, demands sun, wind, and rain no less than the green one. It secretes sap and performs the functions of health. If we choose, we may study the alburnum only. The gnarled stump has as tender a bud as the sapling.

At least let us have healthy books, a stout horse-rake, or a kitchen range which is not cracked. Let not the poet shed tears only for the public weal. He should be as vigorous as a sugar maple, with sap enough to maintain his own verdure, beside what runs into the troughs, and not like a vine, which being cut in the spring bears no fruit, but bleeds to death in the endeavor to heal its wounds. The poet is he that hath fat enough, like bears and marmots, to suck his claws all winter. He hibernates in this world, and feeds on his own marrow. We love to think in winter, as we walk over the snowy pastures, of those happy dreamers that lie under the sod, of dormice and all that race of dormant creatures, which have such a superfluity of life enveloped in thick folds of fur, impervious to cold. Alas, the poet too is in one sense a sort of dormouse gone into winter quarters of deep and serene thoughts, insensible to surrounding circumstances; his words are the relation of his oldest and finest memory, a wisdom drawn from the remotest experience. Other men lead a starved existence, meanwhile, like hawks, that would fain keep on the wing, and trust to pick up a sparrow now and then.

There are already essays and poems, the growth of this land, which are not in vain, all which, however, we could conveniently have stowed in the till of our chest. If the gods permitted their own inspiration to be breathed in vain, these might be overlooked in the crowd, but the accents of truth are as sure to be heard at last on earth as in heaven. They already seem ancient, and in some measure have lost the traces of their modern birth. Here are they who

> "ask for that which is our whole life's light,
> For the perpetual, true, and clear insight."

I remember a few sentences which spring like the sward in its native pasture, where its roots were never disturbed, and not as if spread over a sandy embankment; answering to the poet's prayer, —

> "Let us set so just
> A rate on knowledge, that the world may trust
> The poet's sentence, and not still aver
> Each art is to itself a flatterer."

But, above all, in our native port, did we not frequent the peaceful games of the Lyceum, from which a new era will be dated to New England, as from the games of Greece. For if Herodotus carried his history to Olympia to read, after the cestus and the race, have we not heard such histories recited there, which since our countrymen have read, as made Greece sometimes to be forgotten?

Philosophy, too, has there her grove and portico, not wholly unfrequented in these days.

Lately the victor, whom all Pindars praised, has won another palm, contending with

"Olympian bards who sung
Divine ideas below,
Which always find us young,
And always keep us so."

What earth or sea, mountain or stream, or Muses' spring or grove, is safe from his all-searching, ardent eye, who drives off Phœbus' beaten track, visits unwonted zones, makes the gelid Hyperboreans glow, and the old polar serpent writhe, and many a Nile flow back and hide his head!

That Phaeton of our day,
Who'd make another milky way,
And burn the world up with his ray,

By us an undisputed seer, —
Who'd drive his flaming car so near
Unto our shuddering mortal sphere,

Disgracing all our slender worth,
And scorching up the living earth,
To prove his heavenly birth.

The silver spokes, the golden tire,
Are glowing with unwonted fire,
And ever nigher roll and nigher;

The pins and axle melted are,
The silver radii fly afar,
Ah, he will spoil his Father's car!

Who let him have the steeds he cannot steer?
Henceforth the sun will not shine for a year;
And we shall Ethiops all appear.

From *his*

> "lips of cunning fell
> The thrilling Delphic oracle."

And yet, sometimes, —

> We should not mind if on our ear there fell
> Some less of cunning, more of oracle.

It is Apollo shining in your face. O rare Contemporary, let us have far-off heats. Give us the subtler, the heavenlier, though fleeting beauty, which passes through and through, and dwells not in the verse; even pure water, which but reflects those tints which wine wears in its grain. Let epic trade-winds blow, and cease this waltz of inspirations. Let us oftener feel even the gentle southwest wind upon our cheeks blowing from the Indian's heaven. What though we lose a thousand meteors from the sky, if skyey depths, if star-dust and undissolvable nebulæ remain? What though we lose a thousand wise responses of the oracle, if we may have instead some natural acres of Ionian earth?

Though we know well, —

> "That 't is not in the power of kings [or presidents] to raise
> A spirit for verse that is not born thereto,
> Nor are they born in every prince's days;"

yet spite of all they sang in praise of their "Eliza's reign," we have evidence that poets may be born and sing in *our* day, in the presidency of James K. Polk, —

> "And that the utmost powers of English rhyme,"
> *Were not* "within *her* peaceful reign confined."

The prophecy of the poet Daniel is already how much more than fulfilled!

"And who, in time, knows whither we may vent
　The treasure of our tongue, to what strange shores
　This gain of our best glory shall be sent,
　T' enrich unknowing nations with our stores?
　What worlds in th' yet unformed Occident,
　May come refin'd with th' accents that are ours."

Enough has been said in these days of the charm of fluent writing. We hear it complained of some works of genius that they have fine thoughts, but are irregular and have no flow. But even the mountain peaks in the horizon are, to the eye of science, parts of one range. We should consider that the flow of thought is more like a tidal wave than a prone river, and is the result of a celestial influence, not of any declivity in its channel. The river flows because it runs down hill, and flows the faster, the faster it descends. The reader who expects to float down-stream for the whole voyage may well complain of nauseating swells and choppings of the sea when his frail shore craft gets amidst the billows of the ocean stream, which flows as much to sun and moon as lesser streams to it. But if we would appreciate the flow that is in these books, we must expect to feel it rise from the page like an exhalation, and wash away our critical brains like burr millstones, flowing to higher levels above and behind ourselves. There is many a book which ripples on like a freshet, and flows as glibly as a mill-stream sucking under a causeway; and when their authors are in the full tide of their discourse, Pythagoras and Plato and Jamblichus halt beside them. Their long, stringy, slimy sentences are of that consistency that they naturally flow and run together. They read as if written for military men, for men of business, there is such a dispatch in them. Compared with these, the grave thinkers and philosophers seem not to have got their swaddling-clothes off; they are slower than a Roman army in its march, the rear camping to-night where the van camped last night. The wise Jamblichus eddies and gleams like a watery slough.

> "How many thousands never heard the name
>   Of Sidney, or of Spenser, or their books !
> And yet brave fellows, and presume of fame,
>   And seem to bear down all the world with looks !"

The ready writer seizes the pen and shouts, "Forward! Alamo and Fanning!" and after rolls the tide of war. The very walls and fences seem to travel. But the most rapid trot is no flow after all; and thither, reader, you and I, at least, will not follow.

A perfectly healthy sentence, it is true, is extremely rare. For the most part we miss the hue and fragrance of the thought; as if we could be satisfied with the dews of the morning or evening without their colors, or the heavens without their azure. The most attractive sentences are, perhaps, not the wisest, but the surest and roundest. They are spoken firmly and conclusively, as if the speaker had a right to know what he says, and if not wise, they have at least been well learned. Sir Walter Raleigh might well be studied, if only for the excellence of his style, for he is remarkable in the midst of so many masters. There is a natural emphasis in his style, like a man's tread, and a breathing space between the sentences, which the best of modern writing does not furnish. His chapters are like English parks, or say rather like a Western forest, where the larger growth keeps down the underwood, and one may ride on horseback through the openings. All the distinguished writers of that period possess a greater vigor and naturalness than the more modern, — for it is allowed to slander our own time, — and when we read a quotation from one of them in the midst of a modern author, we seem to have come suddenly upon a greener ground, a greater depth and strength of soil. It is as if a green bough were laid across the page, and we are refreshed as by the sight of fresh grass in midwinter or early spring. You have constantly the warrant of life and experience in what you read. The little that is said is eked out by implication of the much that was done. The sentences are verdurous and blooming as evergreen and flowers, because they are rooted in fact and experience, but our false and florid sentences have only the tints of flowers without their sap or roots. All men are really most attracted by the beauty of plain speech, and they even write in a florid style in imitation of this. They prefer to be misunderstood rather than to come short of its exuberance. Hussein Effendi praised the epistolary style of Ibrahim Pasha to the French traveler Botta, because of "the difficulty of understanding it; there was," he said, "but one person at Jidda who was capable of understanding and explaining the Pasha's correspondence." A man's whole life is taxed for the least thing well done. It is its net result. Every sentence is the result of a long probation. Where shall we look for standard English but to the words of a standard man? The word which is best said came nearest to not being spoken at all, for it is cousin to a

deed which the speaker could have better done. Nay,
almost it must have taken the place of a deed by some
urgent necessity, even by some misfortune, so that the
truest writer will be some captive knight, after all. And
perhaps the fates had such a design, when, having stored
Raleigh so richly with the substance of life and experience, they made him a fast prisoner, and compelled him
to make his words his deeds, and transfer to his expression the emphasis and sincerity of his action.

Men have a respect for scholarship and learning
greatly out of proportion to the use they commonly
serve. We are amused to read how Ben Jonson engaged
that the dull masks with which the royal family and
nobility were to be entertained should be "grounded
upon antiquity and solid learning." Can there be any
greater reproach than an idle learning? Learn to split
wood, at least. The necessity of labor and conversation
with many men and things to the scholar is rarely well
remembered; steady labor with the hands, which en-
grosses the attention also, is unquestionably the best
method of removing palaver and sentimentality out of
one's style, both of speaking and writing. If he has
worked hard from morning till night, though he may
have grieved that he could not be watching the train
of his thoughts during that time, yet the few hasty lines
which at evening record his day's experience will be
more musical and true than his freest but idle fancy could
have furnished. Surely the writer is to address a world of
laborers, and such therefore must be his own discipline.
He will not idly dance at his work who has wood to cut
and cord before nightfall in the short days of winter; but

every stroke will be husbanded, and ring soberly through
the wood; and so will the strokes of that scholar's pen,
which at evening record the story of the day, ring soberly,
yet cheerily, on the ear of the reader, long after the
echoes of his axe have died away. The scholar may be
sure that he writes the tougher truth for the calluses on
his palms. They give firmness to the sentence. Indeed,
the mind never makes a great and successful effort,
without a corresponding energy of the body. We are
often struck by the force and precision of style to which
hard-working men, unpracticed in writing, easily attain
when required to make the effort. As if plainness and
vigor and sincerity, the ornaments of style, were better
learned on the farm and in the workshop than in the
schools. The sentences written by such rude hands are
nervous and tough, like hardened thongs, the sinews of
the deer, or the roots of the pine. As for the graces of
expression, a great thought is never found in a mean
dress; but though it proceed from the lips of the Wolofs,
the nine Muses and the three Graces will have conspired
to clothe it in fit phrase. Its education has always been
liberal, and its implied wit can endow a college. The
world, which the Greeks called Beauty, has been made
such by being gradually divested of every ornament
which was not fitted to endure. The Sibyl, "speaking
with inspired mouth, smileless, inornate, and unper-
fumed, pierces through centuries by the power of the
god." The scholar might frequently emulate the propriety and emphasis of the farmer's call to his team, and
confess that if that were written it would surpass his
labored sentences. Whose are the truly *labored* sentences?

From the weak and flimsy periods of the politician and literary man, we are glad to turn even to the description of work, the simple record of the month's labor in the farmer's almanac, to restore our tone and spirits. A sentence should read as if its author, had he held a plow instead of a pen, could have drawn a furrow deep and straight to the end. The scholar requires hard and serious labor to give an impetus to his thought. He will learn to grasp the pen firmly so, and wield it gracefully and effectively, as an axe or a sword. When we consider the weak and nerveless periods of some literary men, who perchance in feet and inches come up to the standard of their race, and are not deficient in girth also, we are amazed at the immense sacrifice of thews and sinews. What! these proportions, these bones, — and this their work! Hands which could have felled an ox have hewed this fragile matter which would not have tasked a lady's fingers! Can this be a stalwart man's work, who has a marrow in his back and a tendon Achilles in his heel? They who set up the blocks of Stonehenge did somewhat, if they only laid out their strength for once, and stretched themselves.

Yet, after all, the truly efficient laborer will not crowd his day with work, but will saunter to his task, surrounded by a wide halo of ease and leisure, and then do but what he loves best. He is anxious only about the fruitful kernels of time. Though the hen should sit all day, she could lay only one egg, and, besides, would not have picked up materials for another. Let a man take time enough for the most trivial deed, though it be but the paring of his nails. The buds swell imperceptibly, without hurry or confusion, as if the short spring days were an eternity.

> Then spend an age in whetting thy desire,
> Thou need'st not *hasten* if thou dost *stand fast*.

Some hours seem not to be occasion for any deed, but for resolves to draw breath in. We do not directly go about the execution of the purpose that thrills us, but shut our doors behind us and ramble with prepared mind, as if the half were already done. Our resolution is taking root or hold on the earth then, as seeds first send a shoot downward which is fed by their own albumen, ere they send one upward to the light.

There is a sort of homely truth and naturalness in some books which is very rare to find, and yet looks cheap enough. There may be nothing lofty in the sentiment, or fine in the expression, but it is careless country talk. Homeliness is almost as great a merit in a book as in a house, if the reader would abide there. It is next to beauty, and a very high art. Some have this merit only. The scholar is not apt to make his most familiar experience come gracefully to the aid of his expression. Very few men can speak of Nature, for instance, with any truth. They overstep her modesty, somehow or other, and confer no favor. They do not speak a good word for her. Most cry better than they speak, and you can get more nature out of them by pinching than by addressing them. The surliness with which the woodchopper speaks of his woods, handling them as indifferently as his axe, is better than the mealy-mouthed enthusiasm of the lover of nature. Better that the primrose by the river's brim be a yellow primrose, and nothing more, than that it be something less. Aubrey relates of Thomas Fuller that his was " a very working head, insomuch that, walking and meditating before dinner, he would eat up a penny loaf, not knowing that he did it. His natural memory was very great, to which he added the art of memory. He would repeat to you forwards and backwards all the signs from Ludgate to Charing Cross." He says of Mr. John Hales, that " he loved Canarie," and was buried " under an altar monument of black marble . . . with a too long epitaph;" of Edmund Halley, that he " at sixteen could make a dial, and then, he said, he thought himself a brave fellow;" of William Holder, who wrote a book upon his curing one Popham who was deaf and dumb, " he was beholding to no author; did only consult with nature." For the most part, an author consults only with all who have written before him upon a subject, and his book is but the advice of so many. But a good book will never have been forestalled, but the topic itself will in one sense be new, and its author, by consulting with nature, will consult not only with those who have gone before, but with those who may come after. There is always room and occasion enough for a true book on any subject; as there is room for more light the brightest day, and more rays will not interfere with the first.

We thus worked our way up this river, gradually adjusting our thoughts to novelties, beholding from its placid bosom a new nature and new works of men, and, as it were with increasing confidence, finding nature

still habitable, genial, and propitious to us; not following any beaten path, but the windings of the river, as
ever the nearest way for us. Fortunately we had no business in this country. The Concord had rarely been a
river, or *rivus*, but barely *fluvius*, or between *fluvius* and
lacus. This Merrimack was neither *rivus* nor *fluvius* nor
lacus, but rather *amnis* here, a gently swelling and stately
rolling flood approaching the sea. We could even sympathize with its buoyant tide, going to seek its fortune
in the ocean, and, anticipating the time when "being
received within the plain of its freer water," it should
"beat the shores for banks," —

"campoque recepta
Liberioris aquae, pro ripis litora pulsant."

At length we doubled a low shrubby islet, called
Rabbit Island, subjected alternately to the sun and to
the waves, as desolate as if it lay some leagues within the
icy sea, and found ourselves in a narrower part of the
river, near the sheds and yards for picking the stone
known as the Chelmsford granite, which is quarried
in Westford and the neighboring towns. We passed
Wicasuck Island, which contains seventy acres or more,
on our right, between Chelmsford and Tyngsborough.
This was a favorite residence of the Indians. According
to the History of Dunstable, "About 1663, the eldest
son of Passaconaway [Chief of the Penacooks] was
thrown into jail for a debt of £45, due to John Tinker,
by one of his tribe, and which he had promised verbally
should be paid. To relieve him from his imprisonment,
his brother Wannalancet and others, who owned Wicasuck Island, sold it and paid the debt." It was, however,

restored to the Indians by the General Court in 1665.
After the departure of the Indians in 1683, it was granted
to Jonathan Tyng in payment for his services to the
colony, in maintaining a garrison at his house. Tyng's
house stood not far from Wicasuck Falls. Gookin, who,
in his Epistle Dedicatory to Robert Boyle, apologizes
for presenting his "matter clothed in a wilderness dress,"
says that, on the breaking out of Philip's war in 1675,
there were taken up by the Christian Indians and the
English in Marlborough, and sent to Cambridge, seven
"Indians belonging to Narragansett, Long Island, and
Pequod, who had all been at work about seven weeks
with one Mr. Jonathan Tyng, of Dunstable, upon Merrimack River; and, hearing of the war, they reckoned
with their master, and getting their wages, conveyed
themselves away without his privity, and, being afraid,
marched secretly through the woods, designing to go to
their own country." However, they were released soon
after. Such were the hired men in those days. Tyng was
the first permanent settler of Dunstable, which then
embraced what is now Tyngsborough and many other
towns. In the winter of 1675, in Philip's war, every other
settler left the town, but "he," says the historian of
Dunstable, "fortified his house; and, although 'obliged
to send to Boston for his food,' sat himself down in the
midst of his savage enemies, alone, in the wilderness,
to defend his home. Deeming his position an important
one for the defense of the frontiers, in February, 1676,
he petitioned the Colony for aid," humbly showing, as
his petition runs, that, as he lived "in the uppermost
house on Merrimac river, lying open to yᵉ enemy, yet

being so seated that it is, as it were, a watch-house to the neighboring towns," he could render important service to his country if only he had some assistance, "there being," he said, "never an inhabitant left in the town but myself." Wherefore he requests that their "Honors would be pleased to order him *three or four men* to help garrison his said house," which they did. But methinks that such a garrison would be weakened by the addition of a man.

> "Make bandog thy scout watch to bark at a thief,
> Make courage for life, to be captain chief;
> Make trap-door thy bulwark, make bell to begin,
> Make gunstone and arrow show who is within."

Thus he earned the title of first permanent settler. In 1694 a law was passed "that every settler who deserted a town for fear of the Indians should forfeit all his rights therein." But now, at any rate, as I have frequently observed, a man may desert the fertile frontier territories of truth and justice, which are the State's best lands, for fear of far more insignificant foes, without forfeiting any of his civil rights therein. Nay, townships are granted to deserters, and the General Court, as I am sometimes inclined to regard it, is but a deserters' camp itself.

As we rowed along near the shore of Wicasuck Island, which was then covered with wood, in order to avoid the current, two men, who looked as if they had just run out of Lowell, where they had been waylaid by the Sabbath, meaning to go to Nashua, and who now found themselves in the strange, natural, uncultivated, and unsettled part of the globe which intervenes, full of walls and barriers, a rough and uncivil place to them, seeing our boat moving so smoothly up the stream, called out from the high bank above our heads to know if we would take them as passengers, as if this were the street they had missed; that they might sit and chat and drive away the time, and so at last find themselves in Nashua. This smooth way they much preferred. But our boat was crowded with necessary furniture, and sunk low in the water, and moreover required to be worked, for even *it* did not progress against the stream without effort; so we were obliged to deny them passage. As we glided away with even sweeps, while the fates scattered oil in our course, the sun now sinking behind the alders on the distant shore, we could still see them far off over the water, running along the shore and climbing over the rocks and fallen trees like insects, — for they did not know any better than we that they were on an island, — the unsympathizing river ever flowing in an opposite direction; until, having reached the entrance of the island brook, which they had probably crossed upon the locks below, they found a more effectual barrier to their progress. They seemed to be learning much in a little time. They ran about like ants on a burning brand, and once more they tried the river here, and once more there, to see if water still indeed was not to be walked on, as if a new thought inspired them, and by some peculiar disposition of the limbs they could accomplish it. At length sober common sense seemed to have resumed its sway, and they concluded that what they had so long heard must be true, and resolved to ford the shallower stream. When nearly a mile distant we could see them stripping off their clothes and preparing for this experiment; yet it seemed likely that a new dilemma would arise, they were so thoughtlessly throwing away their clothes on the wrong side of the stream, as in the case of the country-man with his corn, his fox, and his goose, which had to be transported one at a time. Whether they got safely through, or went round by the locks, we never learned. We could not help being struck by the seeming, though innocent, indifference of Nature to these men's necessities, while elsewhere she was equally serving others. Like a true benefactress, the secret of her service is unchangeableness. Thus is the busiest merchant, though within sight of his Lowell, put to pilgrim's shifts, and soon comes to staff and scrip and scallop-shell.

We, too, who held the middle of the stream, came near experiencing a pilgrim's fate, being tempted to pursue what seemed a sturgeon or larger fish, for we remembered that this was the Sturgeon River, its dark and monstrous back alternately rising and sinking in midstream. We kept falling behind, but the fish kept his back well out, and did not dive, and seemed to prefer to swim against the stream, so, at any rate, he would not escape us by going out to sea. At length, having got as near as was convenient, and looking out not to get a blow from his tail, now the bow-gunner delivered his charge, while the stern-man held his ground. But the halibut-skinned monster, in one of these swift-gliding pregnant moments, without ever ceasing his bobbing, up and down, saw fit, without a chuckle or other prelude, to proclaim himself a huge imprisoned spar, placed there as a buoy, to warn sailors of sunken rocks. So, each casting some blame upon the other, we withdrew quickly to safer waters.

The Scene-shifter saw fit here to close the drama of this day without regard to any unities which we mortals prize. Whether it might have proved tragedy, or comedy, or tragi-comedy, or pastoral, we cannot tell. This Sunday ended by the going down of the sun, leaving us still on the waves. But they who are on the water enjoy a longer and brighter twilight than they who are on the land, for here the water, as well as the atmosphere, absorbs and reflects the light, and some of the day seems to have sunk down into the waves. The light gradually forsook the deep water, as well as the deeper air, and the gloaming came to the fishes as well as to us, and more dim and gloomy to them, whose day is a perpetual twilight, though sufficiently bright for their weak and watery eyes. Vespers had already rung in many a dim and watery chapel down below, where the shadows of the weeds were extended in length over the sandy floor. The vespertinal pout had already begun to flit on leathern fin, and the finny gossips withdrew from the fluvial street to creeks and coves, and other private haunts, excepting a few of stronger fin, which anchored in the stream, stemming the tide even in their dreams. Meanwhile, like a dark evening cloud, we were wafted over the cope of their sky, deepening the shadows on their deluged fields.

Having reached a retired part of the river where it spread out to sixty rods in width, we pitched our tent on the east side, in Tyngsborough, just above some patches of the beach plum, which was now nearly ripe, where the

sloping bank was a sufficient pillow, and with the bustle
of sailors making the land, we transferred such stores as
were required from boat to tent, and hung a lantern to
the tent-pole, and so our house was ready. With a buffalo
spread on the grass, and a blanket for our covering,
our bed was soon made. A fire crackled merrily before
the entrance, so near that we could tend it without stepping abroad, and when we had supped, we put out the
blaze, and closed the door, and with the semblance of
domestic comfort, sat up to read the Gazetteer, to learn
our latitude and longitude, and write the journal of the
voyage, or listened to the wind and the rippling of the
river till sleep overtook us. There we lay under an
oak on the bank of the stream, near to some farmer's
cornfield, getting sleep, and forgetting where we were; a
great blessing, that we are obliged to forget our enterprises every twelve hours. Minks, muskrats, meadow
mice, woodchucks, squirrels, skunks, rabbits, foxes, and
weasels, all inhabit near, but keep very close while you
are there. The river sucking and eddying away all night
down toward the marts and the seaboard, a great wash
and freshet, and no small enterprise to reflect on.
Instead of the Scythian vastness of the Billerica night,
and its wild musical sounds, we were kept awake by the
boisterous sport of some Irish laborers on the railroad,
wafted to us over the water, still unwearied and unrest-
ing on this seventh day, who would not have done with
whirling up and down the track with ever-increasing
velocity and still reviving shouts, till late in the night.

One sailor was visited in his dreams this night by the
Evil Destinies, and all those powers that are hostile

to human life, which constrain and oppress the minds of men, and make their path seem difficult and narrow, and beset with dangers, so that the most innocent and worthy enterprises appear insolent and a tempting of fate, and the gods go not with us. But the other happily passed a serene and even ambrosial or immortal night, and his sleep was dreamless, or only the atmosphere of pleasant dreams remained, a happy, natural sleep until the morning; and his cheerful spirit soothed and reassured his brother, for whenever they meet, the Good Genius is sure to prevail.

MONDAY

I thynke for to touche also
The worlde whiche neweth everie daie,
So as I can, so as I maie. — GOWER.

The hye sheryfe of Notynghame,
    Hym holde in your mynde. — *Robin Hood Ballads.*

His shoote it was but loosely shott,
    Yet flewe not the arrowe in vaine,
For it mett one of the sheriffe's men,
    And William a Trent was slaine.
                    Robin Hood Ballads.

Gazed on the Heavens for what he missed on Earth.
                    Britannia's Pastorals.

WHEN the first light dawned on the earth, and the
birds awoke, and the brave river was heard rippling
confidently seaward, and the nimble early rising wind
rustled the oak leaves about our tent, all men, having
reinforced their bodies and their souls with sleep, and
cast aside doubt and fear, were invited to unattempted
adventures.

        "All courageous knichtis
        Agains the day dichtis
        The breest-plate that bricht is,
            To feght with their foue.

        The stoned steed stampis
        Throw curage and crampis,
        Syne on the land lampis;
            The night is neir gone."

One of us took the boat over to the opposite shore, which was flat and accessible, a quarter of a mile distant, to empty it of water and wash out the clay, while the other kindled a fire and got breakfast ready. At an early hour we were again on our way, rowing through the fog as before, the river already awake, and a million crisped waves come forth to meet the sun when he should show himself. The countrymen, recruited by their day of rest, were already stirring, and had begun to cross the ferry on the business of the week. This ferry was as busy as a beaver dam, and all the world seemed anxious to get across the Merrimack River at this particular point, waiting to get set over, — children with their two cents done up in paper, jail-birds broke loose and constable with warrant, travelers from distant lands to distant lands, men and women to whom the Merrimack River was a bar. There stands a gig in the gray morning, in the mist, the impatient traveler pacing the wet shore with whip in hand, and shouting through the fog after the regardless Charon and his retreating ark, as if he might throw that passenger overboard and return forthwith for himself; he will compensate him. He is to break his fast at some unseen place on the opposite side. It may be Ledyard or the Wandering Jew. Whence, pray, did he come out of the foggy night? and whither through the sunny day will he go? We observe only his transit; important to us, forgotten by him, transiting all day. There are two of them. Maybe they are Virgil and Dante. But when they crossed the Styx, none were seen bound up or down the stream, that I remember. It is only a *transjectus*, a transitory voyage.

like life itself, none but the long-lived gods bound up or
down the stream.   Many of these Monday men are
ministers, no doubt, reseeking their parishes with hired
horses, with sermons in their valises all read and gutted,
the day after never with them.   They cross each other's
routes all the country over like woof and warp, making
a garment of loose texture; vacation now for six days.
They stop to pick nuts and berries, and gather apples,
by the wayside at their leisure.   Good religious men,
with the love of men in their hearts, and the means to
pay their toll in their pockets.   We got over this ferry
chain without scraping, rowing athwart the tide of travel,
— no toll for us that day.

The fog dispersed, and we rowed leisurely along
through Tyngsborough, with a clear sky and a mild
atmosphere, leaving the habitations of men behind,
and penetrating yet farther into the territory of ancient
Dunstable.   It was from Dunstable, then a frontier
town, that the famous Captain Lovewell, with his company, marched in quest of the Indians on the 18th of
April, 1725. He was the son of "an ensign in the army
of Oliver Cromwell, who came to this country, and settled at Dunstable, where he died at the great age of one
hundred and twenty years."   In the words of the old
nursery tale, sung about a hundred years ago, —

"He and his valiant soldiers did range the woods full wide,
   And hardships they endured to quell the Indian's pride."

In the shaggy pine forest of Pequawket they met the
"rebel Indians," and prevailed, after a bloody fight, and
a remnant returned home to enjoy the fame of their
victory. A township called Lovewell's Town, but now,

for some reason, or perhaps without reason, Pembroke,
was granted them by the State.

> "Of all our valiant English, there were but thirty-four,
>   And of the rebel Indians, there were about four-score;
>   And sixteen of our English did safely home return,
>   The rest were killed and wounded, for which we all must mourn.

> Our worthy Capt. Lovewell among them there did die,
>   They killed Lieut. Robbins, and wounded good young Frye,
>   Who was our English Chaplin; he many Indians slew,
>   And some of them he scalped while bullets round him flew."

Our brave forefathers have exterminated all the Indians, and their degenerate children no longer dwell in
garrisoned houses nor hear any war-whoop in their path.
It would be well, perchance, if many an " English Chap-
lin" in these days could exhibit as unquestionable trophies of his valor as did "good young Frye." We have
need to be as sturdy pioneers still as Miles Standish, or
Church, or Lovewell. We are to follow on another trail,
it is true, but one as convenient for ambushes. What
if the Indians are exterminated, are not savages as grim
prowling about the clearings to-day?

> "And braving many dangers and hardships in the way,
>   They safe arrived at Dunstable the thirteenth (?) day of May."

But they did not all "safe arrive in Dunstable the
thirteenth," or the fifteenth, or the thirtieth "day of
May." Eleazer Davis and Josiah Jones, both of Concord, — for our native town had seven men in this fight,
— Lieutenant Farwell, of Dunstable, and Jonathan Frye,
of Andover, who were all wounded, were left behind,
creeping toward the settlements. "After traveling sev-

eral miles, Frye was left and lost," though a more recent
poet has assigned him company in his last hours.

> "A man he was of comely form,
>   Polished and brave, well learned and kind;
> Old Harvard's learned halls he left
>   Far in the wilds a grave to find.

> "Ah! now his blood-red arm he lifts;
>   His closing lids he tries to raise;
> And speak once more before he dies,
>   In supplication and in praise.

> "He prays kind Heaven to grant success,
>   Brave Lovewell's men to guide and bless,
> And when they've shed their heart-blood true,
>   To raise them all to happiness.
>   .   .   .   .   .   .
> "Lieutenant Farwell took his hand,
>   His arm around his neck he threw,
> And said, 'Brave Chaplain, I could wish
>   That Heaven had made me die for you."

Farwell held out eleven days. "A tradition says,"
as we learn from the History of Concord, "that arriving
at a pond with Lieut. Farwell, Davis pulled off one of
his moccasins, cut it in strings, on which he fastened a
hook, caught some fish, fried and ate them. They refreshed him, but were injurious to Farwell, who died
soon after." Davis had a ball lodged in his body, and
his right hand shot off; but on the whole, he seems to
have been less damaged than his companions. He came
into Berwick after being out fourteen days. Jones also
had a ball lodged in his body, but he likewise got into
Saco after fourteen days, though not in the best condi-

tion imaginable. "He had subsisted," says an old journal, "on the spontaneous vegetables of the forest; and
cranberries which he had eaten came out of wounds he
had received in his body." This was also the case with
Davis. The last two reached home at length, safe if not
sound, and lived many years in a crippled state to enjoy
their pension.

But alas! of the crippled Indians, and their adventures in the woods, —

"For as we are informed, so thick and fast they fell,
  Scarce twenty of their number at night did get home well," —

how many balls lodged with them, how fared their cranberries, what Berwick or Saco they got into, and finally
what pension or township was granted them, there is no
journal to tell.

It is stated in the History of Dunstable that just before his last march, Lovewell was warned to beware of
the ambuscades of the enemy, but "he replied, 'that
he did not care for them,' and bending down a small
elm beside which he was standing into a bow, declared
'that he would treat the Indians in the same way.' This
elm is still standing [in Nashua], a venerable and mag-
nificent tree."

Meanwhile, having passed the Horseshoe Interval
in Tyngsborough, where the river makes a sudden bend
to the northwest, — for our reflections have anticipated
our progress somewhat, — we were advancing farther
into the country and into the day, which last proved almost as golden as the preceding, though the slight bustle
and activity of the Monday seemed to penetrate even

to this scenery. Now and then we had to muster all our
energy to get round a point, where the river broke rippling over rocks, and the maples trailed their branches
in the stream, but there was generally a backwater or
eddy on the side, of which we took advantage. The
river was here about forty rods wide and fifteen feet
deep. Occasionally one ran along the shore, examining the country, and visiting the nearest farmhouses,
while the other followed the windings of the stream
alone, to meet his companion at some distant point,
and hear the report of his adventures; how the farmer
praised the coolness of his well, and his wife offered the
stranger a draught of milk, or the children quarreled
for the only transparency in the window that they might
get sight of the man at the well. For though the country
seemed so new, and no house was observed by us, shut
in between the banks that sunny day, we did not have
to travel far to find where men inhabited, like wild bees,
and had sunk wells in the loose sand and loam of the
Merrimack. There dwelt the subject of the Hebrew
scriptures, and the Esprit des Lois, where a thin, vaporous smoke curled up through the noon. All that is told
of mankind, of the inhabitants of the Upper Nile, and
the Sunderbunds, and Timbuctoo, and the Orinoko,
was experience here. Every race and class of men was
represented. According to Belknap, the historian of
New Hampshire, who wrote sixty years ago, here too,
perchance, dwelt "new lights" and free-thinking men
even then. "The people in general throughout the
State," it is written, "are professors of the Christian religion in some form or other. There is, however, a sort

of *wise men* who pretend to reject it; but they have not
yet been able to substitute a better in its place."

The other voyageur, perhaps, would in the mean
while have seen a brown hawk, or a woodchuck, or a
musquash creeping under the alders.

We occasionally rested in the shade of a maple or a
willow, and drew forth a melon for our refreshment,
while we contemplated at our leisure the lapse of the
river and of human life; and as that current, with its
floating twigs and leaves, so did all things pass in review before us, while far away in cities and marts on
this very stream, the old routine was proceeding still.
There is, indeed, a tide in the affairs of men, as the poet
says, and yet as things flow they circulate, and the ebb
always balances the flow. All streams are but tributary
to the ocean, which itself does not stream, and the shores
are unchanged, but in longer periods than man can
measure. Go where we will, we discover infinite change
in particulars only, not in generals. When I go into a
museum and see the mummies wrapped in their linen
bandages, I see that the lives of men began to need reform as long ago as when they walked the earth. I come
out into the streets, and meet men who declare that the
time is near at hand for the redemption of the race. But
as men lived in Thebes, so do they live in Dunstable to-
day. "Time drinketh up the essence of every great and
noble action which ought to be performed, and is delayed in the execution." So says Veeshnoo Sarma; and
we perceive that the schemers return again and again
to common sense and labor. Such is the evidence of
history.

"Yet I doubt not through the ages one increasing purpose runs,
And the thoughts of men are widened with the process of the Suns."

There are secret articles in our treaties with the gods,
of more importance than all the rest, which the historian
can never know.

There are many skillful apprentices, but few master
workmen. On every hand we observe a truly wise practice, in education, in morals, and in the arts of life, the
embodied wisdom of many an ancient philosopher. Who
does not see that heresies have some time prevailed,
that reforms have already taken place? All this worldly
wisdom might be regarded as the once unamiable heresy
of some wise man. Some interests have got a footing on
the earth which we have not made sufficient allowance
for. Even they who first built these barns and cleared
the land thus, had some valor. The abrupt epochs and
chasms are smoothed down in history as the inequalities
of the plain are concealed by distance. But unless we
do more than simply learn the trade of our time, we
are but apprentices, and not yet masters of the art of
life.

Now that we are casting away these melon seeds,
how can we help feeling reproach? He who eats the
fruit should at least plant the seed; ay, if possible, a
better seed than that whose fruit he has enjoyed. Seeds,
there are seeds enough which need only be stirred in
with the soil where they lie, by an inspired voice or pen,
to bear fruit of a divine flavor. O thou spendthrift!
Defray thy debt to the world; eat not the seed of institutions, as the luxurious do, but plant it rather, while
thou devourest the pulp and tuber for thy subsistence;

that so, perchance, one variety may at last be found
worthy of preservation.

There are moments when all anxiety and stated toil
are becalmed in the infinite leisure and repose of nature. All laborers must have their nooning, and at this
season of the day, we are all, more or less, Asiatics, and
give over all work and reform. While lying thus on our
oars by the side of the stream, in the heat of the day,
our boat held by an osier put through the staple in
its prow, and slicing the melons, which are a fruit of
the East, our thoughts reverted to Arabia, Persia, and
Hindostan, the lands of contemplation and dwelling-
places of the ruminant nations. In the experience of
this noontide we could find some apology even for
the instinct of the opium, betel, and tobacco chewers.
Mount Sabér, according to the French traveler and
naturalist Botta, is celebrated for producing the Kát-
tree, of which " the soft tops of the twigs and tender
leaves are eaten," says his reviewer, " and produce an
agreeable soothing excitement, restoring from fatigue,
banishing sleep, and disposing to the enjoyment of conversation." We thought that we might lead a dignified
Oriental life along this stream as well, and the maple
and alders would be our Kát-trees.

It is a great pleasure to escape sometimes from the
restless class of Reformers. What if these grievances
exist ? So do you and I. Think you that sitting hens are
troubled with ennui these long summer days, sitting on
and on in the crevice of a hay-loft, without active employment ? By the faint cackling in distant barns, I judge
that Dame Nature is interested still to know how many

eggs her hens lay. The Universal Soul, as it is called, has an interest in the stacking of hay, the foddering of cattle, and the draining of peat-meadows. Away in Scythia, away in India, it makes butter and cheese. Suppose that all farms *are* run out, and we youths must buy old land and bring it to, still everywhere the relentless opponents of reform bear a strange resemblance to ourselves; or, perchance, they are a few old maids and bachelors, who sit round the kitchen hearth and listen to the singing of the kettle. "The oracles often give victory to our choice, and not to the order alone of the mundane periods. As, for instance, when they say that our voluntary sorrows germinate in us as the growth of the particular life we lead." The reform which you talk about can be undertaken any morning before unbarring our doors. We need not call any convention. When two neighbors begin to eat corn bread, who before ate wheat, then the gods smile from ear to ear, for it is very pleasant to them. Why do you not try it? Don't let me hinder you.

There are theoretical reformers at all times, and all the world over, living on anticipation. Wolff, traveling in the deserts of Bokhara, says, "Another party of derveeshes came to me and observed, 'The time will come when there shall be no difference between rich and poor, between high and low, when property will be in common, even wives and children.'" But forever I ask of such, What then? The derveeshes in the deserts of Bokhara and the reformers in Marlboro' Chapel sing the same song. "There's a good time coming, boys," but, asked one of the audience, in good faith,

"Can you fix the date?" Said I, "Will you help it along?"

The nonchalance and *dolce-far-niente* air of nature and society hint at infinite periods in the progress of mankind. The States have leisure to laugh from Maine to Texas at some newspaper joke, and New England shakes at the double-entendres of Australian circles, while the poor reformer cannot get a hearing.

Men do not fail commonly for want of knowledge, but for want of prudence to give wisdom the preference. What we need to know in any case is very simple. It is but too easy to establish another durable and harmonious routine. Immediately all parts of nature consent to it. Only make something to take the place of something, and men will behave as if it was the very thing they wanted. They *must* behave, at any rate, and will work up any material. There is always a present and extant life, be it better or worse, which all combine to uphold. We should be slow to mend, my friends, as slow to require mending, "Not hurling, according to the oracle, a transcendent foot towards piety." The language of excitement is at best picturesque merely. You must be calm before you can utter oracles. What was the excitement of the Delphic priestess compared with the calm wisdom of Socrates, — or whoever it was that was wise? Enthusiasm is a supernatural serenity.

> "Men find that action is another thing
>   Than what they in discoursing papers read;
>   The world's affairs require in managing
>   More arts than those wherein you clerks proceed."

As in geology, so in social institutions, we may discover

the causes of all past change in the present invariable
order of society.   The greatest appreciable physical
revolutions are the work of the light-footed air, the
stealthy-paced water, and the subterranean fire.   Aristotle said, " As time never fails, and the universe is eternal, neither the Tanais nor the Nile can have flowed
forever." We are independent of the change we detect.
The longer the lever, the less perceptible its motion.
It is the slowest pulsation which is the most vital. The
hero then will know how to wait, as well as to make
haste. All good abides with him who waiteth *wisely;*
we shall sooner overtake the dawn by remaining here
than by hurrying over the hills of the west. Be assured
that every man's success is in proportion to his *average*
ability. The meadow flowers spring and bloom where
the waters annually deposit their slime, not where they
reach in some freshet only. A man is not his hope, nor
his despair, nor yet his past deed. We know not yet what
we have done, still less what we are doing. Wait till
evening, and other parts of our day's work will shine
than we had thought at noon, and we shall discover the
real purport of our toil. As when the farmer has reached
the end of the furrow and looks back, he can tell best
where the pressed earth shines most.

To one who habitually endeavors to contemplate
the true state of things, the political state can hardly
be said to have any existence whatever. It is unreal,
incredible, and insignificant to him, and for him to
endeavor to extract the truth from such lean material
is like making sugar from linen rags, when sugar-cane

may be had.   Generally speaking, the political news,
whether domestic or foreign, might be written to-day
for the next ten years with sufficient accuracy.   Most
revolutions in society have not power to interest, still less
alarm us; but tell me that our rivers are drying up, or
the genus pine dying out in the country, and I might
attend. Most events recorded in history are more remarkable than important, like eclipses of the sun and
moon, by which all are attracted, but whose effects no
one takes the trouble to calculate.

But will the government never be so well adminis-
tered, inquired one, that we private men shall hear
nothing about it? "The king answered: At all events,
I require a prudent and able man, who is capable of
managing the state affairs of my kingdom. The ex-
minister said: The criterion, O Sire! of a wise and
competent man is, that he will not meddle with such
like matters." Alas that the ex-minister should have
been so nearly right!

In my short experience of human life, the *outward*
obstacles, if there were any such, have not been living
men, but the institutions of the dead. It is grateful to
make one's way through this latest generation as through
dewy grass. Men are as innocent as the morning to the
unsuspicious.

> "And round about good morrows fly,
>   As if day taught humanity."

Not being Reve of this Shire, —

> "The early pilgrim blythe he hailed,
>   That o'er the hills did stray,
> And many an early husbandman,
>   That he met on the way;" —

thieves and robbers all, nevertheless. I have not so surely foreseen that any Cossack or Chippeway would come to disturb the honest and simple commonwealth, as that some monster institution would at length embrace and crush its free members in its scaly folds; for it is not to be forgotten, that while the law holds fast the thief and murderer, it lets itself go loose. When I have not paid the tax which the State demanded for that protection which I did not want, itself has robbed me; when I have asserted the liberty it presumed to declare, itself has imprisoned me. Poor creature! if it knows no better I will not blame it. If it cannot live but by these means, I can. I do not wish, it happens, to be associated with Massachusetts, either in holding slaves or in conquering Mexico. I am a little better than herself in these respects. As for Massachusetts, that huge she Briareus, Argus, and Colchian Dragon conjoined, set to watch the Heifer of the Constitution and the Golden Fleece, we would not warrant our respect for her, like some compositions, to preserve its qualities through all weathers. Thus it has happened, that not the Arch Fiend himself has been in my way, but these toils which tradition says were originally spun to obstruct him. They are cobwebs and trifling obstacles in an earnest man's path, it is true, and at length one even becomes attached to his unswept and undusted garret. I love man — kind, but I hate the institutions of the dead unkind. Men execute nothing so faithfully as the wills of the dead, to the last codicil and letter. *They* rule this world, and the living are but their executors. Such foundation too have our lectures and our sermons, commonly. They are all

Dudleian; and piety derives its origin still from that exploit of *pius Æneas*, who bore his father, Anchises, on his shoulders from the ruins of Troy. Or, rather, like some Indian tribes, we bear about with us the mouldering relics of our ancestors on our shoulders. If, for instance, a man asserts the value of individual liberty over the merely political commonweal, his neighbor still tolerates him, that is, he who is *living near* him, sometimes even sustains him, but never the State. Its officer, as a living man, may have human virtues and a thought in his brain, but as the tool of an institution, a jailer or constable it may be, he is not a whit superior to his prison key or his staff. Herein is the tragedy: that men doing outrage to their proper natures, even those called wise and good, lend themselves to perform the office of inferior and brutal ones. Hence come war and slavery in; and what else may not come in by this opening? But certainly there are modes by which a man may put bread into his mouth which will not prejudice him as a companion and neighbor.

> "Now turn again, turn again, said the pindér,
>   For a wrong way you have gone,
> For you have forsaken the king's highway,
>   And made a path over the corn."

Undoubtedly, countless reforms are called for because society is not animated, or instinct enough with life, but in the condition of some snakes which I have seen in early spring, with alternate portions of their bodies torpid and flexible, so that they could wriggle neither way. All men are partially buried in the grave of custom, and of some we see only the crown of the head above ground. Better are the physically dead, for they more lively rot. Even virtue is no longer such if it be stagnant. A man's life should be constantly as fresh as this river. It should be the same channel, but a new water every instant.

> "Virtues as rivers pass,
> But still remains that virtuous man there was."

Most men have no inclination, no rapids, no cascades, but marshes, and alligators, and miasma instead. We read that when, in the expedition of Alexander, Onesicritus was sent forward to meet certain of the Indian sect of Gymnosophists, and he had told them of those new philosophers of the West, Pythagoras, Socrates, and Diogenes, and their doctrines, one of them, named Dandamis, answered that "they appeared to him to have been men of genius, but to have lived with too passive a regard for the laws." The philosophers of the West are liable to this rebuke still. "They say that Lieou-hia-hoei and Chao-lien did not sustain to the end their resolutions, and that they dishonored their character. Their language was in harmony with reason and justice; while their acts were in harmony with the sentiments of men."

Chateaubriand said: "There are two things which grow stronger in the breast of man, in proportion as he advances in years, — the love of country and religion. Let them be never so much forgotten in youth, they sooner or later present themselves to us arrayed in all their charms, and excite in the recesses of our hearts an attachment justly due to their beauty." It may be so. But even this infirmity of noble minds marks the gradual

decay of youthful hope and faith. It is the allowed infidelity of age. There is a saying of the Wolofs, "He
who was born first has the greatest number of old
clothes ;" consequently M. Chateaubriand has more
old clothes than I have. It is comparatively a faint and
reflected beauty that is admired, not an essential and
intrinsic one. It is because the old are weak, feel their
mortality, and think that they have measured the
strength of man. They will not boast; they will be
frank and humble. Well, let them have the few poor
comforts they can keep. Humility is still a very human
virtue. They look back on life, and so see not into the
future. The prospect of the young is forward and un-
bounded, mingling the future with the present. In the
declining day the thoughts make haste to rest in darkness, and hardly look forward to the ensuing morning.
The thoughts of the old prepare for night and slumber.
The same hopes and prospects are not for him who
stands upon the rosy mountain-tops of life, and him
who expects the setting of his earthly day.

I must conclude that Conscience, if that be the name
of it, was not given us for no purpose, or for a hindrance.
However flattering order and expediency may look, it
is but the repose of a lethargy, and we will choose rather
to be awake, though it be stormy, and maintain ourselves on this earth, and in this life, as we may, without
signing our death-warrant. Let us see if we cannot stay
here, where He has put us, on his own conditions. Does
not his law reach as far as his light? The expedients
of the nations clash with one another: only the absolutely right is expedient for all.

There are some passages in the Antigone of Sophocles, well known to scholars, of which I am reminded in this connection. Antigone has resolved to sprinkle sand on the dead body of her brother Polynices, notwithstanding the edict of King Creon condemning to death that one who should perform this service, which the Greeks deemed so important, for the enemy of his country; but Ismene, who is of a less resolute and noble spirit, declines taking part with her sister in this work, and says,—

" I, therefore, asking those under the earth to consider me, that I am compelled to do thus, will obey those who are placed in office; for to do extreme things is not wise."

Antigone. " I would not ask you, nor would you, if you still wished, do it joyfully with me. Be such as seems good to you. But I will bury him. It is glorious for me doing this to die. I beloved will lie with him beloved, having, like a criminal, done what is holy; since the time is longer which it is necessary for me to please those below, than those here, for there I shall always lie. But if it seems good to you, hold in dishonor things which are honored by the gods."

Ismene. " I indeed do not hold them in dishonor; but to act in opposition to the citizens I am by nature unable."

Antigone being at length brought before King Creon, he asks, —

" Did you then dare to transgress these laws ? "

Antigone. " For it was not Zeus who proclaimed these to me, nor Justice who dwells with the gods below; it was not they who established these laws among men.

Nor did I think that your proclamations were so strong,
as, being a mortal, to be able to transcend the unwritten
and immovable laws of the gods. For not something
now and yesterday, but forever these live, and no one
knows from what time they appeared. I was not about
to pay the penalty of violating these to the gods, fearing
the presumption of any man. For I well knew that I
should die, and why not? even if you had not proclaimed it."

This was concerning the burial of a dead body.

The wisest conservatism is that of the Hindoos.
"Immemorial custom is transcendent law," says Menu.
That is, it was the custom of the gods before men used
it. The fault of our New England custom is that it is
memorial. What is morality but immemorial custom?
Conscience is the chief of conservatives. "Perform
the settled functions," says Kreeshna in the Bhagvat-
Geeta; "action is preferable to inaction. The journey
of thy mortal frame may not succeed from inaction."
"A man's own calling, with all its faults, ought not to be
forsaken. Every undertaking is involved in its faults
as the fire in its smoke." "The man who is acquainted
with the whole should not drive those from their works
who are slow of comprehension, and less experienced
than himself."   "Wherefore, O Arjoon, resolve to
fight," is the advice of the god to the irresolute soldier
who fears to slay his best friends. It is a sublime conservatism; as wide as the world, and as unwearied as
time; preserving the universe with Asiatic anxiety, in
that state in which it appeared to their minds. These

philosophers dwell on the inevitability and unchangeableness of laws, on the power of temperament and constitution, the three *goon*, or qualities, and the circumstances, or birth and affinity. The end is an immense
consolation; eternal absorption in Brahma. Their
speculations never venture beyond their own table-
lands, though they are high and vast as they. Buoyancy, freedom, flexibility, variety, possibility, which
also are qualities of the Unnamed, they deal not with.
The undeserved reward is to be earned by an everlasting
moral drudgery; the incalculable promise of the morrow is, as it were, weighed. And who will say that their
conservatism has not been effectual? "Assuredly,"
says a French translator, speaking of the antiquity
and durability of the Chinese and Indian nations, and
of the wisdom of their legislators, "there are some vestiges of the eternal laws which govern the world."

Christianity, on the other hand, is humane, practical, and, in a large sense, radical. So many years and
ages of the gods those Eastern sages sat contemplating
Brahm, uttering in silence the mystic "Om," being
absorbed into the essence of the Supreme Being, never
going out of themselves, but subsiding farther and
deeper within; so infinitely wise, yet infinitely stagnant; until, at last, in that same Asia, but in the western part of it, appeared a youth, wholly unforetold by
them, — not being absorbed into Brahm, but bringing
Brahm down to earth and to mankind; in whom Brahm
had awaked from his long sleep, and exerted himself,
and the day began, — a new avatar. The Brahman
had never thought to be a brother of mankind as well

as a child of God. Christ is the prince of Reformers
and Radicals. Many expressions in the New Testament come naturally to the lips of all Protestants, and
it furnishes the most pregnant and practical texts.
There is no harmless dreaming, no wise speculation in
it, but everywhere a substratum of good sense. It never
reflects, but it *repents*. There is no poetry in it, we may
say, nothing regarded in the light of beauty merely, but
moral truth is its object. All mortals are convicted
by its conscience.

The New Testament is remarkable for its pure
morality; the best of the Hindoo Scripture, for its pure
intellectuality. The reader is nowhere raised into and
sustained in a higher, purer, or *rarer* region of thought
than in the Bhagvat-Geeta. Warren Hastings, in his
sensible letter recommending the translation of this
book to the Chairman of the East India Company, de-
clares the original to be " of a sublimity of conception,
reasoning, and diction almost unequaled," and that
the writings of the Indian philosophers "will survive
when the British dominion in India shall have long
ceased to exist, and when the sources which it once
yielded of wealth and power are lost to remembrance."
It is unquestionably one of the noblest and most sacred
scriptures which have come down to us. Books are to
be distinguished by the grandeur of their topics even
more than by the manner in which they are treated.
The Oriental philosophy approaches easily loftier
themes than the modern aspires to; and no wonder if
it sometimes prattle about them. It only assigns their
due rank respectively to Action and Contemplation, or

rather does full justice to the latter. Western philosophers have not conceived of the significance of Contemplation in their sense. Speaking of the spiritual discipline to which the Brahmans subjected themselves, and the wonderful power of abstraction to which they attained, instances of which had come under his notice, Hastings says: —

"To those who have never been accustomed to the separation of the mind from the notices of the senses, it may not be easy to conceive by what means such a power is to be attained; since even the most studious men of our hemisphere will find it difficult so to restrain their attention, but that it will wander to some object of present sense or recollection; and even the buzzing of a fly will sometimes have the power to disturb it. But if we are told that there have been men who were successively, for ages past, in the daily habit of abstracted contemplation, begun in the earliest period of youth, and continued in many to the maturity of age, each adding some portion of knowledge to the store accumulated by his predecessors; it is not assuming too much to conclude, that as the mind ever gathers strength, like the body, by exercise, so in such an exercise it may in each have acquired the faculty to which they aspired, and that their collective studies may have led them to the discovery of new tracts and combinations of sentiment, totally different from the doctrines with which the learned of other nations are acquainted; doctrines which, however speculative and subtle, still as they possess the advantage of being derived from a source so free from every adventitious

mixture, may be equally founded in truth with the most
simple of our own."

"The forsaking of works" was taught by Kreeshna
to the most ancient of men, and handed down from
age to age, "until at length, in the course of time, the
mighty art was lost."

"In wisdom is to be found every work without exception," says Kreeshna.

"Although thou wert the greatest of all offenders,
thou shalt be able to cross the gulf of sin with the
bark of wisdom."

"There is not anything in this world to be compared
with wisdom for purity."

"The action stands at a distance inferior to the application of wisdom."

The wisdom of a Moonee "is confirmed, when, like
the tortoise, he can draw in all his members, and restrain them from their wonted purposes."

"Children only, and not the learned, speak of the
speculative and the practical doctrines as two. They
are but one. For both obtain the selfsame end, and
the place which is gained by the followers of the one
is gained by the followers of the other."

"The man enjoyeth not freedom from action, from
the non-commencement of that which he hath to do;
nor doth he obtain happiness from a total inactivity.
No one ever resteth a moment inactive. Every man is
involuntarily urged to act by those principles which
are inherent in his nature. The man who restraineth his
active faculties, and sitteth down with his mind attentive to the objects of his senses, is called one of an

astrayed soul, and the practicer of deceit. So the man
is praised, who, having subdued all his passions, per-
formeth with his active faculties all the functions of
life, unconcerned about the event."

"Let the motive be in the deed and not in the event.
Be not one whose motive for action is the hope of reward. Let not thy life be spent in inaction."

"For the man who doeth that which he hath to do,
without affection, obtaineth the Supreme."

"He who may behold as it were inaction in action,
and action in inaction, is wise amongst mankind. He
is a perfect performer of all duty."

"Wise men call him a *Pandeet*, whose every undertaking is free from the idea of desire, and whose actions
are consumed by the fire of wisdom. He abandoneth
the desire of a reward of his actions; he is always contented and independent; and although he may be engaged in a work, he as it were doeth nothing."

"He is both a Yogee and a Sannyasee who perform-
eth that which he hath to do independent of the fruit
thereof; not he who liveth without the sacrificial fire
and without action."

"He who enjoyeth but the Amreeta which is left of
his offerings obtaineth the eternal spirit of Brahm, the
Supreme."

What, after all, does the practicalness of life amount
to? The things immediate to de done are very trivial.
I could postpone them all to hear this locust sing. The
most glorious fact in my experience is not anything that
I have done or may hope to do, but a transient thought,
or vision, or dream, which I have had. I would give all

the wealth of the world, and all the deeds of all the
heroes, for one true vision. But how can I communicate with the gods, who am a pencil-maker on the earth,
and not be insane?

"I am the same to all mankind," says Kreeshna;
"there is not one who is worthy of my love or hatred."

This teaching is not practical in the sense in which
the New Testament is. It is not always sound sense in
practice. The Brahman never proposes courageously
to assault evil, but patiently to starve it out. His active
faculties are paralyzed by the idea of caste, of impassa-
ble limits of destiny and the tyranny of time. Kreeshna's
argument, it must be allowed, is defective. No sufficient
reason is given why Arjoon should fight. Arjoon may
be convinced, but the reader is not, for his judgment
is *not* "formed upon the speculative doctrines of the
Sankhya Sastra." "Seek an asylum in wisdom alone;"
but what is wisdom to a Western mind? The duty of
which he speaks is an arbitrary one. When was it established? The Brahman's virtue consists in doing, not
right, but arbitrary things. What is that which a man
"hath to do"? What is "action"? What are the "settled functions"? What is "a man's own religion,"
which is so much better than another's? What is "a
man's own particular calling"? What are the duties
which are appointed by one's birth? It is a defense of
the institution of castes, of what is called the "natural
duty" of the Kshetree, or soldier, "to attach himself
to the discipline," "not to flee from the field," and the
like. But they who are unconcerned about the conse-
quences of their actions are not therefore unconcerned
about their actions.

Behold the difference between the Oriental and the Occidental. The former has nothing to do in this world; the latter is full of activity. The one looks in the sun till his eyes are put out; the other follows him prone in his westward course. There is such a thing as caste, even in the West; but it is comparatively faint; it is conservatism here. It says, forsake not your calling, outrage no institution, use no violence, rend no bonds; the State is thy parent. Its virtue or manhood is wholly filial. There is a struggle between the Oriental and Occidental in every nation; some who would be forever contemplating the sun, and some who are hastening toward the sunset. The former class says to the latter, When you have reached the sunset, you will be no nearer to the sun. To which the latter replies, But we so prolong the day. The former "walketh but in that night, when all things go to rest in the night of *time*. The contemplative Moonee sleepeth but in the day of *time*, when all things wake."

To conclude these extracts, I can say, in the words of Sanjay, "As, O mighty Prince! I recollect again and again this holy and wonderful dialogue of Kreeshna and Arjoon, I continue more and more to rejoice; and as I recall to my memory the more than miraculous form of Haree, my astonishment is great, and I marvel and rejoice again and again! Wherever Kreeshna the God of devotion may be, wherever Arjoon the mighty bowman may be, there too, without doubt, are fortune, riches, victory, and good conduct. This is my firm belief."

I would say to the readers of Scriptures, if they wish

for a good book, read the Bhagvat-Geeta, an episode
to the Mahabharat, said to have been written by
Kreeshna Dwypayen Veias, — known to have been
written by ——, more than four thousand years ago, —
it matters not whether three or four, or when, — translated by Charles Wilkins. It deserves to be read with
reverence even by Yankees, as a part of the sacred
writings of a devout people; and the intelligent Hebrew
will rejoice to find in it a moral grandeur and sublimity
akin to those of his own Scriptures.

To an American reader, who, by the advantage of
his position, can see over that strip of Atlantic coast to
Asia and the Pacific, who, as it were, sees the shore
slope upward over the Alps to the Himmaleh Mountains, the comparatively recent literature of Europe
often appears partial and clannish; and, notwithstanding the limited range of his own sympathies and studies,
the European writer who presumes that he is speaking
for the world is perceived by him to speak only for that
corner of it which he inhabits. One of the rarest of
England's scholars and critics, in his classification of
the worthies of the world, betrays the narrowness of his
European culture and the exclusiveness of his reading.
None of her children has done justice to the poets and
philosophers of Persia or of India. They have even
been better known to her merchant scholars than to
her poets and thinkers by profession. You may look in
vain through English poetry for a single memorable
verse inspired by these themes. Nor is Germany to
be excepted, though her philological industry is indi-
rectly serving the cause of philosophy and poetry. Even

Goethe wanted that universality of genius which could
have appreciated the philosophy of India, if he had
more nearly approached it. His genius was more practical, dwelling much more in the regions of the understanding, and was less native to contemplation than
the genius of those sages. It is remarkable that Homer
and a few Hebrews are the most Oriental names which
modern Europe, whose literature has taken its rise since
the decline of the Persian, has admitted into her list of
Worthies, and perhaps the *worthiest* of mankind, and
the fathers of modern thinking, — for the contemplations of those Indian sages have influenced, and still
influence, the intellectual development of mankind, —
whose works even yet survive in wonderful completeness, are, for the most part, not recognized as ever having existed. If the lions had been the painters, it would
have been otherwise. In every one's youthful dreams,
philosophy is still vaguely but inseparably, and with
singular truth, associated with the East, nor do after
years discover its local habitation in the Western world.
In comparison with the philosophers of the East, we
may say that modern Europe has yet given birth to
none. Beside the vast and cosmogonal philosophy of
the Bhagvat-Geeta, even our Shakespeare seems sometimes youthfully green and practical merely. Some of
these sublime sentences, as the Chaldæan oracles of
Zoroaster, still surviving after a thousand revolutions
and translations, alone make us doubt if the poetic
form and dress are not transitory, and not essential to
the most effective and enduring expression of thought.
Ex oriente lux may still be the motto of scholars, for

the Western world has not yet derived from the East all the light which it is destined to receive thence.

It would be worthy of the age to print together the collected Scriptures or Sacred Writings of the several nations, the Chinese, the Hindoos, the Persians, the Hebrews, and others, as the Scripture of mankind. The New Testament is still, perhaps, too much on the lips and in the hearts of men to be called a Scripture in this sense. Such a juxtaposition and comparison might help to liberalize the faith of men. This is a work which Time will surely edit, reserved to crown the labors of the printing-press. This would be the Bible, or Book of Books, which let the missionaries carry to the uttermost parts of the earth.

While engaged in these reflections, thinking ourselves the only navigators of these waters, suddenly a canal-boat, with its sail set, glided round a point before us, like some huge river beast, and changed the scene in an instant; and then another and another glided into sight, and we found ourselves in the current of commerce once more. So we threw our rinds in the water for the fishes to nibble, and added our breath to the life of living men. Little did we think, in the distant garden in which we had planted the seed and reared this fruit, where it would be eaten. Our melons lay at home on the sandy bottom of the Merrimack, and our potatoes in the sun and water at the bottom of the boat looked like a fruit of the country. Soon, however, we were delivered from this fleet of junks, and possessed the river in solitude, once more rowing steadily upward through the noon,

between the territories of Nashua on the one hand and
Hudson, once Nottingham, on the other. From time
to time we scared up a kingfisher or a summer duck,
the former flying rather by vigorous impulses than by
steady and patient steering with that short rudder of
his, sounding his rattle along the fluvial street.

Ere long another scow hove in sight, creeping down
the river; and hailing it, we attached ourselves to its
side, and floated back in company, chatting with the
boatmen, and obtaining a draught of cooler water from
their jug. They appeared to be green hands from far
among the hills, who had taken this means to get to the
seaboard, and see the world; and would possibly visit
the Falkland Isles, and the China seas, before they
again saw the waters of the Merrimack, or, perchance,
they would not return this way forever. They had already embarked the private interests of the landsman
in the larger venture of the race, and were ready to mess
with mankind, reserving only the till of a chest to themselves. But they too were soon lost behind a point, and
we went croaking on our way alone. What grievance
has its root among the New Hampshire hills? we
asked; what is wanting to human life here, that these
men should make haste to the antipodes? We prayed
that their bright anticipations might not be rudely disappointed.

> Though all the fates should prove unkind,
> Leave not your native land behind.
> The ship, becalmed, at length stands still;
> The steed must rest beneath the hill;
> But swiftly still our fortunes pace
> To find us out in every place.

The vessel, though her masts be firm,
Beneath her copper bears a worm;
Around the cape, across the line,
Till fields of ice her course confine;
It matters not how smooth the breeze,
How shallow or how deep the seas,
Whether she bears Manilla twine,
Or in her hold Madeira wine,
Or China teas, or Spanish hides,
In port or quarantine she rides;
Far from New England's blustering shore,
New England's worm her hulk shall bore,
And sink her in the Indian seas,
Twine, wine, and hides, and China teas.

We passed a small desert here on the east bank, between Tyngsborough and Hudson, which was interesting and even refreshing to our eyes in the midst of the almost universal greenness. This sand was indeed somewhat impressive and beautiful to us. A very old inhabitant, who was at work in a field on the Nashua side, told us that he remembered when corn and grain grew there, and it was a cultivated field. But at length the fishermen — for this was a fishing-place — pulled up the bushes on the shore, for greater convenience in hauling their seines, and when the bank was thus broken, the wind began to blow up the sand from the shore, until at length it had covered about fifteen acres several feet deep. We saw near the river, where the sand was blown off down to some ancient surface, the foundation of an Indian wigwam exposed, a perfect circle of burnt stones, four or five feet in diameter, mingled with fine charcoal, and the bones of small animals which had been preserved in the sand. The surrounding sand was sprinkled

with other burnt stones on which their fires had been
built, as well as with flakes of arrowhead stone, and we
found one perfect arrowhead. In one place we noticed
where an Indian had sat to manufacture arrowheads
out of quartz, and the sand was sprinkled with a quart
of small glass-like chips about as big as a fourpence,
which he had broken off in his work. Here, then, the
Indians must have fished before the whites arrived.
There was another similar sandy tract about half a mile
above this.

Still the noon prevailed, and we turned the prow
aside to bathe, and recline ourselves under some buttonwoods, by a ledge of rocks, in a retired pasture sloping to
the water's edge and skirted with pines and hazels, in
the town of Hudson. Still had India, and that old noontide philosophy, the better part of our thoughts.

It is always singular, but encouraging, to meet with
common sense in very old books, as the Heetopades of
Veeshnoo Sarma; a playful wisdom which has eyes
behind as well as before, and oversees itself. It asserts
their health and independence of the experience of later
times. This pledge of sanity cannot be spared in a book,
that it sometimes pleasantly reflect upon itself. The
story and fabulous portion of this book winds loosely
from sentence to sentence as so many oases in a desert,
and is as indistinct as a camel's track between Mourzouk
and Darfour. It is a comment on the flow and freshet
of modern books. The reader leaps from sentence to
sentence, as from one stepping-stone to another, while
the stream of the story rushes past unregarded. The
Bhagvat-Geeta is less sententious and poetic, perhaps.

but still more wonderfully sustained and developed.
Its sanity and sublimity have impressed the minds even
of soldiers and merchants. It is the characteristic of
great poems that they will yield of their sense in due
proportion to the hasty and the deliberate reader. To the
practical they will be common sense, and to the wise
wisdom; as either the traveler may wet his lips, or an
army may fill its water-casks at a full stream.

One of the most attractive of those ancient books
that I have met with is the Laws of Menu. According
to Sir William Jones, " Vyasa, the son of Parasara, has
decided that the Veda, with its Angas, or the six compositions deduced from it, the revealed system of medicine, the Puranas or sacred histories, and the code of
Menu, were four works of supreme authority, which
ought never to be shaken by arguments merely human."
The last is believed by the Hindoos "to have been
promulged in the beginning of time, by Menu, son or
grandson of Brahma," and "first of created beings;"
and Brahma is said to have "taught his laws to Menu in
a hundred thousand verses, which Menu explained to
the primitive world in the very words of the book now
translated." Others affirm that they have undergone
successive abridgments for the convenience of mortals,
" while the gods of the lower heaven and the band of
celestial musicians are engaged in studying the primary
code." "A number of glosses or comments on Menu
were composed by the Munis, or old philosophers, whose
treatises, together with that before us, constitute the
Dherma Sastra, in a collective sense, or Body of Law."
Culluca Bhatta was one of the more modern of these.

Every sacred book, successively, has been accepted in the faith that it was to be the final resting-place of the sojourning soul; but after all, it was but a caravansary which supplied refreshment to the traveler, and directed him farther on his way to Isphahan or Bagdat. Thank God, no Hindoo tyranny prevailed at the framing of the world, but we are freemen of the universe, and not sentenced to any caste.

I know of no book which has come down to us with grander pretensions than this, and it is so impersonal and sincere that it is never offensive nor ridiculous. Compare the modes in which modern literature is advertised with the prospectus of this book, and think what a reading public it addresses, what criticism it expects. It seems to have been uttered from some eastern summit, with a sober morning prescience in the dawn of time, and you cannot read a sentence without being elevated as upon the table-land of the Ghauts. It has such a rhythm as the winds of the desert, such a tide as the Ganges, and is as superior to criticism as the Himmaleh Mountains. Its tone is of such unrelaxed fibre that even at this late day, unworn by time, it wears the English and the Sanskrit dress indifferently; and its fixed sentences keep up their distant fires still, like the stars, by whose dissipated rays this lower world is illumined. The whole book by noble gestures and inclinations renders many words unnecessary. English sense has toiled, but Hindoo wisdom never perspired. Though the sentences open as we read them, unexpensively, and at first almost unmeaningly, as the petals of a flower, they sometimes startle us with that rare kind of wisdom which could

only have been learned from the most trivial experience¦
but it comes to us as refined as the porcelain earth which
subsides to the bottom of the ocean. They are clean and
dry as fossil truths, which have been exposed to the
elements for thousands of years, so impersonally and
scientifically true that they are the ornament of the
parlor and the cabinet. Any *moral* philosophy is exceedingly rare. This of Menu addresses our privacy more
than most. It is a more private and familiar, and at the
same time a more public and universal word, than is
spoken in parlor or pulpit nowadays. As our domestic
fowls are said to have their original in the wild pheasant
of India, so our domestic thoughts have their proto-
types in the thoughts of her philosophers. We are dab-
bling in the very elements of our present conventional
and actual life; as if it were the primeval conventicle,
where how to eat, and to drink, and to sleep, and maintain life with adequate dignity and sincerity, were the
questions to be decided. It is later and more intimate
with us even than the advice of our nearest friends. And
yet it is true for the widest horizon, and read out of doors
has relation to the dim mountain line, and is native and
aboriginal there. Most books belong to the house and
street only, and in the fields their leaves feel very thin.
They are bare and obvious, and have no halo nor haze
about them. Nature lies far and fair behind them all.
But this, as it proceeds from, so it addresses, what is
deepest and most abiding in man. It belongs to the
noontide of the day, the midsummer of the year, and
after the snows have melted, and the waters evaporated
in the spring, still its truth speaks freshly to our experi-

ence. It helps the sun to shine, and his rays fall on its
page to illustrate it. It spends the mornings and the evenings, and makes such an impression on us overnight
as to awaken us before dawn, and its influence lingers
around us like a fragrance late into the day. It conveys
a new gloss to the meadows and the depths of the wood,
and its spirit, like a more subtile ether, sweeps along
with the prevailing winds of a country. The very locusts
and crickets of a summer day are but later or earlier
glosses on the Dherma Sastra of the Hindoos, a continu-
ation of the sacred code. As we have said, there is an
orientalism in the most restless pioneer, and the farthest
west is but the farthest east. While we are reading these
sentences, this fair modern world seems only a reprint of
the Laws of Menu with the gloss of Culluca. Tried by a
New England eye, or the more practical wisdom of modern times, they are the oracles of a race already in its
dotage; but held up to the sky, which is the only impartial and incorruptible ordeal, they are of a piece with its
depth and serenity, and I am assured that they will have
a place and significance as long as there is a sky to test
them by.

Give me a sentence which no intelligence can understand. There must be a kind of life and palpitation to it,
and under its words a kind of blood must circulate forever. It is wonderful that this sound should have come
down to us from so far, when the voice of man can be
heard so little way, and we are not now within earshot of
any contemporary. The woodcutters have here felled an
ancient pine forest, and brought to light to these distant
hills a fair lake in the southwest; and now in an instant

it is distinctly shown to these woods as if its image had
traveled hither from eternity. Perhaps these old stumps
upon the knoll remember when anciently this lake
gleamed in the horizon. One wonders if the bare earth
itself did not experience emotion at beholding again so
fair a prospect. That fair water lies there in the sun thus
revealed, so much the prouder and fairer because its
beauty needed not to be seen. It seems yet lonely, sufficient to itself and superior to observation. So are these
old sentences like serene lakes in the southwest, at length
revealed to us, which have so long been reflecting our
own sky in their bosom.

The great plain of India lies as in a cup between the
Himmaleh and the ocean on the north and south, and
the Brahmapootra and Indus on the east and west,
wherein the primeval race was received. We will not
dispute the story. We are pleased to read in the natural history of the country, of the "pine, larch, spruce,
and silver fir," which cover the southern face of the
Himmaleh range; of the "gooseberry, raspberry, straw-
berry," which from an imminent temperate zone overlook the torrid plains. So did this active modern life
have even then a foothold and lurking-place in the
midst of the stateliness and contemplativeness of those
Eastern plains. In another era the "lily of the valley,
cowslip, dandelion " were to work their way down into
the plain, and bloom in a level zone of their own reaching
round the earth. Already has the era of the temperate
zone arrived, the era of the pine and the oak, for the
palm and the banian do not supply the wants of this age.
The lichens on the summits of the rocks will perchance
find their level ere long.

As for the tenets of the Brahmans, we are not so much concerned to know what doctrines they held, as that they were held by any. We can tolerate all philosophies, Atomists, Pneumatologists, Atheists, Theists, — Plato, Aristotle, Leucippus, Democritus, Pythagoras, Zoroaster, and Confucius. It is the attitude of these men, more than any communication which they make, that attracts us. Between them and their commentators, it is true, there is an endless dispute. But if it comes to this, that you compare notes, then you are all wrong. As it is, each takes us up into the serene heavens, whither the smallest bubble rises as surely as the largest, and paints earth and sky for us. Any sincere thought is irresistible. The very austerity of the Brahmans is tempting to the devotional soul, as a more refined and nobler luxury. Wants so easily and gracefully satisfied seem like a more refined pleasure. Their conception of creation is peaceful as a dream. "When that power awakes, then has this world its full expansion; but when he slumbers with a tranquil spirit, then the whole system fades away." In the very indistinctness of their theogony a sublime truth is implied. It hardly allows the reader to rest in any supreme first cause, but directly it hints at a supremer still which created the last, and the Creator is still behind increate.

Nor will we disturb the antiquity of this Scripture, "From fire, from air, and from the sun," it was "milked out." One might as well investigate the chronology of light and heat. Let the sun shine. Menu understood this matter best, when he said, "Those best know the divisions of days and nights who understand that the day of

Brahma, which endures to the end of a thousand such ages [infinite ages, nevertheless, according to mortal reckoning], gives rise to virtuous exertions; and that his night endures as long as his day." Indeed, the Mussulman and Tartar dynasties are beyond all dating. Methinks I have lived under them myself. In every man's brain is the Sanskrit. The Vedas and their Angas are not so ancient as serene contemplation. Why will we be imposed on by antiquity? Is the babe young? When I behold it, it seems more venerable than the oldest man; it is more ancient than Nestor or the Sibyls, and bears the wrinkles of father Saturn himself. And do we live but in the present? How broad a line is that? I sit now on a stump whose rings number centuries of growth. If I look around I see that the soil is composed of the remains of just such stumps, ancestors to this. The earth is covered with mould. I thrust this stick many æons deep into its surface, and with my heel make a deeper furrow than the elements have ploughed here for a thousand years. If I listen, I hear the peep of frogs which is older than the slime of Egypt, and the distant drumming of a partridge on a log, as if it were the pulse-beat of the summer air. I raise my fairest and freshest flowers in the old mould. Why, what we would fain call new is not skin deep; the earth is not yet stained by it. It is not the fertile ground which we walk on, but the leaves which flutter over our heads. The newest is but the oldest made visible to our senses. When we dig up the soil from a thousand feet below the surface, we call it new, and the plants which spring from it; and when our vision pierces deeper into space, and detects a remoter star, we call that new also. The place where we sit is called Hudson, — once it was Nottingham, — once —

We should read history as little critically as we consider the landscape, and be more interested by the atmospheric tints and various lights and shades which the intervening spaces create than by its groundwork and composition. It is the morning now turned evening and seen in the west, — the same sun, but a new light and atmosphere. Its beauty is like the sunset; not a fresco painting on a wall, flat and bounded, but atmospheric and roving or free. In reality, history fluctuates as the face of the landscape from morning to evening. What is of moment is its hue and color. Time hides no treasures; we want not its *then*, but its *now*. We do not complain that the mountains in the horizon are blue and indistinct; they are the more like the heavens.

Of what moment are facts that can be lost, — which need to be commemorated? The monument of death will outlast the memory of the dead. The Pyramids do not tell the tale which was confided to them; the living fact commemorates itself. Why look in the dark for light? Strictly speaking, the historical societies have not recovered one fact from oblivion, but are themselves instead of the fact that is lost. The researcher is more memorable than the researched. The crowd stood admiring the mist and the dim outlines of the trees seen through it, when one of their number advanced to explore the phenomenon, and with fresh admiration all eyes were turned on his dimly retreating figure. It is

astonishing with how little coöperation of the societies
the past is remembered. Its story has indeed had
another muse than has been assigned it. There is a
good instance of the manner in which all history began, in Alwákidis' Arabian Chronicle: "I was informed
by *Ahmed Almatin Aljorhami*, who had it from *Rephâa
Ebn Kais Alámiri*, who had it from *Saiph Ebn Fabalah
Alchâtquarmi*, who had it from *Thabet Ebn Alkamah*,
who said he was present at the action." These fathers
of history were not anxious to preserve, but to learn the
fact; and hence it was not forgotten. Critical acumen is
exerted in vain to uncover the past; the *past* cannot be
presented; we cannot know what we are not. But one
veil hangs over past, present, and future, and it is the
province of the historian to find out, not what was, but
what is. Where a battle has been fought, you will find
nothing but the bones of men and beasts; where a battle
is being fought, there are hearts beating. We will sit on a
mound and muse, and not try to make these skeletons
stand on their legs again. Does Nature remember, think
you, that they *were* men, or not rather that they *are*
bones ?

Ancient history has an air of antiquity. It should be
more modern. It is written as if the spectator should be
thinking of the backside of the picture on the wall, or
as if the author expected that the dead would be his
readers, and wished to detail to them their own experience. Men seem anxious to accomplish an orderly
retreat through the centuries, earnestly rebuilding the
works behind, as they are battered down by the en-
croachments of time; but while they loiter, they and

their works both fall a prey to the arch enemy. History has neither the venerableness of antiquity, nor the freshness of the modern. It does as if it would go to the beginning of things, which natural history might with reason assume to do; but consider the Universal History, and then tell us, — when did burdock and plantain sprout first? It has been so written, for the most part, that the times it describes are with remarkable propriety called *dark ages*. They are dark, as one has observed, because we are so in the dark about them. The sun rarely shines in history, what with the dust and confusion; and when we meet with any cheering fact which implies the presence of this luminary, we excerpt and modernize it. As when we read in the history of the Saxons that Edwin of Northumbria "caused stakes to be fixed in the highways where he had seen a clear spring," and "brazen dishes were chained to them to refresh the weary sojourner, whose fatigues Edwin had himself experienced." This is worth all Arthur's twelve battles.

"Thro' the shadow of the globe we sweep into the younger day;
Better fifty years of Europe than a cycle of Cathay."
Than fifty years of Europe better one New England ray!

Biography, too, is liable to the same objection; it should be autobiography. Let us not, as the Germans advise, endeavor to go abroad and vex our bowels that we may be somebody else to explain him. If I am not I, who will be?

But it is fit that the Past should be dark; though the darkness is not so much a quality of the past as of tradition. It is not a distance of time, but a distance of relation, which makes thus dusky its memorials. What

is near to the heart of this generation is fair and bright
still. Greece lies outspread fair and sunshiny in floods
of light, for there is the sun and daylight in her literature
and art. Homer does not allow us to forget that the sun
shone, — nor Phidias, nor the Parthenon. Yet no era
has been wholly dark, nor will we too hastily submit to
the historian, and congratulate ourselves on a blaze of
light. If we could pierce the obscurity of those remote
years, we should find it light enough; only *there* is not
our day. Some creatures are made to see in the dark.
There has always been the same amount of light in the
world. The new and missing stars, the comets and
eclipses, do not affect the general illumination, for only
our glasses appreciate them. The eyes of the oldest
fossil remains, they tell us, indicate that the same laws
of light prevailed then as now. Always the laws of light
are the same, but the modes and degrees of seeing vary.
The gods are partial to no era, but steadily shines their
light in the heavens, while the eye of the beholder is
turned to stone. There was but the sun and the eye
from the first. The ages have not added a new ray to the
one, nor altered a fibre of the other.

If we will admit time into our thoughts at all, the
mythologies, those vestiges of ancient poems, wrecks
of poems, so to speak, the world's inheritance, still
reflecting some of their original splendor, like the fragments of clouds tinted by the rays of the departed sun;
reaching into the latest summer day, and allying this
hour to the morning of creation; as the poet sings: —

> "Fragments of the lofty strain
> Float down the tide of years,

As buoyant on the stormy main
A parted wreck appears," —

these are the materials and hints for a history of the
rise and progress of the race; how, from the condition
of ants, it arrived at the condition of men, and arts were
gradually invented. Let a thousand surmises shed some
light on this story. We will not be confined by historical,
even geological periods which would allow us to doubt
of a progress in human affairs. If we rise above this wisdom for the day, we shall expect that this morning of the
race, in which it has been supplied with the simplest
necessaries, with corn, and wine, and honey, and oil,
and fire, and articulate speech, and agricultural and
other arts, reared up by degrees from the condition of
ants to men, will be succeeded by a day of equally pro-
gressive splendor; that, in the lapse of the divine periods,
other divine agents and godlike men will assist to elevate
the race as much above its present condition.

But we do not know much about it.

Thus did one voyageur waking dream, while his companion slumbered on the bank. Suddenly a boatman's
horn was heard echoing from shore to shore, to give
notice of his approach to the farmer's wife with whom
he was to take his dinner, though in that place only
muskrats and kingfishers seemed to hear. The current
of our reflections and our slumbers being thus disturbed,
we weighed anchor once more.

As we proceeded on our way in the afternoon, the
western bank became lower, or receded farther from the
channel in some places, leaving a few trees only to fringe

the water's edge; while the eastern rose abruptly here and there into wooded hills fifty or sixty feet high. The bass (*Tilia Americana*), also called the lime or linden, which was a new tree to us, overhung the water with its broad and rounded leaf, interspersed with clusters of small hard berries now nearly ripe, and made an agreeable shade for us sailors. The inner bark of this genus is the bast, the material of the fisherman's matting, and the ropes and peasant's shoes of which the Russians make so much use, and also of nets and a coarse cloth in some places. According to poets, this was once Philyra, one of the Oceanides. The ancients are said to have used its bark for the roofs of cottages, for baskets, and for a kind of paper called Philyra. They also made bucklers of its wood, "on account of its flexibility, lightness, and resiliency." It was once much used for carving, and is still in demand for sounding-boards of pianofortes and panels of carriages, and for various uses for which toughness and flexibility are required. Baskets and cradles are made of the twigs. Its sap affords sugar, and the honey made from its flowers is said to be preferred to any other. Its leaves are in some countries given to cattle, a kind of chocolate has been made of its fruit, a medicine has been prepared from an infusion of its flowers, and finally, the charcoal made of its wood is greatly valued for gunpowder.

The sight of this tree reminded us that we had reached a strange land to us. As we sailed under this canopy of leaves, we saw the sky through its chinks, and, as it were, the meaning and idea of the tree stamped in a thousand hieroglyphics on the heavens. The universe

is so aptly fitted to our organization that the eye wanders
and reposes at the same time. On every side there is
something to soothe and refresh this sense. Look up at
the tree-tops, and see how finely Nature finishes off her
work there. See how the pines spire without end higher
and higher, and make a graceful fringe to the earth.
And who shall count the finer cobwebs that soar and
float away from their utmost post, and the myriad insects
that dodge between them? Leaves are of more various
forms than the alphabets of all languages put together;
of the oaks alone there are hardly two alike, and each
expresses its own character.

In all her products, Nature only develops her simplest
germs. One would say that it was no great stretch of
invention to create birds. The hawk which now takes
his flight over the top of the wood was at first, perchance,
only a leaf which fluttered in its aisles. From rustling
leaves she came in the course of ages to the loftier flight
and clear carol of the bird.

Salmon Brook comes in from the west under the railroad, a mile and a half below the village of Nashua.
We rowed up far enough into the meadows which border
it to learn its piscatorial history from a haymaker on its
banks. He told us that the silver eel was formerly abundant here, and pointed to some sunken creels at its
mouth. This man's memory and imagination were fer
tile in fishermen's tales of floating isles in bottomless
ponds, and of lakes mysteriously stocked with fishes,
and would have kept us till nightfall to listen, but we
could not afford to loiter in this roadstead, and so stood
out to our sea again. Though we never trod in those

meadows, but only touched their margin with our hands, we still retain a pleasant memory of them.

Salmon Brook, whose name is said to be a translation from the Indian, was a favorite haunt of the aborigines. Here, too, the first white settlers of Nashua planted, and some dents in the earth where their houses stood and the wrecks of ancient apple trees are still visible. About one mile up this stream stood the house of old John Lovewell, who was an ensign in the army of Oliver Cromwell, and the father of "famous Captain Lovewell." He settled here before 1690, and died about 1754, at the age of one hundred and twenty years. He is thought to have been engaged in the famous Narragansett swamp fight, which took place in 1675, before he came here. The Indians are said to have spared him in succeeding wars on account of his kindness to them. Even in 1700 he was so old and gray-headed that his scalp was worth nothing, since the French governor offered no bounty for such. I have stood in the dent of his cellar on the bank of the brook, and talked there with one whose grandfather had — whose father might have — talked with Lovewell. Here also he had a mill in his old age, and kept a small store. He was remembered by some who were recently living, as a hale old man who drove the boys out of his orchard with his cane. Consider the triumphs of the mortal man, and what poor trophies it would have to show, to wit: He cobbled shoes without glasses at a hundred, and cut a handsome swath at a hundred and five! Lovewell's house is said to have been the first which Mrs. Dustan reached on her escape from the Indians. Here, probably, the hero of Pequawket was

born and bred. Close by may be seen the cellar and
the gravestone of Joseph Hassell, who, as is elsewhere
recorded, with his wife Anna, and son Benjamin, and
Mary Marks, "were slain by our Indian enemies on
September 2, [1691], in the evening." As Gookin
observed on a previous occasion, "The Indian rod upon
the English backs had not yet done God's errand."
Salmon Brook near its mouth is still a solitary stream,
meandering through woods and meadows, while the
then uninhabited mouth of the Nashua now resounds
with the din of a manufacturing town.

A stream from Otternic Pond in Hudson comes in just
above Salmon Brook, on the opposite side. There was
a good view of Uncannunuc, the most conspicuous
mountain in these parts, from the bank here, seen rising
over the west end of the bridge above. We soon after
passed the village of Nashua, on the river of the same
name, where there is a covered bridge over the Merrimack. The Nashua, which is one of the largest tributaries, flows from Wachusett Mountain, through Lancaster, Groton, and other towns, where it has formed
well-known elm-shaded meadows, but near its mouth
it is obstructed by falls and factories, and did not tempt
us to explore it.

Far away from here, in Lancaster, with another
companion, I have crossed the broad valley of the
Nashua, over which we had so long looked westward
from the Concord hills without seeing it to the blue
mountains in the horizon. So many streams, so many
meadows and woods and quiet dwellings of men had
lain concealed between us and those Delectable Moun-

tains; — from yonder hill on the road to Tyngsborough you may get a good view of them. There where it seemed uninterrupted forest to our youthful eyes, between two neighboring pines in the horizon, lay the valley of the Nashua, and this very stream was even then winding at its bottom, and then, as now, it was here silently mingling its waters with the Merrimack. The clouds which floated over its meadows and were born there, seen far in the west, gilded by the rays of the setting sun, had adorned a thousand evening skies for us. But as it were by a turf wall this valley was concealed, and in our journey to those hills it was first gradually revealed to us. Summer and winter our eyes had rested on the dim outline of the mountains, to which distance and indistinctness lent a grandeur not their own, so that they served to interpret all the allusions of poets and travelers. Standing on the Concord Cliffs, we thus spoke our mind to them: —

> With frontier strength ye stand your ground,
> With grand content ye circle round,
> Tumultuous silence for all sound,
> Ye distant nursery of rills,
> Monadnock and the Peterborough Hills; —
> Firm argument that never stirs,
> Outcircling the philosophers, —
> Like some vast fleet,
> Sailing through rain and sleet,
> Through winter's cold and summer's heat;
>
> Still holding on upon your high emprise,
> Until ye find a shore amid the skies;
> Not skulking close to land,
> With cargo contraband,

For they who sent a venture out by ye
Have set the Sun to see
Their honesty.
Ships of the line, each one,
Ye westward run,
Convoying clouds,
Which cluster in your shrouds,
Always before the gale,
Under a press of sail,
With weight of metal all untold, —
I seem to feel ye in my firm seat here,
Immeasurable depth of hold,
And breadth of beam, and length of running gear

Methinks ye take luxurious pleasure
In your novel Western leisure;
So cool your brows and freshly blue,
As Time had naught for ye to do:
For ye lie at your length,
An unappropriated strength,
Unhewn primeval timber,
For knees so stiff, for masts so limber;
The stock of which new earths are made,
One day to be our *Western* trade,
Fit for the stanchions of a world
Which through the seas of space is hurled.

While we enjoy a lingering ray,
Ye still o'ertop the western day,
Reposing yonder on God's croft
Like solid stacks of hay;
So bold a line as ne'er was writ
On any page by human wit;
The forest glows as if
An enemy's camp-fires shone
Along the horizon,
Or the day's funeral pyre
Were lighted there;

Edged with silver and with gold,
The clouds hang o'er in damask fold,
And with such depth of amber light
The west is dight,
Where still a few rays slant,
That even Heaven seems extravagant.
Watatic Hill
Lies on the horizon's sill
Like a child's toy left overnight,
And other duds to left and right,
On the earth's edge, mountains and trees
Stand as they were on air graven,
Or as the vessels in a haven
Await the morning breeze.
I fancy even
Through your defiles windeth the way to heaven;
And yonder still, in spite of history's page,
Linger the golden and the silver age;
Upon the laboring gale
The news of future centuries is brought,
And of new dynasties of thought,
From your remotest vale.

But special I remember thee,
Wachusett, who like me
Standest alone without society.
Thy far blue eye,
A remnant of the sky,
Seen through the clearing or the gorge,
Or from the windows of the forge,
Doth leaven all it passes by.
Nothing is true
But stands 'tween me and you,
Thou Western pioneer,
Who know'st not shame nor fear,
By venturous spirit driven
Under the eaves of heaven;
And canst expand thee there,

And breathe enough of air?
Even beyond the West
Thou migratest,
Into unclouded tracts,
Without a pilgrim's axe,
Cleaving thy road on high
With thy well-tempered brow,
And mak'st thyself a clearing in the sky.
Upholding heaven, holding down earth,
Thy pastime from thy birth;
Not steadied by the one, nor leaning on the other,
May I approve myself thy worthy brother!

At length, like Rasselas and other inhabitants of
happy valleys, we had resolved to scale the blue wall
which bounded the western horizon, though not without
misgivings that thereafter no visible fairyland would
exist for us. But it would be long to tell of our adventures, and we have no time this afternoon, transporting
ourselves in imagination up this hazy Nashua valley,
to go over again that pilgrimage. We have since made
many similar excursions to the principal mountains of
New England and New York, and even far in the wilderness, and have passed a night on the summit of many
of them. And now, when we look again westward from
our native hills, Wachusett and Monadnock have re-
treated once more among the blue and fabulous mountains in the horizon, though our eyes rest on the very
rocks on both of them where we have pitched our tent
for a night, and boiled our hasty-pudding amid the
clouds.

As late as 1724 there was no house on the north side
of the Nashua, but only scattered wigwams and grisly

forests between this frontier and Canada. In September of that year, two men who were engaged in making turpentine on that side — for such were the first enterprises in the wilderness — were taken captive and carried to Canada by a party of thirty Indians. Ten of the inhabitants of Dunstable, going to look for them, found the hoops of their barrel cut, and the turpentine spread on the ground. I have been told by an inhabitant of Tyngsborough, who had the story from his ancestors, that one of these captives, when the Indians were about to upset his barrel of turpentine, seized a pine knot and, flourishing it, swore so resolutely that he would kill the first who touched it, that they refrained, and when at length he returned from Canada he found it still standing. Perhaps there was more than one barrel. However this may have been, the scouts knew by marks on the trees, made with coal mixed with grease, that the men were not killed, but taken prisoners. One of the company, named Farwell, perceiving that the turpentine had not done spreading, concluded that the Indians had been gone but a short time, and they accordingly went in instant pursuit. Contrary to the advice of Farwell, following directly on their trail up the Merrimack, they fell into an ambuscade near Thornton's Ferry, in the present town of Merrimack, and nine were killed, only one, Farwell, escaping after a vigorous pursuit. The men of Dunstable went out and picked up their bodies, and carried them all down to Dunstable and buried them. It is almost word for word as in the Robin Hood ballad: —

> "They carried these foresters into fair Nottingham,
>   As many there did know.

They digged them graves in their churchyard,
And they buried them all a-row."

Nottingham is only the other side of the river, and they
were not exactly all a-row. You may read in the churchyard at Dunstable, under the " Memento Mori," and the
name of one of them, how they " departed this life," and

"This man with seven more that lies in
this grave was slew all in a day by
the Indians."

The stones of some others of the company stand around
the common grave with their separate inscriptions.
Eight were buried here, but nine were killed, according
to the best authorities.

"Gentle river, gentle river,
    Lo, thy streams are stained with gore,
Many a brave and noble captain
    Floats along thy willowed shore.

"All beside thy limpid waters,
    All beside thy sands so bright,
Indian Chiefs and Christian warriors
    Joined in fierce and mortal fight."

It is related in the History of Dunstable that on the
return of Farwell the Indians were engaged by a fresh
party, which they compelled to retreat, and pursued as
far as the Nashua, where they fought across the stream
at its mouth. After the departure of the Indians, the
figure of an Indian's head was found carved by them on
a large tree by the shore, which circumstance has given
its name to this part of the village of Nashville, — the
" Indian Head." " It was observed by some judicious,"
says Gookin, referring to Philip's War, "that at the

beginning of the war the English soldiers made a nothing of the Indians, and many spake words to this effect, that one Englishman was sufficient to chase ten Indians; many reckoned it was no other but *Veni, vidi, vici.*" But we may conclude that the judicious would by this time have made a different observation.

Farwell appears to have been the only one who had studied his profession, and understood the business of hunting Indians. He lived to fight another day, for the next year he was Lovewell's lieutenant at Pequawket, but that time, as we have related, he left his bones in the wilderness. His name still reminds us of twilight days and forest scouts on Indian trails, with an uneasy scalp; — an indispensable hero to New England. As the more recent poet of Lovewell's fight has sung, halting a little but bravely still, —

> "Then did the crimson streams that flowed
> Seem like the waters of the brook,
> That brightly shine, that loudly dash,
> Far down the cliffs of Agiochook."

These battles sound incredible to us. I think that posterity will doubt if such things ever were, — if our bold ancestors who settled this land were not struggling rather with the forest shadows, and not with a copper-colored race of men. They were vapors, fever and ague of the unsettled woods. Now, only a few arrowheads are turned up by the plow. In the Pelasgic, the Etruscan, or the British story, there is nothing so shadowy and unreal.

It is a wild and antiquated looking graveyard, overgrown with bushes, on the highroad, about a quarter of a mile from and overlooking the Merrimack, with a deserted mill-stream bounding it on one side, where lie the earthly remains of the ancient inhabitants of Dunstable. We passed it three or four miles below here. You may read there the names of Lovewell, Farwell, and many others whose families were distinguished in Indian warfare. We noticed there two large masses of granite more than a foot thick and rudely squared, lying flat on the ground over the remains of the first pastor and his wife.

It is remarkable that the dead lie everywhere under stones, —

"Strata jacent passim *suo* quaeque sub" *lapide* —

corpora, we might say, if the measure allowed. When the stone is a slight one, it does not oppress the spirits of the traveler to meditate by it; but these did seem a little heathenish to us; and so are all large monuments over men's bodies, from the Pyramids down. A monument should at least be " star-y-pointing," to indicate whither the spirit is gone, and not prostrate, like the body it has deserted. There have been some nations who could do nothing but construct tombs, and these are the only traces which they have left. They are the heathen. But why these stones, so upright and emphatic, like exclamation-points? What was there so remarkable that lived? Why should the monument be so much more enduring than the fame which it is designed to perpetuate, — a stone to a bone? "Here lies," — "Here lies;" — why do they not sometimes write, There rises? Is it

a monument to the body only that is intended ? "Having
reached the term of his *natural* life;" — would it not be
truer to say, Having reached the term of his *unnatural*
life ? The rarest quality in an epitaph is truth. If any
character is given, it should be as severely true as the
decision of the three judges below, and not the partial
testimony of friends. Friends and contemporaries should
supply only the name and date, and leave it to posterity
to write the epitaph.

> Here lies an honest man,
> Rear-Admiral Van.

> Faith, then ye have
> Two in one grave,
> For in his favor,
> Here too lies the Engraver.

Fame itself is but an epitaph; as late, as false, as true.
But they only are the true epitaphs which Old Mortality
retouches.

A man might well pray that he may not taboo or curse
any portion of nature by being buried in it. For the
most part, the best man's spirit makes a fearful sprite to
haunt his grave, and it is therefore much to the credit
of Little John, the famous follower of Robin Hood, and
reflecting favorably on his character, that his grave was
" long celebrous for the yielding of excellent whetstones."
I confess that I have but little love for such collections
as they have at the Catacombs, Père la Chaise, Mount
Auburn, and even this Dunstable graveyard. At any
rate, nothing but great antiquity can make graveyards
interesting to me. I have no friends there. It may be

that I am not competent to write the poetry of the grave.
The farmer who has skimmed his farm might perchance
leave his body to Nature to be plowed in, and in some
measure restore its fertility. We should not retard but
forward her economies.

Soon the village of Nashua was out of sight, and the
woods were gained again, and we rowed slowly on before
sunset, looking for a solitary place in which to spend the
night. A few evening clouds began to be reflected in the
water, and the surface was dimpled only here and there
by a muskrat crossing the stream. We camped at length
near Penichook Brook, on the confines of what is now
Nashville, by a deep ravine, under the skirts of a pine
wood, where the dead pine leaves were our carpet, and
their tawny boughs stretched overhead. But fire and
smoke soon tamed the scene; the rocks consented to
be our walls, and the pines our roof. A woodside was
already the fittest locality for us.

The wilderness is near as well as dear to every man.
Even the oldest villages are indebted to the border of
wild wood which surrounds them, more than to the
gardens of men. There is something indescribably
inspiriting and beautiful in the aspect of the forest
skirting and occasionally jutting into the midst of new
towns, which, like the sand-heaps of fresh fox-burrows,
have sprung up in their midst. The very uprightness
of the pines and maples asserts the ancient rectitude
and vigor of nature. Our lives need the relief of such a
background, where the pine flourishes and the jay still
screams.

We had found a safe harbor for our boat, and as the

sun was setting carried up our furniture, and soon
arranged our house upon the bank, and while the kettle
steamed at the tent door, we chatted of distant friends
and of the sights which we were to behold, and wondered
which way the towns lay from us. Our cocoa was soon
boiled, and supper set upon our chest, and we lengthened
out this meal, like old voyageurs, with our talk. Meanwhile we spread the map on the ground, and read in the
Gazetteer when the first settlers came here and got a
township granted. Then, when supper was done and
we had written the journal of our voyage, we wrapped
our buffaloes about us and lay down with our heads
pillowed on our arms, listening awhile to the distant
baying of a dog, or the murmurs of the river, or to the
wind, which had not gone to rest: —

> The western wind came lumbering in,
> Bearing a faint Pacific din,
> Our evening mail, swift at the call
> Of its Postmaster-General;
> Laden with news from Californ',
> Whate'er transpired hath since morn,
> How wags the world by brier and brake
> From hence to Athabasca Lake; —

or half awake and half asleep, dreaming of a star which
glimmered through our cotton roof. Perhaps at midnight one was awakened by a cricket shrilly singing on
his shoulder, or by a hunting spider in his eye, and was
lulled asleep again by some streamlet purling its way
along at the bottom of a wooded and rocky ravine in our
neighborhood. It was pleasant to lie with our heads so
low in the grass, and hear what a tinkling, ever-busy

laboratory it was. A thousand little artisans beat on their anvils all night long.

Far in the night, as we were falling asleep on the bank of the Merrimack, we heard some tyro beating a drum incessantly, in preparation for a country muster, as we learned, and we thought of the line, —

> " When the drum beat at dead of night."

We could have assured him that his beat would be answered, and the forces be mustered. Fear not, thou drummer of the night ; we too will be there. And still he drummed on in the silence and the dark. This stray sound from a far-off sphere came to our ears from time to time, far, sweet, and significant, and we listened with such an unprejudiced sense as if for the first time we heard at all. No doubt he was an insignificant drummer enough, but his music afforded us a prime and leisure hour, and we felt that we were in season wholly. These simple sounds related us to the stars. Ay, there was a logic in them so convincing that the combined sense of mankind could never make me doubt their conclusions. I stop my habitual thinking, as if the plow had suddenly run deeper in its furrow through the crust of the world. How can I go on, who have just stepped over such a bottomless skylight in the bog of my life ? Suddenly old Time winked at me, — Ah, you know me, you rogue, — and news had come that IT was well. That ancient universe is in such capital health, I think undoubtedly it will never die. Heal yourselves, doctors; by God I live.

> Then idle Time ran gadding by
> And left me with Eternity alone;

> I hear beyond the range of sound,
> I see beyond the verge of sight, —

I see, smell, taste, hear, feel, that everlasting Something to which we are allied, at once our maker, our abode, our destiny, our very Selves; the one historic truth, the most remarkable fact which can become the distinct and uninvited subject of our thought, the actual glory of the universe; the only fact which a human being cannot avoid recognizing, or in some way forget or dispense with.

> It doth expand my privacies
> To all, and leave me single in the crowd.

I have seen how the foundations of the world are laid, and I have not the least doubt that it will stand a good while.

> Now chiefly is my natal hour,
> And only now my prime of life.
> I will not doubt the love untold,
> Which not my worth nor want hath bought,
> Which wooed me young and wooes me old,
> And to this evening hath me brought.

What are ears? what is Time? that this particular series of sounds called a strain of music, an invisible and fairy troop which never brushed the dew from any mead, can be wafted down through the centuries from Homer to me, and he have been conversant with that same aerial and mysterious charm which now so tingles my ears? What a fine communication from age to age, of the fairest and noblest thoughts, the aspirations of ancient men, even such as were never communicated by speech, is music! It is the flower of language, thought colored and curved, fluent and flexible, its crystal foun-

tain tinged with the sun's rays, and its purling ripples
reflecting the grass and the clouds. A strain of music
reminds me of a passage of the Vedas, and I associate
with it the idea of infinite remoteness, as well as of beauty
and serenity, for to the senses that is farthest from us
which addresses the greatest depth within us. It teaches
us again and again to trust the remotest and finest as the
divinest instinct, and makes a dream our only real experience. We feel a sad cheer when we hear it, perchance
because we that hear are not one with that which is
heard.

> Therefore a torrent of sadness deep
> Through the strains of thy triumph is heard to sweep.

The sadness is ours. The Indian poet Calidas says in
the Sacontala: "Perhaps the sadness of men on seeing
beautiful forms and hearing sweet music arises from
some faint remembrance of past joys, and the traces of
connections in a former state of existence." As polishing
expresses the vein in marble, and grain in wood, so
music brings out what of heroic lurks anywhere. The
hero is the sole patron of music. That harmony which
exists naturally between the hero's moods and the universe, the soldier would fain imitate with drum and
trumpet. When we are in health, all sounds fife and
drum for us; we hear the notes of music in the air, or
catch its echoes dying away when we awake in the dawn.
Marching is when the pulse of the hero beats in unison
with the pulse of Nature, and he steps to the measure of
the universe; then there is true courage and invincible
strength.

Plutarch says that "Plato thinks the gods never gave

men music, the science of melody and harmony, for
mere delectation or to tickle the ear; but that the dis-
cordant parts of the circulations and beauteous fabric
of the soul, and that of it that roves about the body,
and many times, for want of tune and air, breaks forth
into many extravagances and excesses, might be sweetly
recalled and artfully wound up to their former consent
and agreement."

Music is the sound of the universal laws promulgated.
It is the only assured tone. There are in it such strains
as far surpass any man's faith in the loftiness of his
destiny. Things are to be learned which it will be worth
the while to learn. Formerly I heard these

RUMORS FROM AN ÆOLIAN HARP

There is a vale which none hath seen,
Where foot of man has never been,
Such as here lives with toil and strife,
An anxious and a sinful life.

There every virtue has its birth,
Ere it descends upon the earth,
And thither every deed returns,
Which in the generous bosom burns.

There love is warm, and youth is young,
And poetry is yet unsung,
For Virtue still adventures there,
And freely breathes her native air.

And ever, if you hearken well,
You still may hear its vesper bell,
And tread of high-souled men go by,
Their thoughts conversing with the sky.

According to Jamblichus, "Pythagoras did not pro-

cure for himself a thing of this kind through instruments
or the voice, but employing a certain ineffable divinity,
and which it is difficult to apprehend, he extended his
ears and fixed his intellect in the sublime symphonies
of the world, he alone hearing and understanding, as it
appears, the universal harmony and consonance of the
spheres, and the stars that are moved through them, and
which produce a fuller and more intense melody than
anything effected by mortal sounds."

Traveling on foot very early one morning due east
from here about twenty miles, from Caleb Harriman's
tavern in Hampstead toward Haverhill, when I reached
the railroad in Plaistow, I heard at some distance a faint
music in the air like an Æolian harp, which I immediately suspected to proceed from the cord of the telegraph
vibrating in the just awakening morning wind, and ap-
plying my ear to one of the posts I was convinced that
it was so. It was the telegraph harp singing its message
through the country, its message sent not by men, but by
gods. Perchance, like the statue of Memnon, it resounds
only in the morning, when the first rays of the sun fall on
it. It was like the first lyre or shell heard on the seashore, — that vibrating cord high in the air over the
shores of earth. So have all things their higher and their
lower uses. I heard a fairer news than the journals ever
print. It told of things worthy to hear, and worthy of
the electric fluid to carry the news of, not of the price
of cotton and flour, but it hinted at the price of the world
itself and of things which are priceless, of absolute truth
and beauty.

Still the drum rolled on, and stirred our blood to fresh

extravagance that night. The clarion sound and clang
of corselet and buckler were heard from many a hamlet
of the soul, and many a knight was arming for the fight
behind the encamped stars.

> "Before each van
> Prick forth the aery knights, and couch their spears
> Till thickest legions close; with feats of arms
> From either end of Heaven the welkin burns."

Away! away! away! away!
  Ye have not kept your secret well,
I will abide that other day,
  Those other lands ye tell.

Has time no leisure left for these,
  The acts that ye rehearse?
Is not eternity a lease
  For better deeds than verse?

'T is sweet to hear of heroes dead,
  To know them still alive,
But sweeter if we earn their bread,
  And in us they survive.

Our life should feed the springs of fame
  With a perennial wave,
As ocean feeds the babbling founts
  Which find in it their grave.

Ye skies, drop gently round my breast,
  And be my corselet blue,
Ye earth, receive my lance in rest,
  My faithful charger you;

Ye stars, my spear-heads in the sky,
  My arrow-tips ye are;
I see the routed foemen fly,
  My bright spears fixèd are.

Give me an angel for a foe,
    Fix now the place and time,
And straight to meet him I will go
    Above the starry chime.

And with our clashing bucklers' clang
    The heavenly spheres shall ring,
While bright the northern lights shall hang
    Beside our tourneying.

And if she lose her champion true,
    Tell Heaven not despair,
For I will be her champion new,
    Her fame I will repair.

There was a high wind this night, which we afterwards learned had been still more violent elsewhere, and had done much injury to the corn-fields far and near; but we only heard it sigh from time to time, as if it had no license to shake the foundations of our tent; the pines murmured, the water rippled, and the tent rocked a little, but we only laid our ears closer to the ground, while the blast swept on to alarm other men, and long before sunrise we were ready to pursue our voyage as usual.

TUESDAY

On either side the river lie
Long fields of barley and of rye,
That clothe the wold and meet the sky;
And through the fields the road runs by
    To many-towered Camelot. — TENNYSON.

Long before daylight we ranged abroad, hatchet in
hand, in search of fuel, and made the yet slumbering
and dreaming wood resound with our blows. Then with
our fire we burned up a portion of the loitering night,
while the kettle sang its homely strain to the morning
star. We tramped about the shore, waked all the muskrats, and scared up the bittern and birds that were
asleep upon their roosts; we hauled up and upset our
boat, and washed it and rinsed out the clay, talking aloud
as if it were broad day, until at length, by three o'clock,
we had completed our preparations and were ready to
pursue our voyage as usual; so, shaking the clay from
our feet, we pushed into the fog.

Though we were enveloped in mist as usual, we
trusted that there was a bright day behind it.

    Ply the oars ! away ! away !
In each dewdrop of the morning
    Lies the promise of a day.

Rivers from the sunrise flow,
    Springing with the dewy morn;
Voyageurs 'gainst time do row,
Idle noon nor sunset know,
    Ever even with the dawn.

Belknap, the historian of this State, says that "in the neighborhood of fresh rivers and ponds, a whitish fog in the morning lying over the water is a sure indication of fair weather for that day; and when no fog is seen, rain is expected before night." That which seemed to us to invest the world was only a narrow and shallow wreath of vapor stretched over the channel of the Merrimack from the seaboard to the mountains. More extensive fogs, however, have their own limits. I once saw the day break from the top of Saddle-back Mountain in Massachusetts, above the clouds. As we cannot distinguish objects through this dense fog, let me tell this story more at length.

I had come over the hills on foot and alone in serene summer days, plucking the raspberries by the wayside, and occasionally buying a loaf of bread at a farmer's house, with a knapsack on my back which held a few traveler's books and a change of clothing, and a staff in my hand. I had that morning looked down from the Hoosack Mountain, where the road crosses it, on the village of North Adams in the valley three miles away under my feet, showing how uneven the earth may sometimes be, and making it seem an accident that it should ever be level and convenient for the feet of man. Putting a little rice and sugar and a tin cup into my knapsack at this village, I began in the afternoon to ascend the mountain, whose summit is three thousand six hundred feet above the level of the sea, and was seven or eight miles distant by the path. My route lay up a long and spacious valley called the Bellows, because the winds rush up or down it with violence in storms, sloping up to the very clouds between the principal range and a lower mountain. There were a few farms scattered along at different elevations, each commanding a fine prospect of the mountains to the north, and a stream ran down the middle of the valley, on which, near the head, there was a mill. It seemed a road for the pilgrim to enter upon who would climb to the gates of heaven. Now I crossed a hayfield, and now over the brook on a slight bridge, still gradually ascending all the while with a sort of awe, and filled with indefinite expectations as to what kind of inhabitants and what kind of nature I should come to at last. It now seemed some advantage that the earth was uneven, for one could not imagine a more noble position for a farmhouse than this vale afforded, farther from or nearer to its head, from a glen-like seclusion overlooking the country at a great elevation between these two mountain walls.

It reminded me of the homesteads of the Huguenots, on Staten Island, off the coast of New Jersey. The hills in the interior of this island, though comparatively low, are penetrated in various directions by similar sloping valleys on a humble scale, gradually narrowing and rising to the centre, and at the head of these the Huguenots, who were the first settlers, placed their houses quite within the land, in rural and sheltered places, in leafy recesses where the breeze played with the poplar and the gum-tree, from which, with equal security in calm and storm, they looked out through a widening vista, over miles of forest and stretching salt marsh, to the Huguenot's Tree, an old elm on the shore, at whose root they had landed, and across the spacious outer bay of New York to Sandy Hook and the Highlands of Neversink, and thence over leagues of the Atlantic, perchance to some faint vessel in the horizon, almost a day's sail on her voyage to that Europe whence they had come. When walking in the interior there, in the midst of rural scenery, where there was as little to remind me of the ocean as amid the New Hampshire hills, I have suddenly, through a gap, a cleft or "clove road," as the Dutch settlers called it, caught sight of a ship under full sail, over a field of corn, twenty or thirty miles at sea. The effect was similar, since I had no means of measuring distances, to seeing a painted ship passed backwards and forwards through a magic lantern.

But to return to the mountain. It seemed as if he must be the most singular and heavenly-minded man whose dwelling stood highest up the valley. The thunder had rumbled at my heels all the way, but the shower passed off in another direction, though if it had not, I half believed that I should get above it. I at length reached the last house but one, where the path to the summit diverged to the right, while the summit itself rose directly in front. But I determined to follow up the valley to its head, and then find my own route up the steep as the shorter and more adventurous way. I had thoughts of returning to this house, which was well kept and so nobly placed, the next day, and perhaps remaining a week there, if I could have entertainment. Its mistress was a frank and hospitable young woman, who stood before me in a dishabille, busily and uncon-

cernedly combing her long black hair while she talked,
giving her head the necessary toss with each sweep of
the comb, with lively, sparkling eyes, and full of interest
in that lower world from which I had come, talking all
the while as familiarly as if she had known me for years,
and reminding me of a cousin of mine. She at first had
taken me for a student from Williamstown, for they
went by in parties, she said, either riding or walking,
almost every pleasant day, and were a pretty wild set of
fellows; but they never went by the way I was going.
As I passed the last house, a man called out to know
what I had to sell, for, seeing my knapsack, he thought
that I might be a peddler who was taking this unusual
route over the ridge of the valley into South Adams. He
told me that it was still four or five miles to the summit
by the path which I had left, though not more than two
in a straight line from where I was, but that nobody ever
went this way; there was no path, and I should find it
as steep as the roof of a house. But I knew that I was
more used to woods and mountains than he, and went
along through his cow-yard, while he, looking at the sun,
shouted after me that I should not get to the top that
night. I soon reached the head of the valley, but as I
could not see the summit from this point, I ascended a
low mountain on the opposite side, and took its bearing with my compass. I at once entered the woods,
and began to climb the steep side of the mountain in
a diagonal direction, taking the bearing of a tree every
dozen rods. The ascent was by no means difficult
or unpleasant, and occupied much less time than
it would have taken to follow the path. Even coun-

try people, I have observed, magnify the difficulty of traveling in the forest, and especially among mountains. They seem to lack their usual common sense in this. I have climbed several higher mountains without guide or path, and have found, as might be expected, that it takes only more time and patience commonly than to travel the smoothest highway. It is very rare that you meet with obstacles in this world which the humblest man has not faculties to surmount. It is true we may come to a perpendicular precipice, but we need not jump off, nor run our heads against it. A man may jump down his own cellar stairs, or dash his brains out against his chimney, if he is mad. So far as my experience goes, travelers generally exaggerate the difficulties of the way. Like most evil, the difficulty is imaginary; for what's the hurry? If a person lost would conclude that after all he is not lost, he is not beside himself, but standing in his own old shoes on the very spot where he is, and that for the time being he will live there; but the places that have known him, *they* are lost, — how much anxiety and danger would vanish. I am not alone if I stand by myself. Who knows where in space this globe is rolling? Yet we will not give ourselves up for lost, let it go where it will.

I made my way steadily upward in a straight line, through a dense undergrowth of mountain laurel, until the trees began to have a scraggy and infernal look, as if contending with frost goblins, and at length I reached the summit, just as the sun was setting. Several acres here had been cleared, and were covered with rocks and stumps, and there was a rude observatory in the middle which overlooked the woods. I had one fair view of the country before the sun went down, but I was too thirsty to waste any light in viewing the prospect, and set out directly to find water. First, going down a well-beaten path for half a mile through the low, scrubby wood, till I came to where the water stood in the tracks of the horses which had carried travelers up, I lay down flat, and drank these dry, one after another, a pure, cold, spring-like water, but yet I could not fill my dipper, though I contrived little siphons of grass stems, and ingenious aqueducts on a small scale; it was too slow a process. Then, remembering that I had passed a moist place near the top, on my way up, I returned to find it again, and here, with sharp stones and my hands, in the twilight, I made a well about two feet deep, which was soon filled with pure cold water, and the birds too came and drank at it. So I filled my dipper, and, making my way back to the observatory, collected some dry sticks, and made a fire on some flat stones which had been placed on the floor for that purpose, and so I soon cooked my supper of rice, having already whittled a wooden spoon to eat it with.

I sat up during the evening, reading by the light of the fire the scraps of newspapers in which some party had wrapped their luncheon, — the prices current in New York and Boston, the advertisements, and the singular editorials which some had seen fit to publish, not foreseeing under what critical circumstances they would be read. I read these things at a vast advantage there, and it seemed to me that the advertisements, or what is called the business part of a paper, were greatly the best, the

most useful, natural, and respectable. Almost all the
opinions and sentiments expressed were so little considered, so shallow and flimsy, that I thought the very
texture of the paper must be weaker in that part and tear
the more easily. The advertisements and the prices
current were more closely allied to nature, and were
respectable in some measure as tide and meteorological
tables are; but the reading-matter, which I remembered
was most prized down below, unless it was some humble
record of science, or an extract from some old classic,
struck me as strangely whimsical, and crude, and one-
idea'd, like a school-boy's theme, such as youths write
and after burn. The opinions were of that kind that are
doomed to wear a different aspect to-morrow, like last
year's fashions; as if mankind were very green indeed,
and would be ashamed of themselves in a few years,
when they had outgrown this verdant period. There
was, moreover, a singular disposition to wit and humor,
but rarely the slightest real success; and the apparent
success was a terrible satire on the attempt; the Evil
Genius of man laughed the loudest at his best jokes.
The advertisements, as I have said, such as were serious,
and not of the modern quack kind, suggested pleasing
and poetic thoughts; for commerce is really as interesting as nature. The very names of the commodities were
poetic, and as suggestive as if they had been inserted in a
pleasing poem, — Lumber, Cotton, Sugar, Hides, Guano,
Logwood. Some sober, private, and original thought
would have been grateful to read there, and as much
in harmony with the circumstances as if it had been
written on a mountain-top; for it is of a fashion which

never changes, and as respectable as hides and logwood,
or any natural product. What an inestimable companion
such a scrap of paper would have been, containing some
fruit of a mature life! What a relic! What a recipe! It
seemed a divine invention, by which not mere shining
coin, but shining and current thoughts, could be brought
up and left there.

As it was cold, I collected quite a pile of wood and lay
down on a board against the side of the building, not
having any blanket to cover me, with my head to the
fire, that I might look after it, which is not the Indian
rule. But as it grew colder towards midnight, I at length
encased myself completely in boards, managing even to
put a board on top of me, with a large stone on it, to keep
it down, and so slept comfortably. I was reminded, it
is true, of the Irish children, who inquired what their
neighbors did who had no door to put over them in winter nights as they had; but I am convinced that there
was nothing very strange in the inquiry. Those who have
never tried it can have no idea how far a door, which
keeps the single blanket down, may go toward making
one comfortable. We are constituted a good deal like
chickens, which, taken from the hen, and put in a basket
of cotton in the chimney-corner, will often peep till they
die, nevertheless; but if you put in a book, or anything
heavy, which will press down the cotton, and feel like the
hen, they go to sleep directly. My only companions were
the mice, which came to pick up the crumbs that had
been left in those scraps of paper; still, as everywhere,
pensioners on man, and not unwisely improving this elevated tract for their habitation. They nibbled what was

for them; I nibbled what was for me. Once or twice in
the night, when I looked up, I saw a white cloud drifting
through the windows, and filling the whole upper story.

This observatory was a building of considerable size,
erected by the students of Williamstown College, whose
buildings might be seen by daylight gleaming far down
in the valley. It would be no small advantage if every
college were thus located at the base of a mountain, as
good at least as one well-endowed professorship. It
were as well to be educated in the shadow of a mountain
as in more classical shades. Some will remember, no
doubt, not only that they went to the college, but that
they went to the mountain. Every visit to its summit
would, as it were, generalize the particular information
gained below, and subject it to more catholic tests.

I was up early and perched upon the top of this tower
to see the daybreak, for some time reading the names
that had been engraved there, before I could distinguish
more distant objects. An "untamable fly" buzzed at
my elbow with the same nonchalance as on a molasses
hogshead at the end of Long Wharf. Even there I must
attend to his stale humdrum. But now I come to the pith
of this long digression. As the light increased, I discovered around me an ocean of mist, which by chance
reached up exactly to the base of the tower, and shut out
every vestige of the earth, while I was left floating on this
fragment of the wreck of a world, on my carved plank, in
cloudland; a situation which required no aid from the
imagination to render it impressive. As the light in the
east steadily increased, it revealed to me more clearly
the new world into which I had risen in the night, the

new *terra firma* perchance of my future life. There was
not a crevice left through which the trivial places we
name Massachusetts or Vermont or New York could be
seen, while I still inhaled the clear atmosphere of a July
morning, — if it were July there. All around beneath
me was spread for a hundred miles on every side, as far
as the eye could reach, an undulating country of clouds,
answering in the varied swell of its surface to the terres-
trial world it veiled. It was such a country as we might
see in dreams, with all the delights of paradise. There
were immense snowy pastures, apparently smooth
shaven and firm, and shady vales between the vaporous
mountains; and far in the horizon I could see where
some luxurious misty timber jutted into the prairie, and
trace the windings of a watercourse, some unimagined
Amazon or Orinoko, by the misty trees on its brink. As
there was wanting the symbol, so there was not the substance of impurity, no spot nor stain. It was a favor for
which to be forever silent to be shown this vision. The
earth beneath had become such a flitting thing of lights
and shadows as the clouds had been before. It was not
merely veiled to me, but it had passed away like the
phantom of a shadow, σκιᾶς ὄναρ, and this new platform was gained. As I had climbed above storm and
cloud, so by successive days' journeys I might reach the
region of eternal day, beyond the tapering shadow of
the earth; ay, —

> "Heaven itself shall slide,
> And roll away like melting stars that glide
> Along their oily threads."

But when its own sun began to rise on this pure world,

I found myself a dweller in the dazzling halls of Aurora,
into which poets have had but a partial glance over the
eastern hills, drifting amid the saffron-colored clouds,
and playing with the rosy fingers of the Dawn, in the
very path of the Sun's chariot, and sprinkled with its
dewy dust, enjoying the benignant smile, and near at
hand the far-darting glances of the god. The inhabitants of earth behold commonly but the dark and
shadowy under side of heaven's pavement; it is only
when seen at a favorable angle in the horizon, morning
or evening, that some faint streaks of the rich lining of
the clouds are revealed. But my muse would fail to convey an impression of the gorgeous tapestry by which I
was surrounded, such as men see faintly reflected afar
off in the chambers of the east. Here, as on earth, I saw
the gracious god

> " Flatter the mountain-tops with sovereign eye,
> .   .   .   .
> Gilding pale streams with heavenly alchemy."

But never here did "Heaven's sun" stain himself.

But, alas, owing, as I think, to some unworthiness in
myself, my private sun did stain himself, and

> "Anon permit the basest clouds to ride
> With ugly wrack on his celestial face," —

for before the god had reached the zenith the heavenly
pavement rose and embraced my wavering virtue, or
rather I sank down again into that "forlorn world,"
from which the celestial sun had hid his visage, —

> "How may a worm that crawls along the dust,
> Clamber the azure mountains, thrown so high,

And fetch from thence thy fair idea just,
That in those sunny courts doth hidden lie,
Clothed with such light as blinds the angel's eye?
　　How may weak mortal ever hope to file
　　His unsmooth tongue, and his deprostrate style?
Oh, raise thou from his corse thy now entombed exile!"

In the preceding evening I had seen the summits of new and yet higher mountains, the Catskills, by which I might hope to climb to heaven again, and had set my compass for a fair lake in the southwest, which lay in my way, for which I now steered, descending the mountain by my own route, on the side opposite to that by which I had ascended, and soon found myself in the region of cloud and drizzling rain, and the inhabitants affirmed that it had been a cloudy and drizzling day wholly.

But now we must make haste back before the fog disperses to the blithe Merrimack water.

　　Since that first "Away! away!"
　　　Many a lengthy reach we've rowed,
　　Still the sparrow on the spray
　　Hastes to usher in the day
　　　With her simple stanza'd ode.

We passed a canal-boat before sunrise, groping its way to the seaboard, and, though we could not see it on account of the fog, the few dull, thumping, stertorous sounds which we heard impressed us with a sense of weight and irresistible motion. One little rill of commerce already awake on this distant New Hampshire river. The fog, as it required more skill in the steering, enhanced the interest of our early voyage, and made the river seem indefinitely broad. A slight mist, through which objects are faintly visible, has the effect of expanding even ordinary streams, by a singular mirage, into arms of the sea or inland lakes. In the present instance, it was even fragrant and invigorating, and we enjoyed it as a sort of earlier sunshine, or dewy and embryo light.

> Low-anchored cloud,
> Newfoundland air,
> Fountain-head and source of rivers,
> Dew-cloth, dream drapery,
> And napkin spread by fays;
> Drifting meadow of the air,
> Where bloom the daisied banks and violets,
> And in whose fenny labyrinth
> The bittern booms and heron wades;
> Spirit of lakes and seas and rivers,
> Bear only perfumes and the scent
> Of healing herbs to just men's fields!

The same pleasant and observant historian whom we quoted above says that "In the mountainous parts of the country, the ascent of vapors, and their formation into clouds, is a curious and entertaining object. The vapors are seen rising in small columns like smoke from many chimneys. When risen to a certain height, they spread, meet, condense, and are attracted to the mountains, where they either distill in gentle dews, and replenish the springs, or descend in showers, accompanied with thunder. After short intermissions, the process is repeated many times in the course of a summer day, affording to travelers a lively illustration of that is observed in the Book of Job, 'They are wet with the showers of the mountains.'"

Fogs and clouds which conceal the overshadowing

mountains lend the breadth of the plains to mountain vales. Even a small-featured country acquires some grandeur in stormy weather when clouds are seen drifting between the beholder and the neighboring hills. When, in traveling toward Haverhill through Hampstead in this State, on the height of land between the Merrimack and the Piscataqua or the sea, you commence the descent eastward, the view toward the coast is so distant and unexpected, though the sea is invisible, that you at first suppose the unobstructed atmosphere to be a fog in the lowlands concealing hills of corresponding elevation to that you are upon; but it is the mist of prejudice alone, which the winds will not disperse. The most stupendous scenery ceases to be sublime when it becomes distinct, or in other words limited, and the imagination is no longer encouraged to exaggerate it. The actual height and breadth of a mountain or a waterfall are always ridiculously small; they are the imagined only that content us. Nature is not made after such a fashion as we would have her. We piously exaggerate her wonders, as the scenery around our home.

Such was the heaviness of the dews along this river that we were generally obliged to leave our tent spread over the bows of the boat till the sun had dried it, to avoid mildew. We passed the mouth of Penichook Brook, a wild salmon stream, in the fog, without seeing it. At length the sun's rays struggled through the mist and showed us the pines on shore dripping with dew, and springs trickling from the moist banks, —

> "And now the taller sons, whom Titan warms,
>   Of unshorn mountains blown with easy winds,

Dandle the morning's childhood in their arms,
And, if they chanced to slip the prouder pines,
The under corylets did catch their shines,
To gild their leaves."

We rowed for some hours between glistening banks
before the sun had dried the grass and leaves, or the day
had established its character. Its serenity at last seemed
the more profound and secure for the denseness of the
morning's fog. The river became swifter, and the scenery more pleasing than before. The banks were steep
and clayey for the most part, and trickling with water,
and where a spring oozed out a few feet above the river
the boatmen had cut a trough out of a slab with their
axes, and placed it so as to receive the water and fill their
jugs conveniently. Sometimes this purer and cooler
water, bursting out from under a pine or a rock, was
collected into a basin close to the edge of and level with
the river, a fountain-head of the Merrimack. So near
along life's stream are the fountains of innocence and
youth making fertile its sandy margin; and the voyageur
will do well to replenish his vessels often at these uncon-
taminated sources. Some youthful spring, perchance,
still empties with tinkling music into the oldest river,
even when it is falling into the sea, and we imagine that
its music is distinguished by the river-gods from the
general lapse of the stream, and falls sweeter on their
ears in proportion as it is nearer to the ocean. As the
evaporations of the river feed thus these unsuspected
springs which filter through its banks, so, perchance,
our aspirations fall back again in springs on the margin
of life's stream to refresh and purify it. The yellow and

tepid river may float his scow, and cheer his eye with its
reflections and its ripples, but the boatman quenches
his thirst at this small rill alone. It is this purer and
cooler element that chiefly sustains his life. The race
will long survive that is thus discreet.

Our course this morning lay between the territories of
Merrimack, on the west, and Litchfield, once called
Brenton's Farm, on the east, which townships were
anciently the Indian Naticook. Brenton was a fur-
trader among the Indians, and these lands were granted
to him in 1656. The latter township contains about five
hundred inhabitants, of whom, however, we saw none,
and but few of their dwellings. Being on the river, whose
banks are always high and generally conceal the few
houses, the country appeared much more wild and
primitive than to the traveler on the neighboring roads.
The river is by far the most attractive highway, and
those boatmen who have spent twenty or twenty-five
years on it must have had a much fairer, more wild and
memorable experience than the dusty and jarring one of
the teamster who has driven, during the same time, on
the roads which run parallel with the stream. As one
ascends the Merrimack he rarely sees a village, but for
the most part alternate wood and pasture lands, and
sometimes a field of corn or potatoes, of rye or oats or
English grass, with a few straggling apple trees, and, at
still longer intervals, a farmer's house. The soil, excepting the best of the interval, is commonly as light and
sandy as a patriot could desire. Sometimes this forenoon the country appeared in its primitive state, and as
if the Indian still inhabited it, and, again, as if many

free, new settlers occupied it, their slight fences straggling down to the water's edge; and the barking of dogs,
and even the prattle of children, were heard, and smoke
was seen to go up from some hearthstone, and the banks
were divided into patches of pasture, mowing, tillage,
and woodland. But when the river spread out broader,
with an uninhabited islet, or a long, low, sandy shore
which ran on single and devious, not answering to its
opposite, but far off as if it were seashore or single coast,
and the land no longer nursed the river in its bosom, but
they conversed as equals, the rustling leaves with rippling
leaves, and few fences were seen, but high oak woods on
one side, and large herds of cattle, and all tracks seemed
to point to one centre behind some statelier grove, — we
imagined that the river flowed through an extensive
manor, and that the few inhabitants were retainers to a
lord, and a feudal state of things prevailed.

When there was a suitable reach, we caught sight of
the Goffstown mountain, the Indian Uncannunuc, rising
before us on the west side. It was a calm and beautiful
day, with only a slight zephyr to ripple the surface of the
water, and rustle the woods on shore, and just warmth
enough to prove the kindly disposition of Nature to her
children. With buoyant spirits and vigorous impulses
we tossed our boat rapidly along into the very middle of
this forenoon. The fish hawk sailed and screamed overhead. The chipping or striped squirrel, *Sciurus striatus*
(*Tamias Lysteri*, Aud.), sat upon the end of some Virginia fence or rider reaching over the stream, twirling a
green nut with one paw, as in a lathe, while the other held
it fast against its incisors as chisels. Like an independent

russet leaf, with a will of its own, rustling whither it could; now under the fence, now over it, now peeping at the voyageurs through a crack with only its tail visible, now at its lunch deep in the toothsome kernel, and now a rod off playing at hide-and-seek, with the nut stowed away in its chaps, where were half a dozen more besides, extending its cheeks to a ludicrous breadth, — as if it were devising through what safe valve of frisk or somerset to let its superfluous life escape; the stream passing harmlessly off, even while it sits, in constant electric flashes through its tail. And now with a chuckling squeak it dives into the root of a hazel, and we see no more of it. Or the larger red squirrel, or chickaree, sometimes called the Hudson Bay squirrel (*Sciurus Hudsonius*), gave warning of our approach by that peculiar alarum of his, like the winding up of some strong clock, in the top of a pine tree, and dodged behind its stem, or leaped from tree to tree with such caution and adroitness, as if much depended on the fidelity of his scout, running along the white pine boughs sometimes twenty rods by our side, with such speed, and by such unerring routes, as if it were some well-worn familiar path to him; and presently, when we have passed, he returns to his work of cutting off the pine cones, and letting them fall to the ground.

We passed Cromwell's Falls, the first we met with on this river, this forenoon, by means of locks, without using our wheels. These falls are the Nesenkeag of the Indians. Great Nesenkeag Stream comes in on the right just above, and Little Nesenkeag some distance below, both in Litchfield. We read in the Gazetteer, under th

head of Merrimack, that "the first house in this town
was erected on the margin of the river [soon after 1665]
for a house of traffic with the Indians. For some time
one Cromwell carried on a lucrative trade with them,
weighing their furs with his foot, till, enraged at his supposed or real deception, they formed the resolution to
murder him. This intention being communicated to
Cromwell, he buried his wealth and made his escape.
Within a few hours after his flight, a party of the Penacook tribe arrived, and, not finding the object of their
resentment, burnt his habitation." Upon the top of the
high bank here, close to the river, was still to be seen his
cellar, now overgrown with trees. It was a convenient
spot for such a traffic, at the foot of the first falls above
the settlements, and commanding a pleasant view up the
river, where he could see the Indians coming down with
their furs. The lock-man told us that his shovel and
tongs had been plowed up here, and also a stone with
his name on it. But we will not vouch for the truth of
this story. In the New Hampshire Historical Collections
for 1815 it says, "Some time after, pewter was found in
the well, and an iron pot and trammel in the sand; the
latter are preserved." These were the traces of the white
trader. On the opposite bank, where it jutted over the
stream cape-wise, we picked up four arrowheads, and a
small Indian tool made of stone, as soon as we had
climbed it, where plainly there had once stood a wigwam of the Indians with whom Cromwell traded, and
who fished and hunted here before he came.

As usual, the gossips have not been silent respecting
Cromwell's buried wealth, and it is said that some years

ago a farmer's plow, not far from here, slid over a flat
stone which emitted a hollow sound, and, on its being
raised, a small hole six inches in diameter was discovered,
stoned about, from which a sum of money was taken.
The lock-man told us another similar story about a
farmer in a neighboring town, who had been a poor man,
but who suddenly bought a good farm, and was well to
do in the world, and, when he was questioned, did not
give a satisfactory account of the matter; how few, alas,
could! This caused his hired man to remember that
one day, as they were plowing together, the plow struck
something, and his employer, going back to look, concluded not to go round again, saying that the sky looked
rather lowering, and so put up his team. The like
urgency has caused many things to be remembered which
never transpired. The truth is, there is money buried
everywhere, and you have only to go to work to find it.

Not far from these falls stands an oak tree, on the
interval, about a quarter of a mile from the river, on the
farm of a Mr. Lund, which was pointed out to us as the
spot where French, the leader of the party which went
in pursuit of the Indians from Dunstable, was killed.
Farwell dodged them in the thick woods near. It did not
look as if men had ever had to run for their lives on this
now open and peaceful interval.

Here, too, was another extensive desert by the side of
the road in Litchfield, visible from the bank of the river
The sand was blown off in some places to the depth of
ten or twelve feet, leaving small grotesque hillocks of
that height, where there was a clump of bushes firmly
rooted. Thirty or forty years ago, as we were told, it was

a sheep-pasture, but the sheep, being worried by the
fleas, began to paw the ground, till they broke the sod,
and so the sand began to blow, till now it had extended
over forty or fifty acres. This evil might easily have
been remedied, at first, by spreading birches with their
leaves on over the sand, and fastening them down with
stakes, to break the wind. The fleas bit the sheep, and
the sheep bit the ground, and the sore had spread to this
extent. It is astonishing what a great sore a little scratch
breedeth. Who knows but Sahara, where caravans and
cities are buried, began with the bite of an African flea?
This poor globe, how it must itch in many places! Will
no god be kind enough to spread a salve of birches over
its sores? Here, too, we noticed where the Indians had
gathered a heap of stones, perhaps for their council-fire,
which, by their weight having prevented the sand under
them from blowing away, were left on the summit of a
mound. They told us that arrowheads, and also bullets
of lead and iron, had been found here. We noticed
several other sandy tracts in our voyage; and the course
of the Merrimack can be traced from the nearest mountain by its yellow sand-banks, though the river itself
is for the most part invisible. Lawsuits, as we hear,
have in some cases grown out of these causes. Railroads
have been made through certain irritable districts,
breaking their sod, and so have set the sand to blowing,
till it has converted fertile farms into deserts, and the
company has had to pay the damages.

This sand seemed to us the connecting link between
land and water. It was a kind of water on which you
could walk, and you could see the ripple-marks on its

surface, produced by the winds, precisely like those at the bottom of a brook or lake. We had read that Mussulmans are permitted by the Koran to perform their ablutions in sand when they cannot get water, a necessary indulgence in Arabia, and we now understood the propriety of this provision.

Plum Island, at the mouth of this river, to whose formation, perhaps, these very banks have sent their contribution, is a similar desert of drifting sand, of various colors, blown into graceful curves by the wind. It is a mere sand-bar exposed, stretching nine miles parallel to the coast, and, exclusive of the marsh on the inside, rarely more than half a mile wide. There are but half a dozen houses on it, and it is almost without a tree, or a sod, or any green thing with which a countryman is familiar. The thin vegetation stands half buried in sand, as in drifting snow. The only shrub, the beach plum, which gives the island its name, grows but a few feet high; but this is so abundant that parties of a hundred at once come from the mainland and down the Merrimack, in September, pitch their tents, and gather the plums, which are good to eat raw and to preserve. The graceful and delicate beach pea, too, grows abundantly amid the sand, and several strange moss-like and succulent plants. The island for its whole length is scalloped into low hills, not more than twenty feet high, by the wind, and, excepting a faint trail on the edge of the marsh, is as trackless as Sahara. There are dreary bluffs of sand and valleys plowed by the wind, where you might expect to discover the bones of a caravan. Schooners come from Boston to load with the sand for masons' uses,

and in a few hours the wind obliterates all traces of their
work. Yet you have only to dig a foot or two anywhere
to come to fresh water; and you are surprised to learn
that woodchucks abound here, and foxes are found,
though you see not where they can burrow or hide themselves. I have walked down the whole length of its broad
beach at low tide, at which time alone you can find a
firm ground to walk on, and probably Massachusetts
does not furnish a more grand and dreary walk. On the
seaside there are only a distant sail and a few coots to
break the grand monotony. A solitary stake stuck up,
or a sharper sand-hill than usual, is remarkable as a
landmark for miles; while for music you hear only the
ceaseless sound of the surf, and the dreary peep of the
beach-birds.

There were several canal-boats at Cromwell's Falls
passing through the locks, for which we waited. In the
forward part of one stood a brawny New Hampshire
man, leaning on his pole, bareheaded and in shirt and
trousers only, a rude Apollo of a man, coming down
from "that vast uplandish country" to the main; of
nameless age, with flaxen hair and vigorous, weather-
bleached countenance, in whose wrinkles the sun still
lodged, as little touched by the heats and frosts and
withering cares of life as a maple of the mountain; an
undressed, unkempt, uncivil man, with whom we par-
leyed awhile, and parted not without a sincere interest
in one another. His humanity was genuine and instinc-
tive, and his rudeness only a manner. He inquired, just
as we were passing out of earshot, if we had killed any-

thing, and we shouted after him that we had shot a *buoy*, and could see him for a long while scratching his head in vain to know if he had heard aright.

There is reason in the distinction of civil and uncivil. The manners are sometimes so rough a rind that we doubt whether they cover any core or sap-wood at all. We sometimes meet uncivil men, children of Amazons, who dwell by mountain paths, and are said to be inhospitable to strangers; whose salutation is as rude as the grasp of their brawny hands, and who deal with men as unceremoniously as they are wont to deal with the elements. They need only to extend their clearings, and let in more sunlight, to seek out the southern slopes of the hills, from which they may look down on the civil plain or ocean, and temper their diet duly with the cereal fruits, consuming less wild meat and acorns, to become like the inhabitants of cities. A true politeness does not result from any hasty and artificial polishing, it is true, but grows naturally in characters of the right grain and quality, through a long fronting of men and events, and rubbing on good and bad fortune. Perhaps I can tell a tale to the purpose while the lock is filling, — for our voyage this forenoon furnishes but few incidents of importance.

Early one summer morning I had left the shores of the Connecticut, and for the livelong day traveled up the bank of a river, which came in from the west; now looking down on the stream, foaming and rippling through the forest a mile off, from the hills over which the road led, and now sitting on its rocky brink and dipping my feet in its rapids, or bathing adventurously in mid-channel. The hills grew more and more frequent, and gradually swelled into mountains as I advanced, hemming in the course of the river, so that at last I could not see where it came from, and was at liberty to imagine the most wonderful meanderings and descents. At noon I slept on the grass in the shade of a maple, where the river had found a broader channel than usual, and was spread out shallow, with frequent sand-bars exposed. In the names of the towns I recognized some which I had long ago read on teamsters' wagons, that had come from far up country; quiet uplandish towns, of mountainous fame. I walked along, musing and enchanted, by rows of sugar maples, through the small and uninquisitive villages, and sometimes was pleased with the sight of a boat drawn up on a sand-bar, where there appeared no inhabitants to use it. It seemed, however, as essential to the river as a fish, and to lend a certain dignity to it. It was like the trout of mountain streams to the fishes of the sea, or like the young of the land crab born far in the interior, who have never yet heard the sound of the ocean's surf. The hills approached nearer and nearer to the stream, until at last they closed behind me, and I found myself just before nightfall in a romantic and retired valley, about half a mile in length, and barely wide enough for the stream at its bottom. I thought that there could be no finer site for a cottage among mountains. You could anywhere run across the stream on the rocks, and its constant murmuring would quiet the passions of mankind forever. Suddenly the road, which seemed aiming for the mountain-side, turned short to the left, and another valley opened, concealing the former, and of the same character with it. It was the most remarkable and pleasing scenery I had ever seen. I found here a few mild and hospitable inhabitants, who, as the day was not quite spent, and I was anxious to improve the light, directed me four or five miles farther on my way to the dwelling of a man whose name was Rice, who occupied the last and highest of the valleys that lay in my path, and who, they said, was a rather rude and uncivil man. But "what is a foreign country to those who have science? Who is a stranger to those who have the habit of speaking kindly?"

At length, as the sun was setting behind the mountains in a still darker and more solitary vale, I reached the dwelling of this man. Except for the narrowness of the plain, and that the stones were solid granite, it was the counterpart of that retreat to which Belphœbe bore the wounded Timias, —

> "In a pleasant glade,
> With mountains round about environed,
> And mighty woods, which did the valley shade,
> And like a stately theatre it made,
> Spreading itself into a spacious plain;
> And in the midst a little river played
> Amongst the pumy stones which seemed to plain,
> With gentle murmur, that his course they did restrain."

I observed, as I drew near, that he was not so rude as I had anticipated, for he kept many cattle, and dogs to watch them, and I saw where he had made maple sugar on the sides of the mountains, and above all distinguished the voices of children mingling with the mur-

mur of the torrent before the door. As I passed his stable,
I met one whom I supposed to be a hired man, attending
to his cattle, and I inquired if they entertained travelers
at that house. "Sometimes we do," he answered gruffly,
and immediately went to the farthest stall from me, and
I perceived that it was Rice himself whom I had addressed. But pardoning this incivility to the wildness of
the scenery, I bent my steps to the house. There was no
sign-post before it, nor any of the usual invitations to the
traveler, though I saw by the road that many went and
came there, but the owner's name only was fastened to
the outside; a sort of implied and sullen invitation, as
I thought. I passed from room to room without meeting
any one, till I came to what seemed the guests' apartment, which was neat, and even had an air of refinement
about it, and I was glad to find a map against the wall
which would direct me on my journey on the morrow.
At length I heard a step in a distant apartment, which
was the first I had entered, and went to see if the landlord had come in; but it proved to be only a child, one of
those whose voices I had heard, probably his son, and
between him and me stood in the doorway a large watch-
dog, which growled at me, and looked as if he would
presently spring, but the boy did not speak to him; and
when I asked for a glass of water, he briefly said, "It
runs in the corner." So I took a mug from the counter
and went out of doors, and searched round the corner of
the house, but could find neither well nor spring, nor any
water but the stream which ran all along the front. I
came back, therefore, and, setting down the mug, asked
the child if the stream was good to drink; whereupon he

seized the mug, and, going to the corner of the room, where a cool spring which issued from the mountain behind trickled through a pipe into the apartment, filled it, and drank, and gave it to me empty again, and, calling to the dog, rushed out of doors. Ere long some of the hired men made their appearance, and drank at the spring, and lazily washed themselves and combed their hair in silence, and some sat down as if weary, and fell asleep in their seats. But all the while I saw no women, though I sometimes heard a bustle in that part of the house from which the spring came.

At length Rice himself came in, for it was now dark, with an ox-whip in his hand, breathing hard, and he too soon settled down into his seat not far from me, as if, now that his day's work was done, he had no farther to travel, but only to digest his supper at his leisure. When I asked him if he could give me a bed, he said there was one ready, in such a tone as implied that I ought to have known it, and the less said about that the better. So far so good. And yet he continued to look at me as if he would fain have me say something further like a traveler. I remarked that it was a wild and rugged country he inhabited, and worth coming many miles to see. "Not so very rough neither," said he, and appealed to his men to bear witness to the breadth and smoothness of his fields, which consisted in all of one small interval, and to the size of his crops; "and if we have some hills," added he, "there's no better pasturage anywhere." I then asked if this place was the one I had heard of, calling it by a name I had seen on the map, or if it was a certain other; and he answered, gruffly, that it was neither the one nor the other; that he had settled it and cultivated it, and made it what it was, and I could know nothing about it. Observing some guns and other implements of hunting hanging on brackets around the room, and his hounds now sleeping on the floor, I took occasion to change the discourse, and inquired if there was much game in that country, and he answered this question more graciously, having some glimmering of my drift; but when I inquired if there were any bears, he answered impatiently that he was no more in danger of losing his sheep than his neighbors; he had tamed and civilized that region. After a pause, thinking of my journey on the morrow, and the few hours of daylight in that hollow and mountainous country, which would require me to be on my way betimes, I remarked that the day must be shorter by an hour there than on the neighboring plains; at which he gruffly asked what I knew about it, and affirmed that he had as much daylight as his neighbors; he ventured to say, the days were longer there than where I lived, as I should find if I stayed; that in some way, I could not be expected to understand how, the sun came over the mountains half an hour earlier, and stayed half an hour later there than on the neighboring plains. And more of like sort he said. He was, indeed, as rude as a fabled satyr. But I suffered him to pass for what he was, — for why should I quarrel with nature? — and was even pleased at the discovery of such a singular natural phenomenon. I dealt with him as if to me all manners were indifferent, and he had a sweet, wild way with him. I would not question nature, and I would rather have him as he was than as I would have him. For I had

come up here not for sympathy, or kindness, or society,
but for novelty and adventure, and to see what nature
had produced here. I therefore did not repel his rudeness, but quite innocently welcomed it all, and knew
how to appreciate it, as if I were reading in an old drama
a part well sustained. He was indeed a coarse and sensual man, and, as I have said, uncivil, but he had his
just quarrel with nature and mankind, I have no doubt,
only he had no artificial covering to his ill-humors. He
was earthy enough, but yet there was good soil in him,
and even a long-suffering Saxon probity at bottom. If
you could represent the case to him, he would not let the
race die out in him, like a red Indian.

At length I told him that he was a fortunate man,
and I trusted that he was grateful for so much light;
and, rising, said I would take a lamp, and that I would
pay him then for my lodging, for I expected to recom-
mence my journey even as early as the sun rose in his
country; but he answered in haste, and this time civilly,
that I should not fail to find some of his household stirring, however early, for they were no sluggards, and I
could take my breakfast with them before I started, if I
chose; and as he lighted the lamp I detected a gleam of
true hospitality and ancient civility, a beam of pure and
even gentle humanity, from his bleared and moist eyes.
It was a look more intimate with me, and more explana-
tory, than any words of his could have been if he had
tried to his dying day. It was more significant than
any Rice of those parts could even comprehend, and
long anticipated this man's culture, — a glance of his
pure genius, which did not much enlighten him, but did

impress and rule him for the moment, and faintly constrain his voice and manner. He cheerfully led the way
to my apartment, stepping over the limbs of his men,
who were asleep on the floor in an intervening chamber,
and showed me a clean and comfortable bed. For many
pleasant hours after the household was asleep I sat at the
open window, for it was a sultry night, and heard the
little river

> "Amongst the pumy stones, which seemed to plain,
>   With gentle murmur, that his course they did restrain."

But I arose as usual by starlight the next morning, before my host, or his men, or even his dogs, were awake;
and, having left a ninepence on the counter, was already
halfway over the mountain with the sun before they
had broken their fast.

Before I had left the country of my host, while the
first rays of the sun slanted over the mountains, as I
stopped by the wayside to gather some raspberries, a
very old man, not far from a hundred, came along with
a milking-pail in his hand, and turning aside began
to pluck the berries near me: —

> "His reverend locks
> In comelye curles did wave;
> And on his aged temples grew
> The blossoms of the grave."

But when I inquired the way, he answered in a low,
rough voice, without looking up or seeming to regard my
presence, which I imputed to his years; and presently,
muttering to himself, he proceeded to collect his cows in
a neighboring pasture; and when he had again returned

near to the wayside, he suddenly stopped, while his cows went on before, and, uncovering his head, prayed aloud in the cool morning air, as if he had forgotten this exercise before, for his daily bread, and also that He who letteth his rain fall on the just and on the unjust, and without whom not a sparrow falleth to the ground, would not neglect the stranger (meaning me), and with even more direct and personal applications, though mainly according to the long-established formula common to lowlanders and the inhabitants of mountains. When he had done praying, I made bold to ask him if he had any cheese in his hut which he would sell me, but he answered without looking up, and in the same low and repulsive voice as before, that they did not make any, and went to milking. It is written, "The stranger who turneth away from a house with disappointed hopes, leaveth there his own offenses, and departeth, taking with him all the good actions of the owner."

Being now fairly in the stream of this week's commerce, we began to meet with boats more frequently, and hailed them from time to time with the freedom of sailors. The boatmen appeared to lead an easy and contented life, and we thought that we should prefer their employment ourselves to many professions which are much more sought after. They suggested how few circumstances are necessary to the well-being and serenity of man, how indifferent all employments are, and that any may seem noble and poetic to the eyes of men, if pursued with sufficient buoyancy and freedom. With liberty and pleasant weather, the simplest occupation, any unquestioned country mode of life which detains us in the open air, is alluring. The man who picks peas steadily for a living is more than respectable, he is even envied by his shop-worn neighbors. We are as happy as the birds when our Good Genius permits us to pursue any outdoor work, without a sense of dissipation. Our penknife glitters in the sun; our voice is echoed by yonder wood; if an oar drops, we are fain to let it drop again.

The canal-boat is of very simple construction, requiring but little ship-timber, and, as we were told, costs about two hundred dollars. They are managed by two men. In ascending the stream they use poles fourteen or fifteen feet long, pointed with iron, walking about one third the length of the boat from the forward end. Going down, they commonly keep in the middle of the stream, using an oar at each end; or if the wind is favorable they raise their broad sail, and have only to steer. They commonly carry down wood or bricks, — fifteen or sixteen cords of wood, and as many thousand bricks, at a time, — and bring back stores for the country, consuming two or three days each way between Concord and Charlestown. They sometimes pile the wood so as to leave a shelter in one part where they may retire from the rain. One can hardly imagine a more healthful employment, or one more favorable to contemplation and the observation of nature. Unlike the mariner, they have the constantly varying panorama of the shore to relieve the monotony of their labor, and it seemed to us that as they thus glided noiselessly from town to town, with all their furniture about them, for their very homestead is a movable, they could comment on the character of the inhabitants with greater advantage and security to themselves than the traveler in a coach, who would be unable to indulge in such broadsides of wit and humor in so small a vessel for fear of the recoil. They are not subject to great exposure, like the lumberers of Maine, in any weather, but inhale the healthfulest breezes, being slightly incumbered with clothing, frequently with the head and feet bare. When we met them at noon, as they were leisurely descending the stream, their busy commerce did not look like toil, but rather like some ancient Oriental game still played on a large scale, as the game of chess, for instance, handed down to this generation. From morning till night, unless the wind is so fair that his single sail will suffice without other labor than steering, the boatman walks backwards and forwards on the side of his boat, now stooping with his shoulder to the pole, then drawing it back slowly to set it again, meanwhile moving steadily forward through an endless valley and an ever-changing scenery, now distinguishing his course for a mile or two, and now shut in by a sudden turn of the river in a small woodland lake. All the phenomena which surround him are simple and grand, and there is something impressive, even majestic, in the very motion he causes, which will naturally be communicated to his own character, and he feels the slow, irresistible movement under him with pride, as if it were his own energy.

The news spread like wildfire among us youths, when formerly, once in a year or two, one of these boats came up the Concord River, and was seen stealing mysteri-

ously through the meadows and past the village. It came
and departed as silently as a cloud, without noise or
dust, and was witnessed by few. One summer day this
huge traveler might be seen moored at some meadow's
wharf, and another summer day it was not there. Where
precisely it came from, or who these men were who
knew the rocks and soundings better than we who bathed
there, we could never tell. We knew some river's bay
only, but they took rivers from end to end. They were a
sort of fabulous rivermen to us. It was inconceivable by
what sort of mediation any mere landsman could hold
communication with them. Would they heave to, to
gratify his wishes? No, it was favor enough to know
faintly of their destination, or the time of their possible
return. I have seen them in the summer, when the
stream ran low, mowing the weeds in mid-channel, and
with hayers' jests cutting broad swaths in three feet of
water, that they might make a passage for their scow,
while the grass in long windrows was carried down the
stream, undried by the rarest hay weather. We admired
unweariedly how their vessel would float, like a huge
chip, sustaining so many casks of lime, and thousands
of bricks, and such heaps of iron ore, with wheelbar-
rows aboard, and that, when we stepped on it, it did not
yield to the pressure of our feet. It gave us confidence in
the prevalence of the law of buoyancy, and we imagined
to what infinite uses it might be put. The men appeared
to lead a kind of life on it, and it was whispered that they
slept aboard. Some affirmed that it carried sail, and that
such winds blew here as filled the sails of vessels on the
ocean; which again others much doubted. They had

been seen to sail across our Fair Haven Bay by lucky
fishers who were out, but unfortunately others were not
there to see. We might then say that our river was navigable, — why not? In after years I read in print, with no
little satisfaction, that it was thought by some that, with
a little expense in removing rocks and deepening the
channel, "there might be a profitable inland navigation." *I* then lived somewhere to tell of.

Such is Commerce, which shakes the cocoanut and
bread-fruit tree in the remotest isle, and sooner or later
dawns on the duskiest and most simple-minded savage.
If we may be pardoned the digression, who can help
being affected at the thought of the very fine and slight,
but positive relation, in which the savage inhabitants
of some remote isle stand to the mysterious white mariner, the child of the sun? — as if *we* were to have deal-
ings with an animal higher in the scale of being than
ourselves. It is a barely recognized fact to the natives
that he exists, and has his home far away somewhere,
and is glad to buy their fresh fruits with his superfluous
commodities. Under the same catholic sun glances his
white ship over Pacific waves into their smooth bays,
and the poor savage's paddle gleams in the air.

> Man's little acts are grand,
> Beheld from land to land,
> There as they lie in time,
> Within their native clime.
> > Ships with the noontide weigh,
> > And glide before its ray
> > To some retired bay,
> > Their haunt,
> > Whence, under tropic sun,

Again they run,
  Bearing gum Senegal and Tragicant.
For this was ocean meant,
For this the sun was sent,
And moon was lent,
And winds in distant caverns pent.

Since our voyage the railroad on the bank has been
extended, and there is now but little boating on the
Merrimack. All kinds of produce and stores were formerly conveyed by water, but now nothing is carried
up the stream, and almost wood and bricks alone are
carried down, and these are also carried on the railroad.
The locks are fast wearing out, and will soon be impass-
able, since the tolls will not pay the expense of repairing
them, and so in a few years there will be an end of
boating on this river. The boating at present is princi-
pally between Merrimack and Lowell, or Hooksett and
Manchester. They make two or three trips in a week,
according to wind and weather, from Merrimack to
Lowell and back, about twenty-five miles each way.
The boatman comes singing in to shore late at night,
and moors his empty boat, and gets his supper and lodging in some house near at hand, and again early in
the morning, by starlight perhaps, he pushes away up-
stream, and, by a shout, or the fragment of a song, gives
notice of his approach to the lock-man, with whom he is
to take his breakfast. If he gets up to his wood-pile
before noon he proceeds to load his boat, with the help
of his single "hand," and is on his way down again
before night. When he gets to Lowell he unloads his
boat, and gets his receipt for his cargo, and, having heard

the news at the public house at Middlesex or elsewhere, goes back with his empty boat and his receipt in his pocket to the owner, and to get a new load. We were frequently advertised of their approach by some faint sound behind us, and looking round saw them a mile off, creeping stealthily up the side of the stream like alligators. It was pleasant to hail these sailors of the Merrimack from time to time, and learn the news which circulated with them. We imagined that the sun shining on their bare heads had stamped a liberal and public character on their most private thoughts.

The open and sunny interval still stretched away from the river sometimes by two or more terraces, to the distant hill-country, and when we climbed the bank, we commonly found an irregular copse-wood skirting the river, the primitive having floated down-stream long ago to ——, the "King's navy." Sometimes we saw the river road a quarter or half a mile distant, and the particolored Concord stage, with its cloud of dust, its van of earnest traveling faces, and its rear of dusty trunks, reminding us that the country had its places of rendezvous for restless Yankee men. There dwelt along at considerable distances on this interval a quiet agricultural and pastoral people, with every house its well, as we sometimes proved, and every household, though never so still and remote it appeared in the noontide, its dinner about these times. There they lived on, those New England people, farmer lives, father and grandfather and great-grandfather, on and on without noise, keeping up tradition, and expecting, beside fair weather and abundant harvests, we did not learn what. They were contented to live, since it was so contrived for them, and where their lines had fallen.

> Our uninquiring corpses lie more low
> Than our life's curiosity doth go.

Yet these men had no need to travel to be as wise as Solomon in all his glory, so similar are the lives of men in all countries, and fraught with the same homely experiences. One half the world *knows* how the other half lives.

About noon we passed a small village in Merrimack at Thornton's Ferry, and tasted of the waters of Naticook Brook on the same side, where French and his companions, whose grave we saw in Dunstable, were ambuscaded by the Indians. The humble village of Litchfield, with its steepleless meeting-house, stood on the opposite or east bank, near where a dense grove of willows backed by maples skirted the shore. There also we noticed some shagbark trees, which, as they do not grow in Concord, were as strange a sight to us as the palm would be, whose fruit only we have seen. Our course now curved gracefully to the north, leaving a low, flat shore on the Merrimack side, which forms a sort of harbor for canal-boats. We observed some fair elms and particularly large and handsome white maples standing conspicuously on this interval; and the opposite shore, a quarter of a mile below, was covered with young elms and maples six inches high, which had probably sprung from the seeds which had been washed across.

Some carpenters were at work here mending a scow on the green and sloping bank. The strokes of their

mallets echoed from shore to shore, and up and down
the river, and their tools gleamed in the sun a quarter of
a mile from us, and we realized that boat-building was
as ancient and honorable an art as agriculture, and that
there might be a naval as well as a pastoral life. The
whole history of commerce was made manifest in that
scow turned bottom upward on the shore. Thus did men
begin to go down upon the sea in ships; *quaeque diu
steterant in montibus altis, Fluctibus ignotis insultavêre
carinae;* "and keels which had long stood on high
mountains careered insultingly (*insultavêre*) over unknown waves." [1]

We thought that it would be well for the traveler to
build his boat on the bank of a stream, instead of finding
a ferry or a bridge. In the Adventures of Henry the fur-
trader, it is pleasant to read that when with his Indians
he reached the shore of Ontario, they consumed two
days in making two canoes of the bark of the elm tree,
in which to transport themselves to Fort Niagara. It is
a worthy incident in a journey, a delay as good as much
rapid traveling. A good share of our interest in Xenophon's story of his retreat is in the manœuvres to get the
army safely over the rivers, whether on rafts of logs or
fagots, or sheepskins blown up. And where could they
better afford to tarry meanwhile than on the banks of a
river?

As we glided past at a distance, these outdoor workmen appeared to have added some dignity to their labor
by its very publicness. It was a part of the industry of
nature, like the work of hornets and mud wasps.

[1] Ovid, *Met.* I. 133.

> The waves slowly beat,
> Just to keep the noon sweet,
> And no sound is floated o'er,
> Save the mallet on shore,
> Which echoing on high
> Seems a-calking the sky.

The haze, the sun's dust of travel, had a Lethean influence on the land and its inhabitants, and all creatures resigned themselves to float upon the inappreciable tides of nature.

> Woof of the sun, ethereal gauze,
> Woven of Nature's richest stuffs,
> Visible heat, air-water, and dry sea,
> Last conquest of the eye;
> Toil of the day displayed, sun-dust,
> Aerial surf upon the shores of earth,
> Ethereal estuary, frith of light,
> Breakers of air, billows of heat,
> Fine summer spray on inland seas;
> Bird of the sun, transparent-winged
> Owlet of noon, soft-pinioned,
> From heath or stubble rising without song;
> Establish thy serenity o'er the fields.

The routine which is in the sunshine and the finest days, as that which has conquered and prevailed, commends itself to us by its very antiquity and apparent solidity and necessity. Our weakness needs it, and our strength uses it. We cannot draw on our boots without bracing ourselves against it. If there were but one erect and solid-standing tree in the woods, all creatures would go to rub against it and make sure of their footing. During the many hours which we spend in this waking sleep, the hand stands still on the face of the clock, and we

grow like corn in the night. Men are as busy as the
brooks or bees, and postpone everything to their business;
as carpenters discuss politics between the strokes of the
hammer while they are shingling a roof.

This noontide was a fit occasion to make some
pleasant harbor, and there read the journal of some
voyageur like ourselves, not too moral nor inquisitive,
and which would not disturb the noon; or else some
old classic, the very flower of all reading, which we had
postponed to such a season

> "Of Syrian peace, immortal leisure."

But, alas, our chest, like the cabin of a coaster, contained only its well-thumbed "Navigator" for all literature, and we were obliged to draw on our memory for
these things.

We naturally remembered Alexander Henry's Adventures here, as a sort of classic among books of American
travel. It contains scenery and rough sketching of men
and incidents enough to inspire poets for many years,
and to my fancy is as full of sounding names as any page
of history, — Lake Winnipeg, Hudson's Bay, Ottaway,
and portages innumerable; Chippeways, Gens de Terres,
Les Pilleurs, The Weepers; with reminiscences of
Hearne's journey, and the like; an immense and shaggy
but sincere country, summer and winter, adorned with
chains of lakes and rivers, covered with snows, with
hemlocks, and fir trees. There is a naturalness, an unpretending and cold life in this traveler, as in a Canadian
winter, what life was preserved through low tempera-
tures and frontier dangers by furs within a stout heart.

He has truth and moderation worthy of the father of history, which belong only to an intimate experience, and he does not defer too much to literature. The unlearned traveler may quote his single line from the poets with as good right as the scholar. He too may speak of the stars, for he sees them shoot perhaps when the astronomer does not. The good sense of this author is very conspicuous. He is a traveler who does not exaggerate, but writes for the information of his readers, for science, and for history. His story is told with as much good faith and directness as if it were a report to his brother traders, or the Directors of the Hudson's Bay Company, and is fitly dedicated to Sir Joseph Banks. It reads like the argument to a great poem on the primitive state of the country and its inhabitants, and the reader imagines what in each case, with the invocation of the Muse, might be sung, and leaves off with suspended interest, as if the full account were to follow. In what school was this fur-trader educated? He seems to travel the immense snowy country with such purpose only as the reader who accompanies him, and to the latter's imagination, it is, as it were, momentarily created to be the scene of his adventures. What is most interesting and valuable in it, however, is not the materials for the history of Pontiac, or Braddock, or the Northwest, which it furnishes; not the *annals* of the country, but the natural facts, or *perennials*, which are ever without date. When out of history the truth shall be extracted, it will have shed its dates like withered leaves.

The Souhegan, or *Crooked* River, as some translate

it, comes in from the west about a mile and a half above Thornton's Ferry. Babboosuck Brook empties into it near its mouth. There are said to be some of the finest water privileges in the country still unimproved on the former stream, at a short distance from the Merrimack. One spring morning, March 22, in the year 1677, an incident occurred on the banks of the river here, which is interesting to us as a slight memorial of an interview between two ancient tribes of men, one of which is now extinct, while the other, though it is still represented by a miserable remnant, has long since disappeared from its ancient hunting-grounds. A Mr. James Parker, at "Mr. Hinchmanne's farme ner Meremack," wrote thus "to the Honred Governer and Council at Bostown, *Hast, Post Hast:*" —

"Sagamore Wanalancet come this morning to informe me, and then went to Mr. Tyng's to informe him, that his son being on ye other sid of Meremack river over against Souhegan upon the 22 day of this instant, about tene of the clock in the morning, he discovered 15 Indians on this sid the river, which he soposed to be Mohokes by ther spech. He called to them; they answered but he could not understand ther spech; and he having a conow ther in the river, he went to breck his conow that they might not have ani ues of it. In the mean time they shot about thirty guns at him, and he being much frighted fled, and come home forthwith to Nahamcock [Pawtucket Falls or Lowell], wher ther wigowames now stand."

Penacooks and Mohawks! *ubique gentium sunt?* In the year 1670, a Mohawk warrior scalped a Naam-

keak or else a Wamesit Indian maiden near where
Lowell now stands. She, however, recovered. Even as
late as 1685, John Hogkins, a Penacook Indian, who
describes his grandfather as having lived "at place
called Malamake rever, other name chef Natukkog and
Panukkog, that one rever great many names," wrote
thus to the governor: —

"May 15th, 1685.

"Honor governor my friend, —

"You my friend I desire your worship and your
power, because I hope you can do som great matters
this one. I am poor and naked and I have no men
at my place because I afraid allwayes Mohogs he will
kill me every day and night. If your worship when
please pray help me you no let Mohogs kill me at my
place at Malamake river called Pannukkog and Natukkog, I will submit your worship and your power.
And now I want pouder and such alminishon shatt
and guns, because I have forth at my hom and I plant
theare.

"This all Indian hand, but pray you do consider your
humble servant,

JOHN HOGKINS."

Signed also by Simon Detogkom, King Hary, Sam
Linis, Mr. Jorge Rodunnonukgus, John Owamosimmin,
and nine other Indians, with their marks against their
names.

But now, one hundred and fifty-four years having
elapsed since the date of this letter, we went unalarmed
on our way without "brecking" our "conow," reading

the New England Gazetteer, and seeing no traces of
" Mohogs " on the banks.

The Souhegan, though a rapid river, seemed to-day
to have borrowed its character from the noon.

> Where gleaming fields of haze
> Meet the voyageur's gaze,
> And above, the heated air
> Seems to make a river there,
> The pines stand up with pride
> By the Souhegan's side,
> And the hemlock and the larch
> With their triumphal arch
> Are waving o'er its march
>   To the sea.
> No wind stirs its waves,
> But the spirits of the braves
>   Hov'ring o'er,
> Whose antiquated graves
> Its still water laves
>   On the shore.
> With an Indian's stealthy tread
> It goes sleeping in its bed,
> Without joy or grief,
> Or the rustle of a leaf,
> Without a ripple or a billow,
> Or the sigh of a willow,
> From the Lyndeboro' hills
> To the Merrimack mills.
> With a louder din
> Did its current begin,
> When melted the snow
> On the far mountain's brow.
> And the drops came together
> In that rainy weather.
> Experienced river,
> Hast thou flowed forever?
> Souhegan soundeth old,

But the half is not told, —
What names hast thou borne,
In the ages far gone,
When the Xanthus and Meander
Commenced to wander,
Ere the black bear haunted
Thy red forest-floor,
Or Nature had planted
The pines by thy shore?

During the heat of the day, we rested on a large island a mile above the mouth of this river, pastured by a herd of cattle, with steep banks and scattered elms and oaks, and a sufficient channel for canal-boats on each side. When we made a fire to boil some rice for our dinner, the flames spreading amid the dry grass, and the smoke curling silently upward and casting grotesque shadows on the ground, seemed phenomena of the noon, and we fancied that we progressed up the stream without effort, and as naturally as the wind and tide went down, not outraging the calm days by unworthy bustle or impatience. The woods on the neighboring shore were alive with pigeons, which were moving south, looking for mast, but now, like ourselves, spending their noon in the shade. We could hear the slight, wiry, winnowing sound of their wings as they changed their roosts from time to time, and their gentle and tremulous cooing. They sojourned with us during the noontide, greater travelers far than we. You may frequently discover a single pair sitting upon the lower branches of the white pine in the depths of the wood, at this hour of the day, so silent and solitary, and with such a hermitlike appearance, as if they had never strayed beyond its skirts, while the acorn which was gathered in the forests of Maine is still undigested in their crops. We obtained one of these handsome birds, which lingered too long upon its perch, and plucked and broiled it here with some other game, to be carried along for our supper; for, beside the provisions which we carried with us, we depended mainly on the river and forest for our supply. It is true, it did not seem to be putting this bird to its right use to pluck off its feathers, and extract its entrails, and broil its carcass on the coals; but we heroically persevered, nevertheless, waiting for further information. The same regard for Nature which excited our sympathy for her creatures nerved our hands to carry through what we had begun. For we would be honorable to the party we deserted; we would fulfill fate, and so at length, perhaps, detect the secret innocence of these incessant tragedies which Heaven allows.

> "Too quick resolves do resolution wrong.
> What, part so soon to be divorced so long?
> Things to be done are long to be debated;
> Heaven is not day'd, Repentance is not dated."

We are double-edged blades, and every time we whet our virtue the return stroke straps our vice. Where is the skillful swordsman who can give clean wounds, and not rip up his work with the other edge?

Nature herself has not provided the most graceful end for her creatures. What becomes of all these birds that people the air and forest for our solacement? The sparrows seem always *chipper*, never infirm. We do not see their bodies lie about. Yet there is a tragedy at the end of each one of their lives. They must perish miserably;

not one of them is translated. True, "not a sparrow falleth to the ground without our Heavenly Father's knowledge," but they do fall, nevertheless.

The carcasses of some poor squirrels, however, the same that frisked so merrily in the morning, which we had skinned and emboweled for our dinner, we abandoned in disgust, with tardy humanity, as too wretched a resource for any but starving men. It was to perpetuate the practice of a barbarous era. If they had been larger, our crime had been less. Their small red bodies, little bundles of red tissue, mere gobbets of venison, would not have "fattened fire." With a sudden impulse we threw them away, and washed our hands, and boiled some rice for our dinner. "Behold the difference between the one who eateth flesh, and him to whom it belonged! The first hath a momentary enjoyment, whilst the latter is deprived of existence!" "Who would commit so great a crime against a poor animal, who is fed only by the herbs which grow wild in the woods, and whose belly is burnt up with hunger?" We remembered a picture of mankind in the hunter age, chasing hares down the mountains; O me miserable! Yet sheep and oxen are but larger squirrels, whose hides are saved and meat is salted, whose souls perchance are not so large in proportion to their bodies.

There should always be some flowering and maturing of the fruits of nature in the cooking process. Some simple dishes recommend themselves to our imaginations as well as palates. In parched corn, for instance, there is a manifest sympathy between the bursting seed and the more perfect developments of vegetable life.

It is a perfect flower with its petals, like the houstonia or anemone. On my warm hearth these cerealian blossoms expanded; here is the bank whereon they grew. Perhaps some such visible blessing would always attend the simple and wholesome repast.

Here was that "pleasant harbor" which we had sighed for, where the weary voyageur could read the journal of some other sailor, whose bark had plowed, perchance, more famous and classic seas. At the tables of the gods, after feasting follow music and song; we will recline now under these island trees, and for our minstrel call on

ANACREON

"Nor has he ceased his charming song, for still that lyre,
Though he is dead, sleeps not in Hades." [1]

I lately met with an old volume from a London book-shop, containing the Greek Minor Poets, and it was a pleasure to read once more only the words Orpheus, Linus, Musæus, — those faint poetic sounds and echoes of a name, dying away on the ears of us modern men; and those hardly more substantial sounds, Mimnermus, Ibycus, Alcæus, Stesichorus, Menander. They lived not in vain. We can converse with these bodiless fames without reserve or personality.

I know of no studies so composing as those of the classical scholar. When we have sat down to them, life seems as still and serene as if it were very far off, and I believe it is not habitually seen from any common platform so truly and unexaggerated as in the light of literature. In serene hours we contemplate the tour of the

[1] Simonides' Epigram on Anacreon.

Greek and Latin authors with more pleasure than the traveler does the fairest scenery of Greece or Italy. Where shall we find a more refined scoiety ? That highway down from Homer and Hesiod to Horace and Juvenal is more attractive than the Appian. Reading the classics or conversing with those old Greeks and Latins in their surviving works, is like walking amid the stars and constellations, a high and by way serene to travel. Indeed, the true scholar will be not a little of an astronomer in his habits. Distracting cares will not be allowed to obstruct the field of his vision, for the higher regions of literature, like astronomy, are above storm and darkness.

But passing by these rumors of bards, let us pause for a moment at the Teian poet.

There is something strangely modern about him. He is very easily turned into English. Is it that our lyric poets have resounded but that lyre, which would sound only light subjects, and which Simonides tells us does not sleep in Hades ? His odes are like gems of pure ivory. They possess an ethereal and evanescent beauty like summer evenings, ὃ χρή σε νοεῖν νόου ἄνθει, — *which you must perceive with the flower of the mind,* — and show how slight a beauty could be expressed. You have to consider them, as the stars of lesser magnitude, with the side of the eye, and look aside from them to behold them. They charm us by their serenity and freedom from exaggeration and passion, and by a certain flower-like beauty, which does not propose itself, but must be approached and studied like a natural object. But perhaps their chief merit consists in the lightness and yet security of their tread, —

> "The young and tender stalk
> Ne'er bends when *they* do walk."

True, our nerves are never strung by them; it is too constantly the sound of the lyre, and never the note of the trumpet; but they are not gross, as has been presumed, but always elevated above the sensual.

These are some of the best that have come down to us.

ON HIS LYRE

I wish to sing the Atridæ,
And Cadmus I wish to sing;
But my lyre sounds
Only love with its chords.
Lately I changed the strings
And all the lyre;
And I began to sing the labors
Of Hercules; but my lyre
Resounded loves.
Farewell, henceforth, for me,
Heroes! for my lyre
Sings only loves.

TO A SWALLOW

Thou indeed, dear swallow,
Yearly going and coming,
In summer weavest thy nest,
And in winter go'st disappearing
Either to Nile or to Memphis.
But Love always weaveth
His nest in my heart. . . .

ON A SILVER CUP

Turning the silver,
Vulcan, make for me,
Not indeed a panoply,
For what are battles to me?

But a hollow cup,
As deep as thou canst.
And make for me in it
Neither stars, nor wagons,
Nor sad Orion;
What are the Pleiades to me?
What the shining Boötes?
Make vines for me,
And clusters of grapes in it,
And of gold Love and Bathyllus
Treading the grapes
With the fair Lyæus.

ON HIMSELF

Thou sing'st the affairs of Thebes,
And he the battles of Troy,
But I of my own defeats.
No horse have wasted me,
Nor foot, nor ships;
But a new and different host,
From eyes smiting me.

TO A DOVE

Lovely dove,
Whence, whence dost thou fly?
Whence, running on air,
Dost thou waft and diffuse
So many sweet ointments?
Who art? What thy errand? —
Anacreon sent me
To a boy, to Bathyllus,
Who lately is ruler and tyrant of all.
Cythere has sold me
For one little song,
And I'm doing this service
For Anacreon.
And now, as you see,
I bear letters from him.

And he says that directly
He 'll make me free,
But though he release me,
His slave will I tarry with him.
For why should I fly
Over mountains and fields,
And perch upon trees,
Eating some wild thing?
Now indeed I eat bread,
Plucking it from the hands
Of Anacreon himself;
And he gives me to drink
The wine which he tastes,
And drinking, I dance,
And shadow my master's
Face with my wings;
And, going to rest,
On the lyre itself I sleep.
That is all; get thee gone.
Thou hast made me more talkative,
Man, than a crow.

ON LOVE

Love walking swiftly,
With hyacinthine staff,
Bade me to take a run with him;
And hastening through swift torrents,
And woody places, and over precipices,
A water-snake stung me.
And my heart leaped up to
My mouth, and I should have fainted;
But Love, fanning my brows
With his soft wings, said,
Surely, thou art not able to love.

ON WOMEN

Nature has given horns
To bulls, and hoofs to horses,

Swiftness to hares,
To lions yawning teeth,
To fishes swimming,
To birds flight,
To men wisdom.
For woman she had nothing beside;
What then does she give? Beauty, —
Instead of all shields,
Instead of all spears;
And she conquers even iron
And fire, who is beautiful.

ON LOVERS

Horses have the mark
Of fire on their sides,
And some have distinguished
The Parthian men by their crests;
So I, seeing lovers,
Know them at once,
For they have a certain slight
Brand on their hearts.

TO A SWALLOW

What dost thou wish me to do to thee, —
What, thou loquacious swallow?
Dost thou wish me taking thee
Thy light pinions to clip?
Or rather to pluck out
Thy tongue from within,
As that Tereus did?
Why with thy notes in the dawn
Hast thou plundered Bathyllus
From my beautiful dreams?

TO A COLT

Thracian colt, why at me
Looking aslant with thy eyes,
Dost thou cruelly flee,
And think that I know nothing wise?

Know I could well
Put the bridle on thee,
And holding the reins, turn
Round the bounds of the course.
But now thou browsest the meads,
And gamboling lightly dost play,
For thou hast no skillful horseman
Mounted upon thy back.

CUPID WOUNDED

Love once among roses
Saw not
A sleeping bee, but was stung;
And being wounded in the finger
Of his hand, cried for pain.
Running as well as flying
To the beautiful Venus,
I am killed, mother, said he,
I am killed, and I die.
A little serpent has stung me,
Winged, which they call
A bee, — the husbandmen.
And she said, If the sting
Of a bee afflicts you,
How, think you, are they afflicted,
Love, whom you smite?

Late in the afternoon, for we had lingered long on the
island, we raised our sail for the first time, and for a short
hour the southwest wind was our ally; but it did not
please Heaven to abet us long. With one sail raised we
swept slowly up the eastern side of the stream, steering
clear of the rocks, while, from the top of a hill which
formed the opposite bank, some lumberers were rolling
down timber to be rafted down the stream. We could see
their axes and levers gleaming in the sun, and the logs

came down with a dust and a rumbling sound, which was reverberated through the woods beyond us on our side, like the roar of artillery. But Zephyr soon took us out of sight and hearing of this commerce. Having passed Read's Ferry, and another island called McGaw's Island, we reached some rapids called Moore's Falls, and entered on "that section of the river, nine miles in extent, converted, by law, into the Union Canal, comprehending in that space six distinct falls; at each of which, and at several intermediate places, work has been done." After passing Moore's Falls by means of locks, we again had recourse to our oars, and went merrily on our way, driving the small sandpiper from rock to rock before us, and sometimes rowing near enough to a cottage on the bank, though they were few and far between, to see the sunflowers, and the seed-vessels of the poppy, like small goblets filled with the water of Lethe, before the door, but without disturbing the sluggish household behind. Thus we held on, sailing or dipping our way along with the paddle up this broad river, smooth and placid, flowing over concealed rocks, where we could see the pickerel lying low in the transparent water, eager to double some distant cape, to make some great bend as in the life of man, and see what new perspective would open; looking far into a new country, broad and serene, the cottages of settlers seen afar for the first time, yet with the moss of a century on their roofs, and the third or fourth generation in their shadows. Strange was it to consider how the sun and the summer, the buds of spring and the seared leaves of autumn, were related to these cabins along the shore; how all the rays which paint the landscape radiate from them, and the flight of the crow and the gyrations of the hawk have reference to their roofs. Still the ever rich and fertile shores accompanied us, fringed with vines and alive with small birds and frisking squirrels, the edge of some farmer's field or widow's wood-lot, or wilder, perchance, where the muskrat, the little medicine of the river, drags itself along stealthily over the alder leaves and mussel shells, and man and the memory of man are banished far.

At length the unwearied, never-sinking shore, still holding on without break, with its cool copses and serene pasture-grounds, tempted us to disembark; and we adventurously landed on this remote coast, to survey it, without the knowledge of any human inhabitant probably to this day. But we still remember the gnarled and hospitable oaks which grew even there for our entertainment, and were no strangers to us, the lonely horse in his pasture, and the patient cows, whose path to the river, so judiciously chosen to overcome the difficulties of the way, we followed, and disturbed their ruminations in the shade; and, above all, the cool, free aspect of the wild apple trees, generously proffering their fruit to us, though still green and crude, — the hard, round, glossy fruit, which, if not ripe, still was not poison, but New English too, brought hither, its ancestors, by ours once. These gentler trees imparted a half-civilized and twilight aspect to the otherwise barbarian land. Still farther on we scrambled up the rocky channel of a brook, which had long served nature for a sluice there, leaping like it from rock to rock, through tangled woods, at the bottom of a ravine, which grew darker and darker, and more and more hoarse the murmurs of the stream, until we reached the ruins of a mill, where now the ivy grew, and the trout glanced through the crumbling flume; and there we imagined what had been the dreams and specu- lations of some early settler. But the waning day com- pelled us to embark once more, and redeem this wasted time with long and vigorous sweeps over the rippling stream.

It was still wild and solitary, except that at intervals of a mile or two the roof of a cottage might be seen over the bank. This region, as we read, was once famous for the manufacture of straw bonnets of the Leghorn kind, of which it claims the invention in these parts; and occasionally some industrious damsel tripped down to the water's edge, to put her straw a-soak, as it ap- peared, and stood awhile to watch the retreating voy- ageurs, and catch the fragment of a boat-song which we had made, wafted over the water.

Thus, perchance, the Indian hunter,
  Many a lagging year agone,
Gliding o'er thy rippling waters,
  Lowly hummed a natural song.

Now the sun's behind the willows,
  Now he gleams along the waves ;
Faintly o'er the wearied billows
  Come the spirits of the braves.

Just before sundown we reached some more falls in the town of Bedford, where some stone-masons were employed repairing the locks in a solitary part of the river. They were interested in our adventure, especially one young man of our own age, who inquired at first if

we were bound up to "'Skeag;" and when he had heard
our story, and examined our outfit, asked us other questions, but temperately still, and always turning to his
work again, though as if it were become his duty. It was
plain that he would like to go with us, and, as he looked
up the river, many a distant cape and wooded shore were
reflected in his eye, as well as in his thoughts. When we
were ready he left his work, and helped us through the
locks with a sort of quiet enthusiasm, telling us that we
were at Coos Falls, and we could still distinguish the
strokes of his chisel for many sweeps after we had left
him.

We wished to camp this night on a large rock in the
middle of the stream, just above these falls, but the want
of fuel, and the difficulty of fixing our tent firmly, prevented us; so we made our bed on the mainland opposite, on the west bank, in the town of Bedford, in a
retired place, as we supposed, there being no house in
sight.

WEDNESDAY

Man is man's foe and destiny. — COTTON.

EARLY this morning, as we were rolling up our buffaloes and loading our boat amid the dew, while our embers were still smoking, the masons who worked at the locks, and whom we had seen crossing the river in their boat the evening before while we were examining the rock, came upon us as they were going to their work, and we found that we had pitched our tent directly in the path to their boat. This was the only time that we were observed on our camping-ground. Thus, far from the beaten highways and the dust and din of travel, we beheld the country privately, yet freely, and at our leisure. Other roads do some violence to Nature, and bring the traveler to stare at her, but the river steals into the scenery it traverses without intrusion, silently creating and adorning it, and is as free to come and go as the zephyr.

As we shoved away from this rocky coast, before sunrise, the smaller bittern, the genius of the shore, was moping along its edge, or stood probing the mud for its food, with ever an eye on us, though so demurely at work, or else he ran along over the wet stones like a wrecker in his storm-coat, looking out for wrecks of snails and cockles. Now away he goes, with a limping flight, uncertain where he will alight, until a rod of clear sand amid the alders invites his feet; and now our steady approach compels him to seek a new retreat. It is a bird

of the oldest Thalesian school, and no doubt believes
in the priority of water to the other elements; the relic
of a twilight antediluvian age which yet inhabits these
bright American rivers with us Yankees. There is something venerable in this melancholy and contemplative
race of birds, which may have trodden the earth while it
was yet in a slimy and imperfect state. Perchance their
tracks, too, are still visible on the stones. It still lingers
into our glaring summers, bravely supporting its fate
without sympathy from man, as if it looked forward to
some second advent of which *he* has no assurance. One
wonders if, by its patient study by rocks and sandy capes,
it has wrested the whole of her secret from Nature yet.
What a rich experience it must have gained, standing on
one leg and looking out from its dull eye so long on sunshine and rain, moon and stars! What could it tell of
stagnant pools and reeds and dank night-fogs! It would
be worth the while to look closely into the eye which has
been open and seeing at such hours, and in such solitudes
its dull, yellowish, greenish eye. Methinks my own soul
must be a bright invisible green. I have seen these birds
stand by the half dozen together in the shallower water
along the shore, with their bills thrust into the mud at
the bottom, probing for food, the whole head being concealed, while the neck and body formed an arch above
the water.

Cohass Brook, the outlet of Massabesic Pond, —
which last is five or six miles distant, and contains fifteen
hundred acres, being the largest body of fresh water in
Rockingham County, — comes in near here from the
east. Rowing between Manchester and Bedford, we

passed, at an early hour, a ferry and some falls, called Goff's Falls, the Indian Cohasset, where there is a small village, and a handsome green islet in the middle of the stream. From Bedford and Merrimack have been boated the bricks of which Lowell is made. About twenty years before, as they told us, one Moore, of Bedford, having clay on his farm, contracted to furnish eight millions of bricks to the founders of that city within two years. He fulfilled his contract in one year, and since then bricks have been the principal export from these towns. The farmers found thus a market for their wood, and when they had brought a load to the kilns, they could cart a load of bricks to the shore, and so make a profitable day's work of it. Thus all parties were benefited. It was worth the while to see the place where Lowell was " dug out." So, likewise, Manchester is being built of bricks made still higher up the river at Hooksett.

There might be seen here on the bank of the Merrimack, near Goff's Falls, in what is now the town of Bedford, famous " for hops and for its fine domestic manufactures," some graves of the aborigines. The land still bears this scar here, and time is slowly crumbling the bones of a race. Yet, without fail, every spring, since they first fished and hunted here, the brown thrasher has heralded the morning from a birch or alder spray, and the undying race of reed-birds still rustles through the withering grass. But these bones rustle not. These mouldering elements are slowly preparing for another metamorphosis, to serve new masters, and what was the Indian's will ere long be the white man's sinew.

We learned that Bedford was not so famous for hops
as formerly, since the price is fluctuating, and poles are
now scarce. Yet if the traveler goes back a few miles
from the river, the hop kilns will still excite his curiosity.

There were few incidents in our voyage this forenoon,
though the river was now more rocky and the falls more
frequent than before. It was a pleasant change, after
rowing incessantly for many hours, to lock ourselves
through in some retired place, — for commonly there
was no lock-man at hand, — one sitting in the boat,
while the other, sometimes with no little labor and heave-
yo-ing, opened and shut the gates, waiting patiently to
see the locks fill. We did not once use the wheels which
we had provided. Taking advantage of the eddy, we
were sometimes floated up to the locks almost in the face
of the falls; and, by the same cause, any floating timber
was carried round in a circle and repeatedly drawn into
the rapids before it finally went down the stream. These
old gray structures, with their quiet arms stretched over
the river in the sun, appeared like natural objects in the
scenery, and the kingfisher and sandpiper alighted on
them as readily as on stakes or rocks.

We rowed leisurely up the stream for several hours,
until the sun had got high in the sky, our thoughts
monotonously beating time to our oars. For outward
variety there was only the river and the receding shores,
a vista continually opening behind and closing before us,
as we sat with our backs upstream; and, for inward,
such thoughts as the muses grudgingly lent us. We were
always passing some low, inviting shore, or some overhanging bank, on which, however, we never landed.

Such near aspects had we
Of our life's scenery.

It might be seen by what tenure men held the earth.
The smallest stream is *mediterranean* sea, a smaller
ocean creek within the land, where men may steer by
their farm bounds and cottage lights. For my own part,
but for the geographers, I should hardly have known
how large a portion of our globe is water, my life has
chiefly passed within so deep a cove. Yet I have sometimes ventured as far as to the mouth of my Snug Harbor.
From an old ruined fort on Staten Island, I have loved
to watch all day some vessel whose name I had read in
the morning through the telegraph glass, when she first
came upon the coast, and her hull heaved up and glis-
tened in the sun, from the moment when the pilot and
most adventurous news-boats met her, past the Hook,
and up the narrow channel of the wide bay, till she was
boarded by the health officer, and took her station at
quarantine, or held on her unquestioned course to the
wharves of New York. It was interesting, too, to watch
the less adventurous newsman, who made his assault as
the vessel swept through the Narrows, defying plague
and quarantine law, and, fastening his little cockboat
to her huge side, clambered up and disappeared in the
cabin. And then I could imagine what momentous news
was being imparted by the captain, which no American
ear had ever heard, that Asia, Africa, Europe — were all
sunk; for which at length he pays the price, and is seen
descending the ship's side with his bundle of newspapers, but not where he first got up, for these arrivers do
not stand still to gossip; and he hastes away with steady

sweeps to dispose of his wares to the highest bidder, and
we shall ere long read something startling, — "By the
latest arrival," — "by the good ship ——." On Sunday I
beheld, from some interior hill, the long procession of
vessels getting to sea, reaching from the city wharves
through the Narrows, and past the Hook, quite to the
ocean stream, far as the eye could reach, with stately
march and silken sails, all counting on lucky voyages,
but each time some of the number, no doubt, destined
to go to Davy's locker, and never come on this coast
again. And, again, in the evening of a pleasant day, it
was my amusement to count the sails in sight. But as
the setting sun continually brought more and more to
light, still farther in the horizon, the last count always
had the advantage, till, by the time the last rays streamed
over the sea, I had doubled and trebled my first number;
though I could no longer class them all under the several
heads of ships, barks, brigs, schooners, and sloops, but
most were faint generic *vessels* only. And then the temperate twilight, perchance, revealed the floating home of
some sailor whose thoughts were already alienated from
this American coast, and directed towards the Europe of
our dreams. I have stood upon the same hilltop, when
a thunder-shower, rolling down from the Catskills and
Highlands, passed over the island, deluging the land;
and, when it had suddenly left us in sunshine, have seen
it overtake successively, with its huge shadow and dark,
descending wall of rain, the vessels in the bay. Their
bright sails were suddenly drooping and dark, like the
sides of barns, and they seemed to shrink before the
storm; while still far beyond them on the sea, through

this dark veil, gleamed the sunny sails of those vessels
which the storm had not yet reached. And at midnight,
when all around and overhead was darkness, I have seen
a field of trembling, silvery light far out on the sea, the
reflection of the moonlight from the ocean, as if beyond
the precincts of our night, where the moon traversed a
cloudless heaven, — and sometimes a dark speck in its
midst, where some fortunate vessel was pursuing its
happy voyage by night.

But to us river sailors the sun never rose out of ocean
waves, but from some green coppice, and went down
behind some dark mountain line. We, too, were but
dwellers on the shore, like the bittern of the morning;
and our pursuit, the wrecks of snails and cockles.
Nevertheless, we were contented to know the better one
fair particular shore.

> My life is like a stroll upon the beach,
>   As near the ocean's edge as I can go;
> My tardy steps its waves sometimes o'erreach,
>   Sometimes I stay to let them overflow.
>
> My sole employment 't is, and scrupulous care,
>   To place my gains beyond the reach of tides,
> Each smoother pebble, and each shell more rare,
>   Which ocean kindly to my hand confides.
>
> I have but few companions on the shore,
>   They scorn the strand who sail upon the sea,
> Yet oft I think the ocean they 've sailed o'er
>   Is deeper known upon the strand to me.
>
> The middle sea contains no crimson dulse,
>   Its deeper waves cast up no pearls to view,
> Along the shore my hand is on its pulse,
>   And I converse with many a shipwrecked crew.

The small houses which were scattered along the river
at intervals of a mile or more were commonly out of
sight to us, but sometimes, when we rowed near the
shore, we heard the peevish note of a hen, or some slight
domestic sound, which betrayed them. The lock-men's
houses were particularly well placed, retired, and high,
always at falls or rapids, and commanding the pleasant-
est reaches of the river, — for it is generally wider and
more lake-like just above a fall, — and there they wait
for boats. These humble dwellings, homely and sincere,
in which a hearth was still the essential part, were more
pleasing to our eyes than palaces or castles would have
been. In the noon of these days, as we have said, we
occasionally climbed the banks and approached these
houses, to get a glass of water and make acquaintance
with their inhabitants. High in the leafy bank, surrounded commonly by a small patch of corn and beans,
squashes and melons, with sometimes a graceful hop-
yard on one side, and some running vine over the windows, they appeared like beehives set to gather honey
for a summer. I have not read of any Arcadian life
which surpasses the actual luxury and serenity of these
New England dwellings. For the outward gilding, at
least, the age is golden enough. As you approach the
sunny doorway, awakening the echoes by your steps,
still no sound from these barracks of repose, and you
fear that the gentlest knock may seem rude to the
Oriental dreamers. The door is opened, perchance, by
some Yankee-Hindoo woman, whose small-voiced but
sincere hospitality, out of the bottomless depths of a
quiet nature, has traveled quite round to the opposite

side, and fears only to obtrude its kindness. You step over the white-scoured floor to the bright "dresser" lightly, as if afraid to disturb the devotions of the household, — for Oriental dynasties appear to have passed away since the dinner-table was last spread here, — and thence to the frequented curb, where you see your long-forgotten, unshaven face at the bottom, in juxtaposition with new-made butter and the trout in the well. "Perhaps you would like some molasses and ginger," suggests the faint noon voice. Sometimes there sits the brother who follows the sea, their representative man; who knows only how far it is to the nearest port, no more distances, all the rest is sea and distant capes, — patting the dog, or dandling the kitten in arms that were stretched by the cable and the oar, pulling against Boreas or the trade-winds. He looks up at the stranger, half pleased, half astonished, with a mariner's eye, as if he were a dolphin within cast. If men will believe it, *sua si bona norint*, there are no more quiet Tempes, nor more poetic and Arcadian lives, than may be lived in these New England dwellings. We thought that the employment of their inhabitants by day would be to tend the flowers and herds, and at night, like the shepherds of old, to cluster and give names to the stars from the river banks.

We passed a large and densely wooded island this forenoon, between Short's and Griffith's Falls, the fairest which we had met with, with a handsome grove of elms at its head. If it had been evening, we should have been glad to camp there. Not long after, one or two more were passed. The boatmen told us that the current had

recently made important changes here. An island always
pleases my imagination, even the smallest, as a small continent and integral portion of the globe. I have a fancy
for building my hut on one. Even a bare, grassy isle,
which I can see entirely over at a glance, has some
undefined and mysterious charm for me. There is
commonly such a one at the junction of two rivers,
whose currents bring down and deposit their respective
sands in the eddy at their confluence, as it were the
womb of a continent. By what a delicate and far-
stretched contribution every island is made! What an
enterprise of Nature thus to lay the foundations of and
to build up the future continent, of golden and silver
sands and the ruins of forests, with ant-like industry.
Pindar gives the following account of the origin of Thera,
whence, in after times, Libyan Cyrene was settled by
Battus. Triton, in the form of Eurypylus, presents a
clod to Euphemus, one of the Argonauts, as they are
about to return home.

> "He knew of our haste,
> And immediately seizing a clod
> With his right hand, strove to give it
> As a chance stranger's gift.
> Nor did the hero disregard him, but leaping on the shore,
> Stretching hand to hand,
> Received the mystic clod.
> But I hear it sinking from the deck,
> Go with the sea brine
> At evening, accompanying the watery sea.
> Often indeed I urged the careless
> Menials to guard it, but their minds forgot.
> And now in this island the imperishable seed of spacious Libya
> Is spilled before its hour."

It is a beautiful fable, also related by Pindar, how
Helius, or the Sun, looked down into the sea one day, —
when perchance his rays were first reflected from some
increasing, glittering sand-bar, — and saw the fair and
fruitful island of Rhodes

> "springing up from the bottom,
> Capable of feeding many men, and suitable for flocks;"

and at the nod of Zeus, —

> "The island sprang from the watery
> Sea; and the genial Father of penetrating beams,
> Ruler of fire-breathing horses, has it."

The shifting islands! who would not be willing that
his house should be undermined by such a foe! The
inhabitant of an island can tell what currents formed
the land which he cultivates; and his earth is still
being created or destroyed. There before his door,
perchance, still empties the stream which brought down
the material of his farm ages before, and is still bringing it down or washing it away, — the graceful, gentle
robber!

Not long after this we saw the Piscataquoag, or
Sparkling Water, emptying in on our left, and heard the
Falls of Amoskeag above. Large quantities of lumber,
as we read in the Gazetteer, were still annually floated
down the Piscataquoag to the Merrimack, and there are
many fine mill privileges on it. Just above the mouth of
this river we passed the artificial falls where the canals
of the Manchester Manufacturing Company discharge
themselves into the Merrimack. They are striking
enough to have a name, and, with the scenery of a Bash-

pish, would be visited from far and near. The water falls thirty or forty feet over seven or eight steep and narrow terraces of stone, probably to break its force, and is converted into one mass of foam. This canal water did not seem to be the worse for the wear, but foamed and fumed as purely, and boomed as savagely and impressively, as a mountain torrent, and, though it came from under a factory, we saw a rainbow here. These are now the Amoskeag Falls, removed a mile down-stream. But we did not tarry to examine them minutely, making haste to get past the village here collected, and out of hearing of the hammer which was laying the foundation of another Lowell on the banks. At the time of our voyage Manchester was a village of about two thousand inhabitants, where we landed for a moment to get some cool water, and where an inhabitant told us that he was accustomed to go across the river into Goffstown for his water. But now, as I have been told, and indeed have witnessed, it contains fourteen thousand inhabitants. From a hill on the road between Goffstown and Hooksett, four miles distant, I have seen a thunder-shower pass over, and the sun break out and shine on a city there, where I had landed nine years before in the fields; and there was waving the flag of its Museum, where "the only perfect skeleton of a Greenland or river whale in the United States" was to be seen, and I also read in its directory of a "Manchester Athenæum and Gallery of the Fine Arts."

According to the Gazetteer, the descent of Amoskeag Falls, which are the most considerable in the Merrimack, is fifty-four feet in half a mile. We locked our-

selves through here with much ado, surmounting the
successive watery steps of this river's staircase in the
midst of a crowd of villagers, jumping into the canal to
their amusement, to save our boat from upsetting, and
consuming much river water in our service. Amoskeag,
or Namaskeak, is said to mean "great fishing-place."
It was hereabouts that the Sachem Wannalancet resided.
Tradition says that his tribe, when at war with the
Mohawks, concealed their provisions in the cavities of
the rocks in the upper part of these falls. The Indians,
who hid their provisions in these holes, and affirmed
"that God had cut them out for that purpose," understood their origin and use better than the Royal Society,
who in their Transactions, in the last century, speaking
of these very holes, declare that "they seem plainly to be
artificial." Similar "pot-holes" may be seen at the Stone
Flume on this river, on the Ottaway, at Bellows Falls on
the Connecticut, and in the limestone rock at Shelburne
Falls on Deerfield River in Massachusetts, and more or
less generally about all falls. Perhaps the most remarkable curiosity of this kind in New England is the well-
known Basin on the Pemigewasset, one of the head-
waters of this river, twenty by thirty feet in extent and
proportionably deep, with a smooth and rounded brim,
and filled with a cold, pellucid, and greenish water. At
Amoskeag the river is divided into many separate tor
rents and trickling rills by the rocks, and its volume is so
much reduced by the drain of the canals that it does not
fill its bed. There are many pot-holes here on a rocky
island which the river washes over in high freshets. As
at Shelburne Falls, where I first observed them, they are

from one foot to four or five in diameter, and as many in depth, perfectly round and regular, with smooth and gracefully curved brims, like goblets. Their origin is apparent to the most careless observer. A stone which the current has washed down, meeting with obstacles, revolves as on a pivot where it lies, gradually sinking in the course of centuries deeper and deeper into the rock, and in new freshets receiving the aid of fresh stones, which are drawn into this trap and doomed to revolve there for an indefinite period, doing Sisyphus-like penance for stony sins, until they either wear out or wear through the bottom of their prison, or else are released by some revolution of nature. There lie the stones of various sizes, from a pebble to a foot or two in diameter, some of which have rested from their labor only since the spring, and some higher up which have lain still and dry for ages, — we noticed some here at least sixteen feet above the present level of the water, — while others are still revolving, and enjoy no respite at any season. In one instance, at Shelburne Falls, they have worn quite through the rock, so that a portion of the river leaks through in anticipation of the fall. Some of these pot-holes at Amoskeag, in a very hard brown-stone, had an oblong, cylindrical stone of the same material loosely fitting them. One, as much as fifteen feet deep and seven or eight in diameter, which was worn quite through to the water, had a huge rock of the same material, smooth but of irregular form, lodged in it. Everywhere there were the rudiments or the wrecks of a dimple in the rock; the rocky shells of whirlpools. As if by force of example and sympathy after so many lessons, the rocks, the hardest material, had been endeavoring to whirl or flow into the forms of the most fluid. The finest workers in stone are not copper or steel tools, but the gentle touches of air and water working at their leisure with a liberal allowance of time.

Not only have some of these basins been forming for countless ages, but others exist which must have been completed in a former geological period. In deepening the Pawtucket Canal, in 1822, the workmen came to ledges with pot-holes in them, where probably was once the bed of the river, and there are some, we are told, in the town of Canaan in this State, with the stones still in them, on the height of land between the Merrimack and Connecticut, and nearly a thousand feet above these rivers, proving that the mountains and the rivers have changed places. There lie the stones which completed their revolutions perhaps before thoughts began to revolve in the brain of man. The periods of Hindoo and Chinese history, though they reach back to the time when the race of mortals is confounded with the race of gods, are as nothing compared with the periods which these stones have inscribed. That which commenced a rock when time was young shall conclude a pebble in the unequal contest. With such expense of time and natural forces are our very paving-stones produced. They teach us lessons, these dumb workers ; verily there are " sermons in stones, and books in the running brooks." In these very holes the Indians hid their provisions; but now there is no bread, but only its old neighbor stones at the bottom. Who knows how many races they have served thus ? By as simple a law, some accidental bylaw, perchance, our system itself was made ready for its inhabitants.

These, and such as these, must be our antiquities, for lack of human vestiges. The monuments of heroes and the temples of the gods which may once have stood on the banks of this river are now, at any rate, returned to dust and primitive soil. The murmur of unchronicled nations has died away along these shores, and once more Lowell and Manchester are on the trail of the Indian.

The fact that Romans once inhabited her reflects no little dignity on Nature herself; that from some particular hill the Roman once looked out on the sea. She need not be ashamed of the vestiges of her children. How gladly the antiquary informs us that their vessels penetrated into this frith, or up that river of some remote isle! Their military monuments still remain on the hills and under the sod of the valleys. The oft-repeated Roman story is written in still legible characters in every quarter of the Old World, and but to-day, perchance, a new coin is dug up whose inscription repeats and confirms their fame. Some " Judæa Capta," with a woman mourning under a palm tree, with silent argument and demonstration confirms the pages of history.

> "Rome living was the world's sole ornament;
> And dead is now the world's sole monument.
>
> . . . .
>
> With her own weight down pressèd now she lies,
> And by her heaps her hugeness testifies."

If one doubts whether Grecian valor and patriotism are not a fiction of the poets, he may go to Athens and see still upon the walls of the temple of Minerva the circular marks made by the shields taken from the enemy in the Persian war, which were suspended there. We have not far to seek for living and unquestionable evidence. The very dust takes shape and confirms some story which we had read. As Fuller said, commenting on the zeal of Camden, "A broken urn is a whole evidence; or an old gate still surviving out of which the city is run out." When Solon endeavored to prove that Salamis had formerly belonged to the Athenians, and not to the Megareans, he caused the tombs to be opened, and showed that the inhabitants of Salamis turned the faces of their dead to the same side with the Athenians, but the Megareans to the opposite side. There they were to be interrogated.

Some minds are as little logical or argumentative as nature; they can offer no reason or "guess," but they exhibit the solemn and incontrovertible fact. If a historical question arises, they cause the tombs to be opened. Their silent and practical logic convinces the reason and the understanding at the same time. Of such sort is always the only pertinent question and the only satisfactory reply .

Our own country furnishes antiquities as ancient and durable, and as useful, as any; rocks at least as well covered with lichens, and a soil which, if it is virgin, is but virgin mould, the very dust of nature. What if we cannot read Rome or Greece, Etruria or Carthage, or Egypt or Babylon, on these; are our cliffs bare? The lichen on the rocks is a rude and simple shield which beginning and imperfect Nature suspended there. Still hangs her wrinkled trophy. And here, too, the poet's

eye may still detect the brazen nails which fastened
Time's inscriptions, and if he has the gift, decipher them
by this clue. The walls that fence our fields, as well as
modern Rome, and not less the Parthenon itself, are
all built of *ruins*. Here may be heard the din of rivers,
and ancient winds which have long since lost their
names sough through our woods, — the first faint
sounds of spring, older than the summer of Athenian
glory, the titmouse lisping in the wood, the jay's scream,
and bluebird's warble, and the hum of

> "bees that fly
> About the laughing blossoms of sallowy."

Here is the gray dawn for antiquity, and our to-morrow's
future should be at least paulo-post to theirs which we
have put behind us. There are the red maple and birchen
leaves, old runes which are not yet deciphered; catkins,
pine cones, vines, oak leaves, and acorns; the very
things themselves, and not their forms in stone, — so
much the more ancient and venerable. And even to the
current summer there has come down tradition of a
hoary-headed master of all art, who once filled every
field and grove with statues and godlike architecture, of
every design which Greece has lately copied; whose
ruins are now mingled with the dust, and not one block
remains upon another. The century sun and unwearied
rain have wasted them, till not one fragment from that
quarry now exists; and poets perchance will feign that
gods sent down the material from heaven.

What though the traveler tell us of the ruins of Egypt,
are we so sick or idle that we must sacrifice our America
and to day to some man's ill-remembered and indolent

story? Carnac and Luxor are but names, or if their skeletons remain, still more desert sand and at length a wave of the Mediterranean Sea are needed to wash away the filth that attaches to their grandeur. Carnac! Carnac! here is Carnac for me. I behold the columns of a larger and purer temple.

> This is my Carnac, whose unmeasured dome
> Shelters the measuring art and measurer's home.
> Behold these flowers, let us be up with time,
> Not dreaming of three thousand years ago,
> Erect ourselves and let those columns lie,
> Not stoop to raise a foil against the sky.
> Where is the spirit of that time but in
> This present day, perchance the present line?
> Three thousand years ago are not agone,
> They are still lingering in this summer morn,
> And Memnon's Mother sprightly greets us now,
> Wearing her youthful radiance on her brow.
> If Carnac's columns still stand on the plain,
> To enjoy our opportunities they remain.

In these parts dwelt the famous Sachem Pasaconaway, who was seen by Gookin "at Pawtucket, when he was about one hundred and twenty years old." He was reputed a wise man and a powwow, and restrained his people from going to war with the English. They believed "that he could make water burn, rocks move, and trees dance, and metamorphose himself into a flaming man; that in winter he could raise a green leaf out of the ashes of a dry one, and produce a living snake from the skin of a dead one, and many similar miracles." In 1660, according to Gookin, at a great feast and dance, he made his farewell speech to his people, in which he said that as he was not likely to see them met together

again, he would leave them this word of advice, to take
heed how they quarreled with their English neighbors,
for though they might do them much mischief at first,
it would prove the means of their own destruction. He
himself, he said, had been as much an enemy to the
English at their first coming as any, and had used all his
arts to destroy them, or at least to prevent their settlement, but could by no means effect it. Gookin thought
that he " possibly might have such a kind of spirit upon
him as was upon Balaam, who, in Numbers xxiii. 23,
said, 'Surely, there is no enchantment against Jacob,
neither is there any divination against Israel.' " His son
Wannalancet carefully followed his advice, and when
Philip's war broke out, he withdrew his followers to
Penacook, now Concord in New Hampshire, from the
scene of the war. On his return afterwards, he visited
the minister of Chelmsford, and, as is stated in the history of that town, " wished to know whether Chelmsford
had suffered much during the war; and being informed
that it had not, and that God should be thanked for it,
Wannalancet replied, 'Me next.' "

Manchester was the residence of John Stark, a hero
of two wars, and survivor of a third, and at his death the
last but one of the American generals of the Revolution.
He was born in the adjoining town of Londonderry,
then Nutfield, in 1728. As early as 1752, he was taken
prisoner by the Indians while hunting in the wilderness
near Baker's River; he performed notable service as
a captain of rangers in the French war: commanded a
regiment of the New Hampshire militia at the battle of
Bunker Hill; and fought and won the battle of Benning·

ton in 1777. He was past service in the last war, and died here in 1822, at the age of ninety-four. His monument stands upon the second bank of the river, about a mile and a half above the falls, and commands a prospect several miles up and down the Merrimack. It suggested how much more impressive in the landscape is the tomb of a hero than the dwellings of the inglorious living. Who is most dead, — a hero by whose monument you stand, or his descendants of whom you have never heard?

The graves of Pasaconaway and Wannalancet are marked by no monument on the bank of their native river.

Every town which we passed, if we may believe the Gazetteer, had been the residence of some great man. But though we knocked at many doors, and even made particular inquiries, we could not find that there were any now living. Under the head of Litchfield we read: —

"The Hon. Wyseman Clagett closed his life in this town." According to another, "He was a classical scholar, a good lawyer, a wit, and a poet." We saw his old gray house just below Great Nesenkeag Brook. — Under the head of Merrimack: "Hon. Mathew Thornton, one of the signers of the Declaration of American Independence, resided many years in this town." His house too we saw from the river. — "Dr. Jonathan Gove, a man distinguished for his urbanity, his talents and professional skill, resided in this town [Goffstown]. He was one of the oldest practitioners of medicine in the county. He was many years an active member of the

legislature." — " Hon. Robert Means, who died January 24, 1823, at the age of 80, was for a long period a
resident in Amherst. He was a native of Ireland. In
1764 he came to this country, where, by his industry and
application to business, he acquired a large property,
and great respect." — " William Stinson [one of the first
settlers of Dunbarton], born in Ireland, came to Londonderry with his father. He was much respected and was a
useful man. James Rogers was from Ireland, and father
to Major Robert Rogers. He was shot in the woods,
being mistaken for a bear." — " Rev. Matthew Clark,
second minister of Londonderry, was a native of Ireland,
who had in early life been an officer in the army, and
distinguished himself in the defense of the city of Londonderry, when besieged by the army of King James II.,
A. D. 1688–89. He afterwards relinquished a military
life for the clerical profession. He possessed a strong
mind, marked by a considerable degree of eccentricity.
He died January 25, 1735, and was borne to the grave,
at his particular request, by his former companions
in arms, of whom there were a considerable number
among the early settlers of this town; several of them
had been made free from taxes throughout the British
dominions by King William, for their bravery in that
memorable siege." — Colonel George Reid and Captain David M'Clary, also citizens of Londonderry, were
" distinguished and brave " officers. — " Major Andrew
M'Clary, a native of this town [Epsom], fell at the battle
of Breed's Hill." Many of these heroes, like the illustri-
ous Roman, were plowing when the news of the massacre
at Lexington arrived, and straightway left their plows in

the furrow, and repaired to the scene of action. Some miles from where we now were, there once stood a guide-post on which were the words, " 3 miles to Squire Mac-Gaw's."

But, generally speaking, the land is now, at any rate, very barren of men, and we doubt if there are as many hundreds as we read of. It may be that we stood too near.

Uncannunuc Mountain in Goffstown was visible from Amoskeag, five or six miles westward. It is the north-easternmost in the horizon which we see from our native town, but seen from there is too ethereally blue to be the same which the like of us have ever climbed. Its name is said to mean " The Two Breasts," there being two eminences some distance apart. The highest, which is about fourteen hundred feet above the sea, probably affords a more extensive view of the Merrimack valley and the adjacent country than any other hill, though it is somewhat obstructed by woods. Only a few short reaches of the river are visible, but you can trace its course far down-stream by the sandy tracts on its banks.

A little south of Uncannunuc, about sixty years ago, as the story goes, an old woman who went out to gather pennyroyal tripped her foot in the bail of a small brass kettle in the dead grass and bushes. Some say that flints and charcoal and some traces of a camp were also found. This kettle, holding about four quarts, is still preserved and used to dye thread in. It is supposed to have belonged to some old French or Indian hunter, who was killed in one of his hunting or scouting excursions, and so never returned to look after his kettle.

But we were most interested to hear of the penny-royal; it is soothing to be reminded that wild nature produces anything ready for the use of man. Men know that *something* is good. One says that it is yellow dock, another that it is bittersweet, another that it is slippery-elm bark, burdock, catnip, calamint, elecampane, thoroughwort, or pennyroyal. A man may esteem himself happy when that which is his food is also his medicine. There is no kind of herb, but somebody or other says that it is good. I am very glad to hear it. It reminds me of the first chapter of Genesis. But how should they know that it is good? That is the mystery to me. I am always agreeably disappointed; it is incredible that they should have found it out. Since all things are good, men fail at last to distinguish which is the bane and which the antidote. There are sure to be two prescriptions diametrically opposite. Stuff a cold and starve a cold are but two ways. They are the two practices, both always in full blast. Yet you must take advice of the one school as if there was no other. In respect to religion and the healing art, all nations are still in a state of barbarism. In the most civilized countries the priest is still but a Powwow, and the physician a Great Medicine. Consider the deference which is everywhere paid to a doctor's opinion. Nothing more strikingly betrays the credulity of mankind than medicine. Quackery is a thing universal, and universally successful. In this case it becomes literally true that no imposition is too great for the credulity of men. Priests and physicians should never look one another in the face. They have no common ground, nor is there any to mediate between them. When the one comes, the other goes. They could not come together without laughter, or a significant silence, for the one's profession is a satire on the other's, and either's success would be the other's failure. It is wonderful that the physician should ever die, and that the priest should ever live. Why is it that the priest is never called to consult with the physician? Is it because men believe practically that matter is independent of spirit? But what is quackery? It is commonly an attempt to cure the diseases of a man by addressing his body alone. There is need of a physician who shall minister to both soul and body at once, that is, to man. Now he falls between two stools.

After passing through the locks, we had poled ourselves through the canal here, about half a mile in length, to the boatable part of the river. Above Amoskeag the river spreads out into a lake reaching a mile or two without a bend. There were many canal-boats here bound up to Hooksett, about eight miles, and as they were going up empty, with a fair wind, one boatman offered to take us in tow if we would wait. But when we came alongside, we found that they meant to take us on board, since otherwise we should clog their motions too much; but as our boat was too heavy to be lifted aboard, we pursued our way up the stream, as before, while the boatmen were at their dinner, and came to anchor at length under some alders on the opposite shore, where we could take our lunch. Though far on one side, every sound was wafted over to us from the opposite bank, and from the harbor of the canal, and we could see everything that passed. By and by came several canal-boats, at intervals of a quarter of a mile, standing up to Hooksett with a light breeze, and one by one disappeared round a point above. With their broad sails set, they moved slowly up the stream in the sluggish and fitful breeze, like one-winged antediluvian birds, and as if impelled by some mysterious counter-current. It was a grand motion, so slow and stately, this "standing out," as the phrase is, expressing the gradual and steady progress of a vessel, as if it were by mere rectitude and disposition, without shuffling. Their sails, which stood so still, were like chips cast into the current of the air, to show which way it set. At length the boat which we had spoken came along, keeping the middle of the stream, and when within speaking distance, the steersman called out ironically to say that if we could come alongside now, he would take us in tow; but not heeding his taunt, we still loitered in the shade till we had finished our lunch, and when the last boat had disappeared round the point with flapping sail, for the breeze had now sunk to a zephyr, with our own sails set, and plying our oars, we shot rapidly up the stream in pursuit, and as we glided close alongside, while they were vainly invoking Æolus to their aid, we returned their compliment by proposing, if they would throw us a rope, to "take them in tow," to which these Merrimack sailors had no suitable answer ready. Thus we gradually overtook and passed each boat in succession until we had the river to ourselves again.

Our course this afternoon was between Manchester and Goffstown.

While we float here, far from that tributary stream

on whose banks our Friends and kindred dwell, our
thoughts, like the stars, come out of their horizon still;
for there circulates a finer blood than Lavoisier has
discovered the laws of, — the blood, not of kindred
merely, but of kindness, whose pulse still beats at any
distance and forever.

> True kindness is a pure divine affinity,
> Not founded upon human consanguinity.
> It is a spirit, not a blood relation,
> Superior to family and station.

After years of vain familiarity, some distant gesture or
unconscious behavior, which we remember, speaks to us
with more emphasis than the wisest or kindest words.
We are sometimes made aware of a kindness long
passed, and realize that there have been times when our
Friends' thoughts of us were of so pure and lofty a character that they passed over us like the winds of heaven
unnoticed; when they treated us not as what we were,
but as what we aspired to be. There has just reached us,
it may be, the nobleness of some such silent behavior,
not to be forgotten, not to be remembered, and we shud-
der to think how it fell on us cold, though in some true
but tardy hour we endeavor to wipe off these scores.

In my experience, persons, when they are made the
subject of conversation, though with a Friend, are commonly the most prosaic and trivial of facts. The universe seems bankrupt as soon as we begin to discuss the
character of individuals. Our discourse all runs to
slander, and our limits grow narrower as we advance.
How is it that we are impelled to treat our old Friends so
ill when we obtain new ones? The housekeeper says, I

never had any new crockery in my life but I began **to**
break the old. I say, let us speak of mushrooms and
forest trees rather. Yet we can sometimes afford **to**
remember them in private.

Lately, alas, I knew a gentle boy,
  Whose features all were cast in Virtue's mould,
As one she had designed for Beauty's toy,
  But after manned him for her own stronghold.

On every side he open was as day,
  That you might see no lack of strength within,
For walls and ports do only serve alway
  For a pretense to feebleness and sin.

Say not that Cæsar was victorious,
  With toil and strife who stormed the House of **Fame,**
In other sense this youth was glorious,
  Himself a kingdom wheresoe'er he came.

No strength went out to get him victory,
  When all was income of its own accord;
For where he went none other was to see,
  But all were parcel of their noble lord.

He forayed like the subtile haze of summer,
  That stilly shows fresh landscapes to our **eyes,**
And revolutions works without a murmur,
  Or rustling of a leaf beneath the skies.

So was I taken unawares by this,
  I quite forgot my homage to confess;
Yet now am forced to know, though hard it **is,**
  I might have loved him had I loved him less.

Each moment as we nearer drew to each,
  A stern respect withheld us farther yet,
So that we seemed beyond each other's reach,
  And less acquainted than when first we **met**

We two were one while we did sympathize,
   So could we not the simplest bargain drive;
And what avails it now that we are wise,
   If absence doth this doubleness contrive?

Eternity may not the chance repeat,
   But I must tread my single way alone,
In sad remembrance that we once did meet,
   And know that bliss irrevocably gone.

The spheres henceforth my elegy shall sing,
   For elegy has other subject none;
Each strain of music in my ears shall ring
   Knell of departure from that other one.

Make haste and celebrate my tragedy;
   With fitting strain resound ye woods and fields;
Sorrow is dearer in such case to me
   Than all the joys other occasion yields.

———

Is 't then too late the damage to repair?
   Distance, forsooth, from my weak grasp hath reft
The empty husk, and clutched the useless tare,
   But in my hands the wheat and kernel left.

If I but love that virtue which he is,
   Though it be scented in the morning air,
Still shall we be truest acquaintances,
   Nor mortals know a sympathy more rare.

Friendship is evanescent in every man's experience
and remembered like heat lightning in past summers.
Fair and flitting like a summer cloud, — there is always
some vapor in the air, no matter how long the drought;
there are even April showers. Surely from time to time,
for its vestiges never depart, it floats through our atmosphere. It takes place, like vegetation in so many mate-

cials, because there is such a law, but always without
permanent form, though ancient and familiar as the sun
and moon, and as sure to come again. The heart is forever inexperienced. They silently gather as by magic,
these never failing, never quite deceiving visions, like the
bright and fleecy clouds in the calmest and clearest days.
The Friend is some fair floating isle of palms eluding the
mariner in Pacific seas. Many are the dangers to be en-
countered, equinoctial gales and coral reefs, ere he may
sail before the constant trades. But who would not sail
through mutiny and storm, even over Atlantic waves,
to reach the fabulous retreating shores of some continent
man? The imagination still clings to the faintest tradition of

THE ATLANTIDES

The smothered streams of love, which flow
More bright than Phlegethon, more low,
Island us ever, like the sea,
In an Atlantic mystery.
Our fabled shores none ever reach,
No mariner has found our beach,
Scarcely our mirage now is seen,
And neighboring waves with floating green,
Yet still the oldest charts contain
Some dotted outline of our main;
In ancient times midsummer days
Unto the western islands' gaze,
To Teneriffe and the Azores,
Have shown our faint and cloud-like shores.

But sink not yet, ye desolate isles,
Anon your coast with commerce smiles,
And richer freights ye'll furnish far
Than Africa or Malabar.

Be fair, be fertile evermore,
Ye rumored but untrodden shore,
Princes and monarchs will contend
Who first unto your land shall send,
And pawn the jewels of the crown
To call your distant soil their own.

Columbus has sailed westward of these isles by the mariner's compass, but neither he nor his successors have found them. We are no nearer than Plato was. The earnest seeker and hopeful discoverer of this New World always haunts the outskirts of his time, and walks through the densest crowd uninterrupted, and, as it were, in a straight line.

Sea and land are but his neighbors,
And companions in his labors,
Who on the ocean's verge and firm land's end
Doth long and truly seek his Friend.
Many men dwell far inland,
But he alone sits on the strand.
Whether he ponders men or books
Always still he seaward looks,
Marine news he ever reads,
And the slightest glances heeds,
Feels the sea breeze on his cheek,
At each word the landsmen speak,
In every companion's eye
A sailing vessel doth descry;
In the ocean's sullen roar
From some distant port he hears
Of wrecks upon a distant shore,
And the ventures of past years.

Who does not walk on the plain as amid the columns of Tadmore of the desert? There is on the earth no institution which Friendship has established; it is not

taught by any religion; no scripture contains its max-
ims. It has no temple, nor even a solitary column.
There goes a rumor that the earth is inhabited, but the
shipwrecked mariner has not seen a footprint on the
shore. The hunter has found only fragments of pottery
and the monuments of inhabitants.

However, our fates at least are social. Our courses
do not diverge; but as the web of destiny is woven it is
fulled, and we are cast more and more into the centre.
Men naturally, though feebly, seek this alliance, and
their actions faintly foretell it. We are inclined to lay
the chief stress on likeness and not on difference, and
in foreign bodies we admit that there are many degrees of warmth below blood heat, but none of cold
above it.

Mencius says: " If one loses a fowl or a dog, he knows
well how to seek them again; if one loses the sentiments
of his heart, he does not know how to seek them again.
. . . The duties of practical philosophy consist only in
seeking after those sentiments of the heart which we
have lost; that is all."

One or two persons come to my house from time to
time, there being proposed to them the faint possibility
of intercourse. They are as full as they are silent, and
wait for my plectrum to stir the strings of their lyre. If
they could ever come to the length of a sentence, or hear
one, on that ground they are dreaming of! They speak
faintly, and do not obtrude themselves. They have heard
some news, which none, not even they themselves, can
impart. It is a wealth they can bear about them which

can be expended in various ways. What came they out to seek?

No word is oftener on the lips of men than Friendship, and indeed no thought is more familiar to their aspirations. All men are dreaming of it, and its drama, which is always a tragedy, is enacted daily. It is the secret of the universe. You may thread the town, you may wander the country, and none shall ever speak of it, yet thought is everywhere busy about it, and the idea of what is possible in this respect affects our behavior toward all new men and women, and a great many old ones. Nevertheless, I can remember only two or three essays on this subject in all literature. No wonder that the Mythology, and Arabian Nights, and Shakespeare, and Scott's novels entertain us, — we are poets and fablers and dramatists and novelists ourselves. We are continually acting a part in a more interesting drama than any written. We are dreaming that our Friends are our *Friends*, and that we are our Friends' *Friends*. Our actual Friends are but distant relations of those to whom we are pledged. We never exchange more than three words with a Friend in our lives on that level to which our thoughts and feelings almost habitually rise. One goes forth prepared to say, "Sweet Friends!" and the salutation is, "Damn your eyes!" But never mind; faint heart never won true Friend. O my Friend, may it come to pass once, that when you are my Friend I may be yours.

Of what use the friendliest dispositions even, if there are no hours given to Friendship, if it is forever postponed to unimportant duties and relations? Friendship is first, Friendship last. But it is equally impossible to forget our Friends, and to make them answer to our ideal. When they say farewell, then indeed we begin to keep them company. How often we find ourselves turning our backs on our actual Friends, that we may go and meet their ideal cousins. I would that I were worthy to be any man's Friend.

What is commonly honored with the name of Friendship is no very profound or powerful instinct. Men do not, after all, *love* their Friends greatly. I do not often see the farmers made seers and wise to the verge of insanity by their Friendship for one another. They are not often transfigured and translated by love in each other's presence. I do not observe them purified, refined, and elevated by the love of a man. If one abates a little the price of his wood, or gives a neighbor his vote at town-meeting, or a barrel of apples, or lends him his wagon frequently, it is esteemed a rare instance of Friendship. Nor do the farmers' wives lead lives consecrated to Friendship. I do not see the pair of farmer Friends of either sex prepared to stand against the world. There are only two or three couples in history. To say that a man is your Friend means commonly no more than this, that he is not your enemy. Most contemplate only what would be the accidental and trifling advantages of Friendship, so that the Friend can assist in time of need, by his substance, or his influence, or his counsel; but he who foresees such advantages in this relation proves himself blind to its real advantage, or indeed wholly inexperienced in the relation itself. Such services are particular and menial, compared with the perpetual and all-embracing service which it is. Even the utmost good-will and harmony and practical kindness are not sufficient for Friendship, for Friends do not live in harmony merely, as some say, but in melody. We do not wish for Friends to feed and clothe our bodies, — neighbors are kind enough for that, — but to do the like office to our spirits. For this few are rich enough, however well disposed they may be. For the most part we stupidly confound one man with another. The dull distinguish only races or nations, or at most classes, but the wise man, individuals. To his Friend a man's peculiar character appears in every feature and in every action, and it is thus drawn out and improved by him.

Think of the importance of Friendship in the education of men.

> "He that hath love and judgment too,
> Sees more than any other doe."

It will make a man honest; it will make him a hero; it will make him a saint. It is the state of the just dealing with the just, the magnanimous with the magnanimous, the sincere with the sincere, man with man.

And it is well said by another poet, —

> "Why love among the virtues is not known,
> It is that love contracts them all in one."

All the abuses which are the object of reform with the philanthropist, the statesman, and the housekeeper are unconsciously amended in the intercourse of Friends. A Friend is one who incessantly pays us the compliment of expecting from us all the virtues, and who can appreciate them in us. It takes two to speak the truth, — one to speak, and another to hear. How can one treat with

magnanimity mere wood and stone? If we dealt only
with the false and dishonest, we should at last forget
how to speak truth. Only lovers know the value and
magnanimity of truth, while traders prize a cheap honesty, and neighbors and acquaintance a cheap civility.
In our daily intercourse with men, our nobler faculties
are dormant and suffered to rust. None will pay us the
compliment to expect nobleness from us. Though we
have gold to give, they demand only copper. We ask our
neighbor to suffer himself to be dealt with truly, sincerely,
nobly; but he answers no by his deafness. He does not
even hear this prayer. He says practically, I will be content if you treat me as " no better than I should be," as
deceitful, mean, dishonest, and selfish. For the most
part, we are contented so to deal and to be dealt with,
and we do not think that for the mass of men there is any
truer and nobler relation possible. A man may have
good neighbors, so called, and acquaintances, and even
companions, wife, parents, brothers, sisters, children,
who meet himself and one another on this ground only.
The state does not demand justice of its members, but
thinks that it succeeds very well with the least degree
of it, hardly more than rogues practice; and so do the
neighborhood and the family. What is commonly called
Friendship even is only a little more honor among rogues.

But sometimes we are said to *love* another, that is,
to stand in a true relation to him, so that we give the best
to, and receive the best from, him. Between whom there
is hearty truth, there is love; and in proportion to our
truthfulness and confidence in one another, our lives
are divine and miraculous, and answer to our ideal.

There are passages of affection in our intercourse with mortal men and women, such as no prophecy had taught us to expect, which transcend our earthly life, and anticipate Heaven for us. What is this Love that may come right into the middle of a prosaic Goffstown day, equal to any of the gods ? that discovers a new world, fair and fresh and eternal, occupying the place of the old one, when to the common eye a dust has settled on the universe ? which world cannot else be reached, and does not exist. What other words, we may almost ask, are memorable and worthy to be repeated than those which love has inspired ? It is wonderful that they were ever uttered. They are few and rare indeed, but, like a strain of music, they are incessantly repeated and modulated by the memory. All other words crumble off with the stucco which overlies the heart. We should not dare to repeat these now aloud. We are not competent to hear them at all times.

The books for young people say a great deal about the *selection* of Friends; it is because they really have nothing to say about *Friends*. They mean associates and confidants merely. " Know that the contrariety of foe and Friend proceeds from God." Friendship takes place between those who have an affinity for one another, and is a perfectly natural and inevitable result. No professions nor advances will avail. Even speech, at first, necessarily has nothing to do with it; but it follows after silence, as the buds in the graft do not put forth into leaves till long after the graft has taken. It is a drama in which the parties have no part to act. We are all Mussulmans and fatalists in this respect. Impatient and uncertain lovers think that they must say or do something kind whenever they meet; they must never be cold. But they who are Friends do not do what they *think* they must, but what they *must*. Even their Friendship is to some extent but a sublime phenomenon to them.

The true and not despairing Friend will address his Friend in some such terms as these.

"I never asked thy leave to let me love thee, — I have a right. I love thee not as something private and personal, which is *your own*, but as something universal and worthy of love, *which I have found*. Oh, how I think of you! You are purely good, — you are infinitely good. I can trust you forever. I did not think that humanity was so rich. Give me an opportunity to live."

"You are the fact in a fiction, — you are the truth more strange and admirable than fiction. Consent only to be what you are. I alone will never stand in your way."

"This is what I would like, — to be as intimate with you as our spirits are intimate, — respecting you as I respect my ideal. Never to profane one another by word or action, even by a thought. Between us, if necessary, let there be no acquaintance."

"I have discovered you; how can you be concealed from me?"

The Friend asks no return but that his Friend will religiously accept and wear and not disgrace his apotheosis of him. They cherish each other's hopes. They are kind to each other's dreams.

Though the poet says, "'T is the preëminence of Friendship to impute excellence," yet we can never praise our Friend, nor esteem him praiseworthy, nor let him think that he can please us by any *behavior*, or ever *treat* us well enough. That kindness which has so good a reputation elsewhere can least of all consist with this relation, and no such affront can be offered to a Friend as a conscious good-will, a friendliness which is not a necessity of the Friend's nature.

The sexes are naturally most strongly attracted to one another by constant constitutional differences, and are most commonly and surely the complements of each other. How natural and easy it is for man to secure the attention of woman to what interests himself! Men and women of equal culture, thrown together, are sure to be of a certain value to one another, more than men to men. There exists already a natural disinterestedness and liberality in such society, and I think that any man will more confidently carry his favorite books to read to some circle of intelligent women, than to one of his own sex. The visit of man to man is wont to be an interruption, but the sexes naturally expect one another. Yet Friendship is no respecter of sex; and perhaps it is more rare between the sexes than between two of the same sex.

Friendship is, at any rate, a relation of perfect equality. It cannot well spare any outward sign of equal obligation and advantage. The nobleman can never have a Friend among his retainers, nor the king among his subjects. Not that the parties to it are in all respects equal, but they are equal in all that respects or affects their Friendship. The one's love is exactly balanced and represented by the other's. Persons are only the vessels which contain the nectar, and the hydrostatic paradox is the symbol of love's law. It finds its level and rises to its fountain-head in all breasts, and its slenderest column balances the ocean.

> "And love as well the shepherd can
> As can the mighty nobleman."

The one sex is not, in this respect, more tender than the other. A hero's love is as delicate as a maiden's.

Confucius said, "Never contract Friendship with a man who is not better than thyself." It is the merit and preservation of Friendship, that it takes place on a level higher than the actual characters of the parties would seem to warrant. The rays of light come to us in such a curve that every man whom we meet appears to be taller than he actually is. Such foundation has civility. My Friend is that one whom I can associate with my choicest thought. I always assign to him a nobler employment in my absence than I ever find him engaged in; and I imagine that the hours which he devotes to me were snatched from a higher society. The sorest insult which I ever received from a Friend was when he behaved with the license which only long and cheap acquaintance allows to one's faults, in my presence, without shame, and still addressed me in friendly accents. Beware, lest thy Friend learn at last to tolerate one frailty of thine, and so an obstacle be raised to the progress of thy love. There are times when we have had enough even of our Friends, when we begin inevitably to profane one another, and must withdraw religiously into solitude and silence, the better to prepare ourselves for a loftier intimacy. Silence is the ambrosial night in the intercourse of Friends, in which their sincerity is recruited and takes deeper root.

Friendship is never established as an understood relation. Do you demand that I be less your Friend that you may know it? Yet what right have I to think that another cherishes so rare a sentiment for me? It is a miracle which requires constant proofs. It is an exercise of the purest imagination and the rarest faith. It says by a silent but eloquent behavior, "I will be so related to thee as thou canst imagine; even so thou mayest believe. I will spend truth, — all my wealth on thee," — and the Friend responds silently through his nature and life, and treats his Friend with the same divine courtesy. He knows us literally through thick and thin. He never asks for a sign of love, but can distinguish it by the features which it naturally wears. We never need to stand upon ceremony with him with regard to his visits. Wait not till I invite thee, but observe that I am glad to see thee when thou comest. It would be paying too dear for thy visit to ask for it. Where my Friend lives there are all riches and every attraction, and no slight obstacle can keep me from him. Let me never have to tell thee what I have not to tell. Let our intercourse be wholly above ourselves, and draw us up to it.

The language of Friendship is not words, but meanings. It is an intelligence above language. One imagines endless conversations with his Friend, in which the tongue shall be loosed, and thoughts be spoken without hesitancy or end; but the experience is commonly far otherwise. Acquaintances may come and go, and have a word ready for every occasion; but what puny word shall he utter whose very breath is thought and meaning?

Suppose you go to bid farewell to your Friend who is setting out on a journey; what other outward sign do you know than to shake his hand? Have you any palaver ready for him then? any box of salve to commit to his pocket? any particular message to send by him? any statement which you had forgotten to make? — as if you could forget anything. No, it is much that you take his hand and say Farewell; that you could easily omit; so far custom has prevailed. It is even painful, if he is to go, that he should linger so long. If he must go, let him go quickly. Have you any *last* words? Alas, it is only the word of words, which you have so long sought and found not; *you* have not a *first* word yet. There are few even whom I should venture to call earnestly by their most proper names. A name pronounced is the recognition of the individual to whom it belongs. He who can pronounce my name aright, he can call me, and is entitled to my love and service. Yet reserve is the freedom and abandonment of lovers. It is the reserve of what is hostile or indifferent in their natures, to give place to what is kindred and harmonious.

The violence of love is as much to be dreaded as that of hate. When it is durable it is serene and equable. Even its famous pains begin only with the ebb of love, for few are indeed lovers, though all would fain be. It is one proof of a man's fitness for Friendship that he is able to do without that which is cheap and passionate. A true Friendship is as wise as it is tender. The parties to it yield implicitly to the guidance of their love, and know no other law nor kindness. It is not extravagant and insane, but what it says is something established

henceforth, and will bear to be stereotyped. It is a truer
truth, it is better and fairer news, and no time will ever
shame it, or prove it false. This is a plant which thrives
best in a temperate zone, where summer and winter
alternate with one another. The Friend is a *necessarius*,
and meets his Friend on homely ground; not on carpets
and cushions, but on the ground and on rocks they will
sit, obeying the natural and primitive laws. They will
meet without any outcry, and part without loud sorrow.
Their relation implies such qualities as the warrior
prizes; for it takes a valor to open the hearts of men as
well as the gates of castles. It is not an idle sympathy
and mutual consolation merely, but a heroic sympathy
of aspiration and endeavor.

> "When manhood shall be matched so
> That fear can take no place,
> Then weary *works* make warriors
> Each other to embrace."

The Friendship which Wawatam testified for Henry
the fur-trader, as described in the latter's "Adventures,"
so almost bare and leafless, yet not blossomless nor fruit-
less, is remembered with satisfaction and security. The
stern, imperturbable warrior, after fasting, solitude, and
mortification of body, comes to the white man's lodge,
and affirms that he is the white brother whom he saw in
his dream, and adopts him henceforth. He buries the
hatchet as it regards his friend, and they hunt and feast
and make maple-sugar together. "Metals unite from
fluxility; birds and beasts from motives of convenience;
fools from fear and stupidity; and just men at sight."
If Wawatam would taste the "white man's milk" with

his tribe, or take his bowl of human broth made of the trader's fellow-countrymen, he first finds a place of safety for his Friend, whom he has rescued from a similar fate. At length, after a long winter of undisturbed and happy intercourse in the family of the chieftain in the wilderness, hunting and fishing, they return in the spring to Michilimackinac to dispose of their furs; and it becomes necessary for Wawatam to take leave of his Friend at the Isle aux Outardes, when the latter, to avoid his enemies, proceeded to the Sault de Sainte Marie, supposing that they were to be separated for a short time only. "We now exchanged farewells," says Henry, "with an emotion entirely reciprocal. I did not quit the lodge without the most grateful sense of the many acts of goodness which I had experienced in it, nor without the sincerest respect for the virtues which I had witnessed among its members. All the family accompanied me to the beach; and the canoe had no sooner put off than Wawatam commenced an address to the Kichi Manito, beseeching him to take care of me, his brother, till we should next meet. We had proceeded to too great a distance to allow of our hearing his voice, before Wawatam had ceased to offer up his prayers." We never hear of him again.

Friendship is not so kind as is imagined; it has not much human blood in it, but consists with a certain disregard for men and their erections, the Christian duties and humanities, while it purifies the air like electricity. There may be the sternest tragedy in the relation of two more than usually innocent and true to their highest instincts. We may call it an essentially heathenish intercourse, free and irresponsible in its nature, and practicing all the virtues gratuitously. It is not the highest sympathy merely, but a pure and lofty society, a fragmentary and godlike intercourse of ancient date, still kept up at intervals, which, remembering itself, does not hesitate to disregard the humbler rights and duties of humanity. It requires immaculate and godlike qualities full-grown, and exists at all only by condescension and anticipation of the remotest future. We love nothing which is merely good and not fair, if such a thing is possible. Nature puts some kind of blossom before every fruit, not simply a calyx behind it. When the Friend comes out of his heathenism and superstition, and breaks his idols, being converted by the precepts of a newer testament; when he forgets his mythology, and treats his Friend like a Christian, or as he can afford, — then Friendship ceases to be Friendship, and becomes charity; that principle which established the almshouse is now beginning with its charity at home, and establishing an almshouse and pauper relations there.

As for the number which this society admits, it is at any rate to be begun with one, the noblest and greatest that we know, and whether the world will ever carry it further, — whether, as Chaucer affirms, —

> "There be mo sterres in the skie than a pair,"

remains to be proved; —

> "And certaine he is well begone
> Among a thousand that findeth one."

We shall not surrender ourselves heartily to any while

we are conscious that another is more deserving of our
love. Yet Friendship does not stand for numbers; the
Friend does not count his Friends on his fingers; they
are not numerable. The more there are included by this
bond, if they are indeed included, the rarer and diviner
the quality of the love that binds them. I am ready to
believe that as private and intimate a relation may exist
by which three are embraced, as between two. Indeed,
we cannot have too many friends; the virtue which we
appreciate we to some extent appropriate, so that thus
we are made at last more fit for every relation of life. A
base Friendship is of a narrowing and exclusive tendency, but a noble one is not exclusive; its very superfluity and dispersed love is the humanity which sweetens
society, and sympathizes with foreign nations; for
though its foundations are private, it is, in effect, a public affair and a public advantage, and the Friend, more
than the father of a family, deserves well of the state.

The only danger in Friendship is that it will end. It
is a delicate plant, though a native. The least unworthiness, even if it be unknown to one's self, vitiates it. Let
the Friend know that those faults which he observes in
his Friend his own faults attract. There is no rule more
invariable than that we are paid for our suspicions by
finding what we suspected. By our narrowness and
prejudices we say, I will have so much and such of you,
my Friend, no more. Perhaps there are none charitable,
none disinterested, none wise, noble, and heroic enough,
for a true and lasting Friendship.

I sometimes hear my Friends complain finely that
I do not appreciate their fineness. I shall not tell them

whether I do or not. As if they expected a vote of thanks
for every fine thing which they uttered or did. Who
knows but it was finely appreciated? It may be that your
silence was the finest thing of the two. There are some
things which a man never speaks of, which are much
finer kept silent about. To the highest communications
we only lend a silent ear. Our finest relations are not
simply kept silent about, but buried under a positive
depth of silence never to be revealed. It may be that
we are not even yet acquainted. In human intercourse
the tragedy begins, not when there is misunderstanding
about words, but when silence is not understood. Then
there can never be an explanation. What avails it that
another loves you, if he does not understand you? Such
love is a curse. What sort of companions are they who
are presuming always that their silence is more expressive than yours? How foolish, and inconsiderate, and
unjust, to conduct as if you were the only party ag-
grieved! Has not your Friend always equal ground of
complaint? No doubt my Friends sometimes speak to
me in vain, but they do not know what things I hear
which they are not aware that they have spoken. I know
that I have frequently disappointed them by not giving
them words when they expected them, or such as they
expected. Whenever I see my Friend I speak to him;
but the expecter, the man with the ears, is not he. They
will complain too that you are hard. O ye that would
have the cocoanut wrong side outwards, when next I
weep I will let you know. They ask for words and deeds,
when a true relation is word and deed. If they know not
of these things, how can they be informed? We often

forbear to confess our feelings, not from pride, but for fear that we could not continue to love the one who required us to give such proof of our affection.

I know a woman who possesses a restless and intelligent mind, interested in her own culture, and earnest to enjoy the highest possible advantages, and I meet her with pleasure as a natural person who not a little provokes me, and I suppose is stimulated in turn by myself. Yet our acquaintance plainly does not attain to that degree of confidence and sentiment which women, which all, in fact, covet. I am glad to help her, as I am helped by her; I like very well to know her with a sort of stranger's privilege, and hesitate to visit her often, like her other Friends. My nature pauses here, I do not well know why. Perhaps she does not make the highest demand on me, a religious demand. Some, with whose prejudices or peculiar bias I have no sympathy, yet inspire me with confidence, and I trust that they confide in me also as a religious heathen at least, — a good Greek. I, too, have principles as well founded as their own. If this person could conceive that, without willfulness, I associate with her as far as our destinies are coincident, as far as our Good Geniuses permit, and still value such intercourse, it would be a grateful assurance to me. I feel as if I appeared careless, indifferent, and without principle to her, not expecting more, and yet not content with less. If she could know that I make an infinite demand on myself, as well as on all others, she would see that this true though incomplete intercourse is infinitely better than a more unreserved but falsely grounded one, without the principle of growth in it. For a companion, I require one who will make an equal demand on me with my own genius. Such a one will always be rightly tolerant. It is suicide, and corrupts good manners, to welcome any less than this. I value and trust those who love and praise my aspiration rather than my performance. If you would not stop to look at me, but look whither I am looking, and farther, then my education could not dispense with your company.

My love must be as free
As is the eagle's wing,
Hovering o'er land and sea
And everything.

I must not dim my eye
In thy saloon,
I must not leave my sky
And nightly moon.

Be not the fowler's net
Which stays my flight,
And craftily is set
T' allure the sight.

But be the favoring gale
That bears me on,
And still doth fill my sail
When thou art gone.

I cannot leave my sky
For thy caprice,
True love would soar as high
As heaven is.

The eagle would not brook
Her mate thus won,
Who trained his eye to look
Beneath the sun.

Few things are more difficult than to help a Friend in matters which do not require the aid of Friendship, but only a cheap and trivial service, if your Friendship wants the basis of a thorough practical acquaintance. I stand in the friendliest relation, on social and spiritual grounds, to one who does not perceive what practical skill I have, but when he seeks my assistance in such matters, is wholly ignorant of that one with whom he deals; does not use my skill, which in such matters is much greater than his, but only my hands. I know another, who, on the contrary, is remarkable for his discrimination in this respect; who knows how to make use of the talents of others when he does not possess the same; knows when not to look after or oversee, and stops short at his man. It is a rare pleasure to serve him, which all laborers know. I am not a little pained by the other kind of treatment. It is as if, after the friendliest and most ennobling intercourse, your Friend should use you as a hammer, and drive a nail with your head, all in good faith; notwithstanding that you are a tolerable carpenter, as well as his good Friend, and would use a hammer cheerfully in his service. This want of perception is a defect which all the virtues of the heart cannot supply: —

> The Good how can we trust?
> Only the Wise are just.
> The Good we use,
> The Wise we cannot choose.
> These there are none above;
> The Good they know and love,
> But are not known again
> By those of lesser ken

> They do not charm us with their eyes,
> But they transfix with their advice;
> No partial sympathy they feel,
> With private woe or private weal,
> But with the universe joy and sigh,
> Whose knowledge is their sympathy.

Confucius said: "To contract ties of Friendship with any one is to contract Friendship with his virtue. There ought not to be any other motive in Friendship." But men wish us to contract Friendship with their vice also. I have a Friend who wishes me to see that to be right which I know to be wrong. But if Friendship is to rob me of my eyes, if it is to darken the day, I will have none of it. It should be expansive and inconceivably liberalizing in its effects. True Friendship can afford true knowledge. It does not depend on darkness and ignorance. A want of discernment cannot be an ingredient in it. If I can see my Friend's virtues more distinctly than another's, his faults too are made more conspicuous by contrast. We have not so good a right to hate any as our Friend. Faults are not the less faults because they are invariably balanced by corresponding virtues, and for a fault there is no excuse, though it may appear greater than it is in many ways. I have never known one who could bear criticism, who could not be flattered, who would not bribe his judge, or was content that the truth should be loved always better than himself.

If two travelers would go their way harmoniously together, the one must take as true and just a view of things as the other, else their path will not be strewn with roses. Yet you can travel profitably and pleasantly even with a blind man, if he practices common courtesy, and when you converse about the scenery will remember that he is blind but that you can see; and you will not forget that his sense of hearing is probably quickened by his want of sight. Otherwise you will not long keep company. A blind man and a man in whose eyes there was no defect were walking together, when they came to the edge of a precipice. " Take care, my friend," said the latter, "here is a steep precipice; go no farther this way." " I know better," said the other, and stepped off.

It is impossible to say all that we think, even to our truest Friend. We may bid him farewell forever sooner than complain, for our complaint is too well grounded to be uttered. There is not so good an understanding between any two, but the exposure by the one of a serious fault in the other will produce a misunderstanding in proportion to its heinousness. The constitutional differences which always exist, and are obstacles to a perfect Friendship, are forever a forbidden theme to the lips of Friends. They advise by their whole behavior. Nothing can reconcile them but love. They are fatally late when they undertake to explain and treat with one another like foes. Who will take an apology for a Friend ? They must apologize like dew and frost, which are off again with the sun, and which all men know in their hearts to be beneficent. The necessity itself for explanation, — what explanation will atone for that ?

True love does not quarrel for slight reasons, such mistakes as mutual acquaintances can explain away, but, alas, however slight the apparent cause, only for adequate and fatal and everlasting reasons, which can never be set aside. Its quarrel, if there is any, is ever recurring, notwithstanding the beams of affection which invariably come to gild its tears; as the rainbow, however beautiful and unerring a sign, does not promise fair weather forever, but only for a season. I have known two or three persons pretty well, and yet I have never known advice to be of use but in trivial and transient matters. One may know what another does not, but the utmost kindness cannot impart what is requisite to make the advice useful. We must accept or refuse one another as we are. I could tame a hyena more easily than my Friend. He is a material which no tool of mine will work. A naked savage will fell an oak with a firebrand, and wear a hatchet out of a rock by friction, but I cannot hew the smallest chip out of the character of my Friend, either to beautify or deform it.

The lover learns at last that there is no person quite transparent and trustworthy, but every one has a devil in him that is capable of any crime in the long run. Yet, as an Oriental philosopher has said, "Although Friendship between good men is interrupted, their principles remain unaltered. The stalk of the lotus may be broken, and the fibres remain connected."

Ignorance and bungling with love are better than wisdom and skill without. There may be courtesy, there may be even temper, and wit, and talent, and sparkling conversation, there may be good-will even, — and yet the humanest and divinest faculties pine for exercise. Our life without love is like coke and ashes. Men may be pure as alabaster and Parian marble, elegant as a Tuscan villa, sublime as Niagara, and yet if there is no milk mingled with the wine at their entertainments, better is the hospitality of Goths and Vandals.

My Friend is not of some other race or family of men, but flesh of my flesh, bone of my bone. He is my real brother. I see his nature groping yonder so like mine. We do not live far apart. Have not the fates associated us in many ways? It says, in the Vishnu Purana, "Seven paces together is sufficient for the friendship of the virtuous, but thou and I have dwelt together." Is it of no significance that we have so long partaken of the same loaf, drank at the same fountain, breathed the same air summer and winter, felt the same heat and cold; that the same fruits have been pleased to refresh us both, and we have never had a thought of different fibre the one from the other?

> Nature doth have her dawn each day,
>   But mine are far between;
> Content, I cry, for, sooth to say,
>   Mine brightest are, I ween.
>
> For when my sun doth deign to rise,
>   Though it be her noontide,
> Her fairest field in shadow lies
>   Nor can my light abide.
>
> Sometimes I bask me in her day,
>   Conversing with my mate,
> But if we interchange one ray,
>   Forthwith her heats abate.
>
> Through his discourse I climb and see,
>   As from some eastern hill,
> A brighter morrow rise to me
>   Than lieth in her skill.

As't were two summer days in one,
Two Sundays come together,
Our rays united make one sun,
With fairest summer weather.

As surely as the sunset in my latest November shall translate me to the ethereal world, and remind me of the ruddy morning of youth; as surely as the last strain of music which falls on my decaying ear shall make age to be forgotten, or, in short, the manifold influences of nature survive during the term of our natural life, so surely my Friend shall forever be my Friend, and reflect a ray of God to me, and time shall foster and adorn and consecrate our Friendship, no less than the ruins of temples. As I love nature, as I love singing birds, and gleaming stubble, and flowing rivers, and morning and evening, and summer and winter, I love thee, my Friend.

But all that can be said of Friendship is like botany to flowers. How can the understanding take account of its friendliness?

Even the death of Friends will inspire us as much as their lives. They will leave consolation to the mourners, as the rich leave money to defray the expenses of their funerals, and their memories will be incrusted over with sublime and pleasing thoughts, as monuments of other men are overgrown with moss; for our Friends have no place in the graveyard.

This to our cis-Alpine and cis-Atlantic Friends.

Also this other word of entreaty and advice to the large and respectable nation of Acquaintances, beyond the mountains; — Greeting.

My most serene and irresponsible neighbors, let us
see that we have the whole advantage of each other;
we will be useful, at least, if not admirable, to one another. I know that the mountains which separate us
are high, and covered with perpetual snow, but despair
not. Improve the serene winter weather to scale them.
If need be, soften the rocks with vinegar. For here lie
the verdant plains of Italy ready to receive you. Nor
shall I be slow on my side to penetrate to your Provence.
Strike then boldly at head or heart or any vital part.
Depend upon it, the timber is well seasoned and tough,
and will bear rough usage; and if it should crack, there
is plenty more where it came from. I am no piece of
crockery that cannot be jostled against my neighbor
without danger of being broken by the collision, and
must needs ring false and jarringly to the end of my
days, when once I am cracked; but rather one of the
old-fashioned wooden trenchers, which one while stands
at the head of the table, and at another is a milking-
stool, and at another a seat for children, and finally goes
down to its grave not unadorned with honorable scars,
and does not die till it is worn out. Nothing can shock a
brave man but dullness. Think how many rebuffs every
man has experienced in his day; perhaps has fallen into
a horse-pond, eaten fresh-water clams, or worn one shirt
for a week without washing. Indeed, you cannot receive
a shock unless you have an electric affinity for that which
shocks you. Use me, then, for I am useful in my way,
and stand as one of many petitioners, from toadstool and
henbane up to dahlia and violet, supplicating to be put
to my use, if by any means ye may find me serviceable:

whether for a medicated drink or bath, as balm and lavender; or for fragrance, as verbena and geranium; or for sight, as cactus; or for thoughts, as pansy. These humbler, at least, if not those higher uses.

Ah, my dear Strangers and Enemies, I would not forget you. I can well afford to welcome you. Let me subscribe myself Yours ever and truly, — your much obliged servant. We have nothing to fear from our foes; God keeps a standing army for that service; but we have no ally against our Friends, those ruthless Vandals.

Once more to one and all, —

"Friends, Romans, Countrymen, and Lovers."

Let such pure hate still underprop
Our love, that we may be
Each other's conscience,
And have our sympathy
Mainly from thence.

We'll one another treat like gods,
And all the faith we have
In virtue and in truth, bestow
On either, and suspicion leave
To gods below.

Two solitary stars, —
Unmeasured systems far
Between us roll,
But by our conscious light we are
Determined to one pole.

What need confound the sphere? —
Love can afford to wait,
For it no hour's too late
That witnesseth one duty's end,
Or to another doth beginning lend.

It will subserve no use,
More than the tints of flowers,
Only the independent guest
Frequents its bowers,
Inherits its bequest.

No speech though kind has it,
But kinder silence doles
Unto its mates,
By night consoles,
By day congratulates.

What saith the tongue to tongue?
What heareth ear of ear?
By the decrees of fate
From year to year,
Does it communicate.

Pathless the gulf of feeling yawns,
No trivial bridge of words,
Or arch of boldest span,
Can leap the moat that girds
The sincere man.

No show of bolts and bars
Can keep the foeman out,
Or 'scape his secret mine
Who entered with the doubt
That drew the line.

No warder at the gate
Can let the friendly in,
But, like the sun, o'er all
He will the castle win,
And shine along the wall.

There's nothing in the world I know
That can escape from love,
For every depth it goes below,
And every height above.

It waits as waits the sky,
Until the clouds go by,
Yet shines serenely on
With an eternal day,
Alike when they are gone,
And when they stay.

Implacable is Love, —
Foes may be bought or teased
From their hostile intent,
But he goes unappeased
Who is on kindness bent.

Having rowed five or six miles above Amoskeag before sunset, and reached a pleasant part of the river, one of us landed to look for a farmhouse, where we might replenish our stores, while the other remained cruising about the stream, and exploring the opposite shores to find a suitable harbor for the night. In the mean while the canal-boats began to come round a point in our rear, poling their way along close to the shore, the breeze having quite died away. This time there was no offer of assistance, but one of the boatmen only called out to say as the truest revenge for having been the losers in the race, that he had seen a wood duck, which we had scared up, sitting on a tall, white pine, half a mile down-stream; and he repeated the assertion several times, and seemed really chagrined at the apparent suspicion with which this information was received. But there sat the summer duck still, undisturbed by us.

By and by the other voyageur returned from his inland expedition, bringing one of the natives with him, a little flaxen-headed boy, with some tradition, or small edition, of Robinson Crusoe in his head, who had been

charmed by the account of our adventures, and asked
his father's leave to join us. He examined, at first from
the top of the bank, our boat and furniture, with sparkling eyes, and wished himself already his own man. He
was a lively and interesting boy, and we should have
been glad to ship him; but Nathan was still his father's
boy, and had not come to years of discretion.

We had got a loaf of home-made bread, and musk and
water melons for dessert. For this farmer, a clever and
well-disposed man, cultivated a large patch of melons
for the Hooksett and Concord markets. He hospitably
entertained us the next day, exhibiting his hop-fields and
kiln and melon-patch, warning us to step over the tight
rope which surrounded the latter at a foot from the
ground, while he pointed to a little bower at one corner,
where it connected with the lock of a gun ranging with
the line, and where, as he informed us, he sometimes
sat in pleasant nights to defend his premises against
thieves. We stepped high over the line, and sympathized
with our host's on the whole quite human, if not humane,
interest in the success of his experiment. That night
especially thieves were to be expected, from rumors in
the atmosphere, and the priming was not wet. He was a
Methodist man, who had his dwelling between the river
and Uncannunuc Mountain; who there belonged, and
stayed at home there, and by the encouragement of
distant political organizations, and by his own tenacity,
held a property in his melons, and continued to plant.
We suggested melon seeds of new varieties and fruit of
foreign flavor to be added to his stock. We had come
away up here among the hills to learn the impartial and

unbribable beneficence of Nature. Strawberries and melons grow as well in one man's garden as another's, and the sun lodges as kindly under his hillside, — when we had imagined that she inclined rather to some few earnest and faithful souls whom we know.

We found a convenient harbor for our boat on the opposite or east shore, still in Hooksett, at the mouth of a small brook which emptied into the Merrimack, where it would be out of the way of any passing boat in the night, — for they commonly hug the shore if bound upstream, either to avoid the current or touch the bottom with their poles, — and where it would be accessible without stepping on the clayey shore. We set one of our largest melons to cool in the still water among the alders at the mouth of this creek, but when our tent was pitched and ready, and we went to get it, it had floated out into the stream, and was nowhere to be seen. So taking the boat in the twilight, we went in pursuit of this property, and at length, after long straining of the eyes, its green disk was discovered far down the river, gently floating seaward with many twigs and leaves from the mountains that evening, and so perfectly balanced that it had not keeled at all, and no water had run in at the tap which had been taken out to hasten its cooling.

As we sat on the bank eating our supper, the clear light of the western sky fell on the eastern trees, and was reflected in the water, and we enjoyed so serene an evening as left nothing to describe. For the most part we think that there are few degrees of sublimity, and that the highest is but little higher than that which we now behold; but we are always deceived. Sublimer visions appear, and the former pale and fade away. We are grateful when we are reminded by interior evidence of the permanence of universal laws; for our faith is but faintly remembered, indeed, is not a remembered assurance, but a use and enjoyment of knowledge. It is when we do not have to believe, but come into actual contact with Truth, and are related to her in the most direct and intimate way. Waves of serener life pass over us from time to time, like flakes of sunlight over the fields in cloudy weather. In some happier moment, when more sap flows in the withered stalk of our life, Syria and India stretch away from our present as they do in history. All the events which make the annals of the nations are but the shadows of our private experiences. Suddenly and silently the eras which we call history awake and glimmer in us, and *there* is room for Alexander and Hannibal to march and conquer. In short, the history which we read is only a fainter memory of events which have happened in our own experience. Tradition is a more interrupted and feebler memory.

This world is but canvas to our imaginations. I see men with infinite pains endeavoring to realize to their bodies, what I, with at least equal pains, would realize to my imagination, — its capacities; for certainly there is a life of the mind above the wants of the body, and independent of it. Often the body is warmed, but the imagination is torpid; the body is fat, but the imagination is lean and shrunk. But what avails all other wealth if this is wanting? "Imagination is the air of mind," in which it lives and breathes. All things are as I am. Where is the House of Change? The past is only so

heroic as we see it. It is the canvas on which our idea
of heroism is painted, and so, in one sense, the dim
prospectus of our future field. Our circumstances
answer to our expectations and the demand of our
natures. I have noticed that if a man thinks that he
needs a thousand dollars, and cannot be convinced that
he does not, he will commonly be found to have them;
if he lives and thinks, a thousand dollars will be forth-
coming, though it be to buy shoe-strings with. A thousand mills will be just as slow to come to one who finds
it equally hard to convince himself that he needs *them*.

> Men are by birth equal in this, that given
> Themselves and their condition, they are even.

I am astonished at the singular pertinacity and
endurance of our lives. The miracle is, that what is *is*,
when it is so difficult, if not impossible, for anything else
to be; that we walk on in our particular paths so far,
before we fall on death and fate, merely because we
must walk in some path; that every man can get a
living, and so few can do anything more. So much only
can I accomplish ere health and strength are gone, and
yet this suffices. The bird now sits just out of gunshot. I
am never rich in money, and I am never meanly poor.
If debts are incurred, why, debts are in the course of
events canceled, as it were, by the same law by which
they were incurred. I heard that an engagement was
entered into between a certain youth and a maiden, and
then I heard that it was broken off, but I did not know
the reason in either case. We are hedged about, we
think, by accident and circumstance; now we creep as
in a dream, and now again we run, as if there were a fate

in it, and all things thwarted or assisted. I cannot change my clothes but when I do, and yet I do change them, and soil the new ones. It is wonderful that this gets done, when some admirable deeds which I could mention do not get done. Our particular lives seem of such fortune and confident strength and durability as piers of solid rock thrown forward into the tide of circumstance. When every other path would fail, with singular and unerring confidence we advance on our particular course. What risks we run! famine and fire and pestilence, and the thousand forms of a cruel fate, — and yet every man lives till he — dies. How did he manage that? Is there no immediate danger? We wonder superfluously when we hear of a somnambulist walking a plank securely, — we have walked a plank all our lives up to this particular string-piece where we are. My life will wait for nobody, but is being matured still without delay, while I go about the streets, and chaffer with this man and that to secure it a living. It is as indifferent and easy meanwhile as a poor man's dog, and making acquaintance with its kind. It will cut its own channel like a mountain stream, and by the longest ridge is not kept from the sea at last. I have found all things thus far, persons and inanimate matter, elements and seasons, strangely adapted to my resources. No matter what imprudent haste in my career; I am permitted to be rash. Gulfs are bridged in a twinkling, as if some unseen baggage train carried pontoons for my convenience, and while from the heights I scan the tempting but unexplored Pacific Ocean of Futurity, the ship is being carried over the mountains piecemeal on

the backs of mules and llamas, whose keel shall plow its
waves, and bear me to the Indies. Day would not dawn
if it were not for

THE INWARD MORNING

Packed in my mind lie all the clothes
    Which outward nature wears,
And in its fashion's hourly change
    It all things else repairs.

In vain I look for change abroad,
    And can no difference find,
Till some new ray of peace uncalled
    Illumes my inmost mind.

What is it gilds the trees and clouds,
    And paints the heavens so gay,
But yonder fast-abiding light
    With its unchanging ray?

Lo, when the sun streams through the wood,
    Upon a winter's morn,
Where'er his silent beams intrude
    The murky night is gone.

How could the patient pine have known
    The morning breeze would come,
Or humble flowers anticipate
    The insect's noonday hum, —

Till the new light with morning cheer
    From far streamed through the aisles,
And nimbly told the forest trees
    For many stretching miles?

I've heard within my inmost soul
    Such cheerful morning news,
In the horizon of my mind
    Have seen such orient hues,

As in the twilight of the dawn,
When the first birds awake,
Are heard within some silent wood,
Where they the small twigs break,

Or in the eastern skies are seen,
Before the sun appears,
The harbingers of summer heats
Which from afar he bears.

Whole weeks and months of my summer life slide away in thin volumes like mist and smoke, till at length, some warm morning, perchance, I see a sheet of mist blown down the brook to the swamp, and I float as high above the fields with it. I can recall to mind the stillest summer hours, in which the grasshopper sings over the mulleins, and there is a valor in that time the bare memory of which is armor that can laugh at any blow of fortune. For our lifetime the strains of a harp are heard to swell and die alternately, and death is but " the pause when the blast is recollecting itself."

We lay awake a long while listening to the murmurs of the brook, in the angle formed by whose bank with the river our tent was pitched, and there was a sort of man interest in its story, which ceases not in freshet or in drought the livelong summer, and the profounder lapse of the river was quite drowned by its din. But the rill, whose

"Silver sands and pebbles sing
Eternal ditties with the spring,"

is silenced by the first frosts of winter, while mightier streams, on whose bottom the sun never shines, clogged with sunken rocks and the ruins of forests, from whose surface comes up no murmur, are strangers to the icy fetters which bind fast a thousand contributory rills.

I dreamed this night of an event which had occurred long before. It was a difference with a Friend, which had not ceased to give me pain, though I had no cause to blame myself. But in my dream ideal justice was at length done me for his suspicions, and I received that compensation which I had never obtained in my waking hours. I was unspeakably soothed and rejoiced, even after I awoke, because in dreams we never deceive ourselves, nor are deceived, and this seemed to have the authority of a final judgment.

We bless and curse ourselves. Some dreams are divine, as well as some waking thoughts. Donne sings of one

"Who dreamt devoutlier than most use to pray."

Dreams are the touchstones of our characters. We are scarcely less afflicted when we remember some unworthiness in our conduct in a dream, than if it had been actual, and the intensity of our grief, which is our atonement, measures the degree by which this is separated from an actual unworthiness. For in dreams we but act a part which must have been learned and rehearsed in our waking hours, and no doubt could discover some waking consent thereto. If this meanness had not its foundation in us, why are we grieved at it? In dreams we see ourselves naked and acting out our real characters, even more clearly than we see others awake. But an unwavering and commanding virtue would compel

even its most fantastic and faintest dreams to respect its
ever-wakeful authority; as we are accustomed to say
carelessly, we should never have *dreamed* of such a thing.
Our truest life is when we are in dreams awake.

> "And, more to lulle him in his slumber soft,
>   A trickling streame from high rock tumbling downe,
>   And ever-drizzling raine upon the loft,
>   Mixt with a murmuring winde, much like the sowne
>   Of swarming bees, did cast him in a swowne,
>   No other noyse, nor people's troublous cryes,
>   As still are wont t' annoy the walled towne,
>   Might there be heard; but careless Quiet lyes
>   Wrapt in eternall silence farre from enemyes."

THURSDAY

He trode the unplanted forest floor, whereon
The all-seeing sun for ages hath not shone;
Where feeds the moose, and walks the surly bear,
And up the tall mast runs the woodpecker.

.   .   .   .

Where darkness found him he lay glad at night;
There the red morning touched him with its light.

.   .   .   .

Go where he will, the wise man is at home,
His hearth the earth, — his hall the azure dome;
Where his clear spirit leads him, there 's his road,
By God's own light illumined and foreshowed.

EMERSON.

W HEN we awoke this morning, we heard the faint,
deliberate, and ominous sound of raindrops on our
cotton roof. The rain had pattered all night, and now
the whole country wept, the drops falling in the river,
and on the alders, and in the pastures, and instead of
any bow in the heavens, there was the trill of the hair-
bird all the morning. The cheery faith of this little
bird atoned for the silence of the whole woodland
choir beside. When we first stepped abroad, a flock of
sheep, led by their rams, came rushing down a ravine
in our rear, with heedless haste and unreserved frisking, as if unobserved by man, from some higher pasture where they had spent the night, to taste the herbage
by the riverside ; but when their leaders caught sight

of our white tent through the mist, struck with sudden astonishment, with their fore feet braced, they sustained the rushing torrent in their rear, and the whole flock stood stock-still, endeavoring to solve the mystery in their sheepish brains. At length, concluding that it boded no mischief to them, they spread themselves out quietly over the field. We learned afterward that we had pitched our tent on the very spot which a few summers before had been occupied by a party of Penobscots. We could see rising before us through the mist a dark conical eminence called Hooksett Pinnacle, a landmark to boatmen, and also Uncannunuc Mountain, broad off on the west side of the river.

This was the limit of our voyage, for a few hours more in the rain would have taken us to the last of the locks, and our boat was too heavy to be dragged around the long and numerous rapids which would occur. On foot, however, we continued up along the bank, feeling our way with a stick through the showery and foggy day, and climbing over the slippery logs in our path with as much pleasure and buoyancy as in brightest sunshine ; scenting the fragrance of the pines and the wet clay under our feet, and cheered by the tones of invisible waterfalls ; with visions of toadstools, and wandering frogs, and festoons of moss hanging from the spruce trees, and thrushes flitting silent under the leaves ; our road still holding together through that wettest of weather, like faith, while we confidently followed its lead. We managed to keep our thoughts dry, however, and only our clothes were wet. It was altogether a cloudy and drizzling day, with occasional brightenings in the mist, when the trill of the tree sparrow seemed to be ushering in sunny hours.

" Nothing that naturally happens to man can *hurt* him, earthquakes and thunder-storms not excepted," said a man of genius, who at this time lived a few miles farther on our road. When compelled by a shower to take shelter under a tree, we may improve that opportunity for a more minute inspection of some of Nature's works. I have stood under a tree in the woods half a day at a time, during a heavy rain in the summer, and yet employed myself happily and profitably there prying with microscopic eye into the crevices of the bark or the leaves of the fungi at my feet. " Riches are the attendants of the miser; and the heavens rain plenteously upon the mountains." I can fancy that it would be a luxury to stand up to one's chin in some retired swamp a whole summer day, scenting the wild honeysuckle and bilberry blows, and lulled by the minstrelsy of gnats and mosquitoes ! A day passed in the society of those Greek sages, such as described in the Banquet of Xenophon, would not be comparable with the dry wit of decayed cranberry vines, and the fresh Attic salt of the moss-beds. Say twelve hours of genial and familiar converse with the leopard frog ; the sun to rise behind alder and dog-wood, and climb buoyantly to his meridian of two hands' breadth, and finally sink to rest behind some bold western hummock. To hear the evening chant of the mosquito from a thousand green chapels, and the bittern begin to boom from some concealed fort like a sunset gun ! Surely one may as profitably be soaked in

the juices of a swamp for one day as pick his way dry-
shod over sand. Cold and damp, — are they not as rich
experience as warmth and dryness?

At present, the drops come trickling down the stubble while we lie drenched on a bed of withered wild
oats, by the side of a bushy hill; and the gathering in
of the clouds, with the last rush and dying breath of
the wind, and then the regular dripping of twigs and
leaves the country over, enhance the sense of inward
comfort and sociableness. The birds draw closer and
are more familiar under the thick foliage, seemingly
composing new strains upon their roots against the
sunshine. What were the amusements of the drawing-
room and the library in comparison, if we had them
here? We should still sing as of old, —

> My books I'd fain cast off, I cannot read;
> 'Twixt every page my thoughts go stray at large
> Down in the meadow, where is richer feed,
> And will not mind to hit their proper targe.
>
> Plutarch was good, and so was Homer too,
> Our Shakespeare's life were rich to live again;
> What Plutarch read, that was not good nor true,
> Nor Shakespeare's books, unless his books were men.
>
> Here while I lie beneath this walnut bough,
> What care I for the Greeks or for Troy town,
> If juster battles are enacted now
> Between the ants upon this hummock's crown?
>
> Bid Homer wait till I the issue learn,
> If red or black the gods will favor most,
> Or yonder Ajax will the phalanx turn,
> Struggling to heave some rock against the host.

Tell Shakespeare to attend some leisure hour,
For now I've business with this drop of dew,
And see you not, the clouds prepare a shower, —
I'll meet him shortly when the sky is blue.

This bed of herd's-grass and wild oats was spread
Last year with nicer skill than monarchs use,
A clover tuft is pillow for my head,
And violets quite overtop my shoes.

And now the cordial clouds have shut all in,
And gently swells the wind to say all's well,
The scattered drops are falling fast and thin,
Some in the pool, some in the flower-bell.

I am well drenched upon my bed of oats;
But see that globe come rolling down its stem;
Now like a lonely planet there it floats,
And now it sinks into my garment's hem.

Drip, drip the trees for all the country round,
And richness rare distills from every bough,
The wind alone it is makes every sound,
Shaking down crystals on the leaves below.

For shame the sun will never show himself,
Who could not with his beams e'er melt me so,
My dripping locks, — they would become an elf,
Who in a beaded coat does gayly go.

The Pinnacle is a small wooded hill which rises very abruptly to the height of about two hundred feet, near the shore at Hooksett Falls. As Uncannunuc Mountain is perhaps the best point from which to view the valley of the Merrimack, so this hill affords the best view of the river itself. I have sat upon its summit, a precipitous rock only a few rods long, in fairer weather, when the sun was setting and filling the river valley with a flood of light. You can see up and down the Merrimack several miles each way. The broad and straight river, full of light and life, with its sparkling and foaming falls, the islet which divides the stream, the village of Hooksett on the shore almost directly under your feet, so near that you can converse with its inhabitants or throw a stone into its yards, the woodland lake at its western base, and the mountains in the north and northeast, make a scene of rare beauty and completeness, which the traveler should take pains to behold.

We were hospitably entertained in Concord, New Hampshire, which we persisted in calling *New* Concord, as we had been wont, to distinguish it from our native town, from which we had been told that it was named and in part originally settled. This would have been the proper place to conclude our voyage, uniting Concord with Concord by these meandering rivers, but our boat was moored some miles below its port.

The richness of the intervals at Penacook, now Concord, New Hampshire, had been observed by explorers, and, according to the historian of Haverhill, in the " year 1726, considerable progress was made in the settlement, and a road was cut through the wilderness from Haverhill to Penacook. In the fall of 1727, the first family, that of Captain Ebenezer Eastman, moved into the place. His team was driven by Jacob Shute, who was by birth a Frenchman, and he is said to have been the first person who drove a team through the wilderness. Soon after,

says tradition, one Ayer, a lad of eighteen, drove a team
consisting of ten yoke of oxen to Penacook, swam the
river, and ploughed a portion of the interval. He is
supposed to have been the first person who ploughed
land in that place. After he had completed his work,
he started on his return at sunrise, drowned a yoke of
oxen while recrossing the river, and arrived at Haverhill about midnight. The crank of the first saw-mill
was manufactured in Haverhill, and carried to Penacook on a horse."

But we found that the frontiers were not this way
any longer. This generation has come into the world
fatally late for some enterprises. Go where we will on
the *surface* of things, men have been there before us.
We cannot now have the pleasure of erecting the *last*
house; that was long ago set up in the suburbs of Astoria
City, and our boundaries have literally been run to the
South Sea, according to the old patents. But the lives
of men, though more extended laterally in their range,
are still as shallow as ever. Undoubtedly, as a Western
orator said, " Men generally live over about the same
surface ; some live long and narrow, and others live
broad and short;" but it is all superficial living. A
worm is as good a traveler as a grasshopper or a cricket,
and a much wiser settler. With all their activity these
do not hop away from drought nor forward to summer. We do not avoid evil by fleeing before it, but by
rising above or diving below its plane ; as the worm
escapes drought and frost by boring a few inches
deeper. The frontiers are not east or west, north or
south; but wherever a man *fronts* a fact, though that

fact be his neighbor, there is an unsettled wilderness
between him and Canada, between him and the setting
sun, or, farther still, between him and *it*. Let him
build himself a log house with the bark on where he is,
fronting IT, and wage there an Old French war for
seven or seventy years, with Indians and Rangers, or
whatever else may come between him and the reality,
and save his scalp if he can.

We now no longer sailed or floated on the river, but
trod the unyielding land like pilgrims. Sadi tells who
may travel ; among others, " A common mechanic,
who can earn a subsistence by the industry of his
hand, and shall not have to stake his reputation for
every morsel of bread, as philosophers have said."
He may travel who can subsist on the wild fruits and
game of the most cultivated country. A man may
travel fast enough and earn his living on the road. I
have at times been applied to, to do work when on a
journey; to do tinkering and repair clocks, when I had
a knapsack on my back. A man once applied to me
to go into a factory, stating conditions and wages, observing that I succeeded in shutting the window of
a railroad car in which we were traveling, when the
other passengers had failed. " Hast thou not heard of
a Sufi, who was hammering some nails into the sole
of his sandal; an officer of cavalry took him by the
sleeve, saying, Come along and shoe my horse." Farmers have asked me to assist them in haying when I
was passing their fields. A man once applied to me
to mend his umbrella, taking me for an umbrella-

mender, because, being on a journey, I carried an umbrella in my hand while the sun shone. Another wished to buy a tin cup of me, observing that I had one strapped to my belt, and a sauce-pan on my back. The cheapest way to travel, and the way to travel the farthest in the shortest distance, is to go afoot, carrying a dipper, a spoon, and a fish line, some Indian meal, some salt, and some sugar. When you come to a brook or a pond, you can catch fish and cook them ; or you can boil a hasty-pudding ; or you can buy a loaf of bread at a farmer's house for fourpence, moisten it in the next brook that crosses the road, and dip it into your sugar, — this alone will last you a whole day; — or, if you are accustomed to heartier living, you can buy a quart of milk for two cents, crumb your bread or cold pudding into it, and eat it with your own spoon out of your own dish. Any one of these things I mean, not all together. I have traveled thus some hundreds of miles without taking any meal in a house, sleeping on the ground when convenient, and found it cheaper, and in many respects more profitable, than staying at home. So that some have inquired why it would not be best to travel always. But I never thought of traveling simply as a means of getting a livelihood. A simple woman down in Tyngsborough, at whose house I once stopped to get a draught of water, when I said, recognizing the bucket, that I had stopped there nine years before for the same purpose, asked if I was not a traveler, supposing I had been traveling ever since, and had now come round again; that traveling was one of the professions,

more or less productive, which her husband did not
follow. But continued traveling is far from productive.
It begins with wearing away the soles of the shoes, and
making the feet sore, and ere long it will wear a man
clean up, after making his heart sore into the bargain.
I have observed that the after life of those who have
traveled much is very pathetic. True and sincere traveling is no pastime, but it is as serious as the grave, or
any part of the human journey, and it requires a long
probation to be broken into it. I do not speak of those
that travel sitting, the sedentary travelers whose legs
hang dangling the while, mere idle symbols of the fact,
any more than when we speak of sitting hens we mean
those that sit standing, but I mean those to whom traveling is life for the legs, and death too, at last. The
traveler must be born again on the road, and earn a
passport from the elements, the principal powers that
be for him. He shall experience at last that old threat
of his mother fulfilled, that he shall be skinned alive.
His sores shall gradually deepen themselves that they
may heal inwardly, while he gives no rest to the sole
of his foot, and at night weariness must be his pillow,
that so he may acquire experience against his rainy
days. So was it with us.

Sometimes we lodged at an inn in the woods, where
trout-fishers from distant cities had arrived before us,
and where, to our astonishment, the settlers dropped in
at nightfall to have a chat and hear the news, though
there was but one road, and no other house was visible,
— as if they had come out of the earth. There we
sometimes read old newspapers, who never before read

new ones, and in the rustle of their leaves heard the
dashing of the surf along the Atlantic shore, instead of
the sough of the wind among the pines. But then walking had given us an appetite even for the least palatable
and nutritious food.

Some hard and dry book in a dead language, which
you have found it impossible to read at home, but for
which you have still a lingering regard, is the best to
carry with you on a journey. At a country inn, in the
barren society of ostlers and travelers, I could undertake
the writers of the silver or the brazen age with confidence. Almost the last regular service which I performed in the cause of literature was to read the works
of

AULUS PERSIUS FLACCUS.

If you have imagined what a divine work is spread
out for the poet, and approach this author too, in the
hope of finding the field at length fairly entered on, you
will hardly dissent from the words of the prologue, —

> "Ipse semipaganus
> Ad sacra Vatum carmen affero nostrum."

> I half pagan
> Bring my verses to the shrine of the poets.

Here is none of the interior dignity of Virgil, nor
the elegance and vivacity of Horace, nor will any sibyl
be needed to remind you that from those older Greek
poets there is a sad descent to Persius. You can scarcely
distinguish one harmonious sound amid this unmusical
bickering with the follies of men.

One sees that music has its place in thought, but

hardly as yet in language. When the Muse arrives, we wait for her to remould language, and impart to it her own rhythm. Hitherto the verse groans and labors with its load, and goes not forward blithely, singing by the way. The best ode may be parodied, indeed is itself a parody, and has a poor and trivial sound, like a man stepping on the rounds of a ladder. Homer and Shakespeare and Milton and Marvell and Wordsworth are but the rustling of leaves and crackling of twigs in the forest, and there is not yet the sound of any bird. The Muse has never lifted up her voice to sing. Most of all, satire will not be sung. A Juvenal or Persius do not marry music to their verse, but are measured faultfinders at best ; stand but just outside the faults they condemn, and so are concerned rather about the monster which they have escaped than the fair prospect before them. Let them live on an age, and they will have traveled out of his shadow and reach, and found other objects to ponder.

As long as there is satire, the poet is, as it were, *particeps criminis*. One sees not but he had best let bad take care of itself, and have to do only with what is beyond suspicion. If you light on the least vestige of truth, and it is the weight of the whole body still which stamps the faintest trace, an eternity will not suffice to extol it, while no evil is so huge, but you grudge to bestow on it a moment of hate. Truth never turns to rebuke falsehood; her own straightforwardness is the severest correction. Horace would not have written satire so well if he had not been inspired by it, as by a passion, and fondly cherished his vein. In his odes, the love always exceeds the hate, so that the severest satire still sings itself, and the poet is satisfied, though the folly be not corrected.

A sort of necessary order in the development of Genius is, first, Complaint; second, Plaint; third, Love. Complaint, which is the condition of Persius, lies not in the province of poetry. Ere long the enjoyment of a superior good would have changed his disgust into regret. We can never have much sympathy with the complainer ; for after searching nature through, we conclude that he must be both plaintiff and defendant too, and so had best come to a settlement without a hearing. He who receives an injury is to some extent an accomplice of the wrong-doer.

Perhaps it would be truer to say, that the highest strain of the muse is essentially plaintive. The saint's are still *tears* of joy. Who has ever heard the *Innocent* sing ?

But the divinest poem, or the life of a great man, is the severest satire ; as impersonal as Nature herself, and like the sighs of her winds in the woods, which convey ever a slight reproof to the hearer. The greater the genius, the keener the edge of the satire.

Hence we have to do only with the rare and fragmentary traits, which least belong to Persius, or shall we say, are the properest utterances of his muse; since that which he says best at any time is what he can best say at all times. The Spectators and Ramblers have not failed to cull some quotable sentences from this garden too, so pleasant is it to meet even the most familiar truth in a new dress, when, if our neigh-

bor had said it, we should have passed it by as hack-
neyed. Out of these six satires, you may perhaps select
some twenty lines, which fit so well as many thoughts,
that they will recur to the scholar almost as readily as
a natural image; though when translated into familiar
language, they lose that insular emphasis which fitted
them for quotation. Such lines as the following, translation cannot render commonplace. Contrasting the
man of true religion with those who, with jealous privacy, would fain carry on a secret commerce with the
gods, he says: —

"Haud cuivis promptum est, murmurque humilesque susurros
Tollere de templis; et aperto vivere voto."

It is not easy for every one to take murmurs and low
Whispers out of the temples, and live with open vow.

To the virtuous man, the universe is the only *sanc-
tum sanctorum*, and the penetralia of the temple are the
broad noon of his existence. Why should he betake
himself to a subterranean crypt, as if it were the only
holy ground in all the world which he had left un-
profaned? The obedient soul would only the more discover and familiarize things, and escape more and more
into light and air, as having henceforth done with secrecy, so that the universe shall not seem open enough
for it. At length, it is neglectful even of that silence
which is consistent with true modesty, but by its independence of all confidence in its disclosures makes that
which it imparts so private to the hearer, that it becomes
the care of the whole world that modesty be not in-
fringed.

To the man who cherishes a secret in his breast, there
is a still greater secret unexplored. Our most indifferent acts may be matter for secrecy, but whatever we
do with the utmost truthfulness and integrity, by virtue
of its pureness, must be transparent as light.

In the third satire, he asks: —

> "Est aliquid quo tendis, et in quod dirigis arcum?
> An passim sequeris corvos, testave, lutove,
> Securus quo pes ferat, atque ex tempore vivis?"

Is there anything to which thou tendest, and against which thou
        directest thy bow?
Or dost thou pursue crows, at random, with pottery or clay,
Careless whither thy feet bear thee, and live *ex tempore*?

The bad sense is always a secondary one. Language
does not appear to have justice done it, but is obviously
cramped and narrowed in its significance, when any
meanness is described. The truest construction is not
put upon it. What may readily be fashioned into a rule
of wisdom is here thrown in the teeth of the sluggard,
and constitutes the front of his offense. Universally,
the innocent man will come forth from the sharpest
inquisition and lecturing, the combined din of reproof
and commendation, with a faint sound of eulogy in his
ears. Our vices always lie in the direction of our virtues, and in their best estate are but plausible imitations
of the latter. Falsehood never attains to the dignity of
entire falseness, but is only an inferior sort of truth; if
it were more thoroughly false, it would incur danger of
becoming true.

> "Securus quo pes ferat, atque ex tempore *vivit*"

is then the motto of a wise man. For first, as the subtle discernment of the language would have taught us, with all his negligence he is still secure; but the sluggard, notwithstanding his heedlessness, is insecure.

The life of a wise man is most of all extemporaneous, for he lives out of an eternity which includes all time. The cunning mind travels further back than Zoroaster each instant, and comes quite down to the present with its revelation. The utmost thrift and industry of thinking give no man any stock in life; his credit with the inner world is no better, his capital no larger. He must try his fortune again to-day as yesterday. All questions rely on the present for their solution. Time measures nothing but itself. The word that is written may be postponed, but not that on the lip. If this is what the occasion says, let the occasion say it. All the world is forward to prompt him who gets up to live without his creed in his pocket.

In the fifth satire, which is the best, I find, —

> "Stat contra ratio, et secretam garrit in aurem,
>   Ne liceat facere id, quod quis vitiabit agendo."

> Reason opposes, and whispers in the secret ear,
>   That it is not lawful to do that which one will spoil by doing.

Only they who do not see how anything might be better done are forward to try their hand on it. Even the master workman must be encouraged by the reflection that his awkwardness will be incompetent to do that thing harm, to which his skill may fail to do justice. Here is no apology for neglecting to do many things from a sense of our incapacity, — for what deed does not fall maimed and imperfect from our hands ? — but only a warning to bungle less.

The satires of Persius are the furthest possible from inspired, — evidently a chosen, not imposed subject. Perhaps I have given him credit for more earnestness than is apparent ; but it is certain that that which alone we can call Persius, which is forever independent and consistent, *was* in earnest, and so sanctions the sober consideration of all. The artist and his work are not to be separated. The most willfully foolish man cannot stand aloof from his folly, but the deed and the doer together make ever one sober fact. There is but one stage for the peasant and the actor. The buffoon cannot bribe you to laugh always at his grimaces ; they shall sculpture themselves in Egyptian granite, to stand heavy as the pyramids on the ground of his character.

Suns rose and set and found us still on the dank forest path which meanders up the Pemigewasset, now more like an otter's or a marten's trail, or where a beaver had dragged his trap, than where the wheels of travel raise a dust ; where towns begin to serve as gores, only to hold the earth together. The wild pigeon sat secure above our heads, high on the dead limbs of naval pines, reduced to a robin's size. The very yards of our hostelries inclined upon the skirts of mountains, and, as we passed, we looked up at a steep angle at the stems of maples waving in the clouds.

Far up in the country, — for we would be faithful to our experience, — in Thornton, perhaps, we met a sol-

dier lad in the woods, going to muster in full regiment-
als, and holding the middle of the road ; deep in the
forest, with shouldered musket and military step, and
thoughts of war and glory all to himself. It was a sore
trial to the youth, tougher than many a battle, to get
by us creditably and with soldier-like bearing. Poor
man! He actually shivered like a reed in his thin military pants, and by the time we had got up with him,
all the sternness that becomes the soldier had forsaken
his face, and he skulked past as if he were driving his
father's sheep under a sword-proof helmet. It was too
much for him to carry any extra armor then, who
could not easily dispose of his natural arms. And for
his legs, they were like heavy artillery in boggy places;
better to cut the traces and forsake them. His greaves
chafed and wrestled one with another for want of other
foes. But he did get by and get off with all his muni-
tions, and lived to fight another day ; and I do not
record this as casting any suspicion on his honor and
real bravery in the field.

Wandering on through notches which the streams
had made, by the side and over the brows of hoar hills
and mountains, across the stumpy, rocky, forested, and
bepastured country, we at length crossed on prostrate
trees over the Amonoosuck, and breathed the free air
of Unappropriated Land. Thus, in fair days as well as
foul, we had traced up the river to which our native
stream is a tributary, until from Merrimack it became
the Pemigewasset that leaped by our side, and when
we had passed its fountain-head, the Wild Amonoosuck, whose puny channel was crossed at a stride,

guiding us toward its distant source among the mountains, at length, without its guidance, we were enabled to reach the summit AGIOCOCHOOK.

> "Sweet day, so cool, so calm, so bright,
> The bridal of the earth and sky,
> The dew shall weep thy fall to-night,
> For thou must die." — HERBERT.

When we returned to Hooksett, a week afterward, the melon man, in whose corn-barn we had hung our tent and buffaloes and other things to dry, was already picking his hops, with many women and children to help him. We bought one watermelon, the largest in his patch, to carry with us for ballast. It was Nathan's, which he might sell if he wished, having been conveyed to him in the green state, and owned daily by his eyes. After due consultation with "Father," the bargain was concluded, — we to buy it at a venture on the vine, green or ripe, our risk, and pay "what the gentleman pleased." It proved to be ripe; for we had had honest experience in selecting this fruit.

Finding our boat safe in its harbor, under Uncannunuc Mountain, with a fair wind and the current in our favor, we commenced our return voyage at noon, sitting at our ease and conversing, or in silence watching for the last trace of each reach in the river as a bend concealed it from our view. As the season was further advanced, the wind now blew steadily from the north, and with our sail set we could occasionally lie on our oars without loss of time. The lumbermen throwing down wood from the top of the high bank, thirty or forty feet above the water, that it might be sent downstream, paused in their work to watch our retreating sail. By this time, indeed, we were well known to the boatmen, and were hailed as the Revenue Cutter of the stream. As we sailed rapidly down the river, shut in between two mounds of earth, the sounds of this timber rolled down the bank enhanced the silence and vastness of the noon, and we fancied that only the primeval echoes were awakened. The vision of a distant scow just heaving in sight round a headland also increased by contrast the solitude.

Through the din and desultoriness of noon, even in the most Oriental city, is seen the fresh and primitive and savage nature, in which Scythians and Ethiopians and Indians dwell. What is echo, what are light and shade, day and night, ocean and stars, earthquake and eclipse, there? The works of man are everywhere swallowed up in the immensity of nature. The Ægean Sea is but Lake Huron still to the Indian. Also there is all the refinement of civilized life in the woods under a sylvan garb. The wildest scenes have an air of domesticity and homeliness even to the citizen, and when the flicker's cackle is heard in the clearing, he is reminded that civilization has wrought but little change there. Science is welcome to the deepest recesses of the forest, for there too nature obeys the same old civil laws. The little red bug on the stump of a pine, — for it the wind shifts and the sun breaks through the clouds. In the wildest nature, there is not only the material of the most cultivated life, and a sort of anticipation of the last result, but a greater refinement already than is ever attained by man. There is papyrus by the riverside, and rushes for light, and the goose only flies overhead, ages before the studious are born or letters invented, and that literature which the former suggest, and even from the first have rudely served, it may be man does not yet use them to express. Nature is prepared to welcome into her scenery the finest work of human art, for she is herself an art so cunning that the artist never appears in his work.

Art is not tame, and Nature is not wild, in the ordinary sense. A perfect work of man's art would also be wild or natural in a good sense. Man tames Nature only that he may at last make her more free even than he found her, though he may never yet have succeeded.

With this propitious breeze, and the help of our oars, we soon reached the Falls of Amoskeag, and the mouth of the Piscataquoag, and recognized, as we swept rapidly by, many a fair bank and islet on which our eyes had rested in the upward passage. Our boat was like that which Chaucer describes in his Dream, in which the knight took his departure from the island, —

> "To journey for his marriage,
> And returne with such an host,
> That wedded might be least and most. . . .
> Which barge was as a man's thought,
> After his pleasure to him brought,
> The queene herselfe accustomed aye

In the same barge to play,
It needeth neither mast ne rother,
I have not heard of such another,
No maister for the governaunce,
Hie sayled by thought and pleasaunce,
Without labour, east and west,
Alle was one, calme or tempest."

So we sailed this afternoon, thinking of the saying of Pythagoras, though we had no peculiar right to remember it, " It is beautiful when prosperity is present with intellect, and when sailing as it were with a prosperous wind, actions are performed looking to virtue; just as a pilot looks to the motions of the stars." All the world reposes in beauty to him who preserves equipoise in his life, and moves serenely on his path without secret violence ; as he who sails down a stream, he has only to steer, keeping his bark in the middle, and carry it round the falls. The ripples curled away in our wake, like ringlets from the head of a child, while we steadily held on our course, and under the bows we watched

"The swaying soft,
Made by the delicate wave parted in front,
As through the gentle element we move
Like shadows gliding through untroubled realms."

The forms of beauty fall naturally around the path of him who is in the performance of his proper work; as the curled shavings drop from the plane, and borings cluster around the auger. Undulation is the gentlest and most ideal of motions, produced by one fluid falling on another. Rippling is a more graceful flight.

From a hill-top you may detect in it the wings of birds endlessly repeated. The two waving lines which represent the flight of birds appear to have been copied from the ripple.

The trees made an admirable fence to the landscape, skirting the horizon on every side. The single trees and the groves left standing on the interval appeared naturally disposed, though the farmer had consulted only his convenience, for he too falls into the scheme of Nature. Art can never match the luxury and superfluity of Nature. In the former all is seen; it cannot afford concealed wealth, and is niggardly in comparison; but Nature, even when she is scant and thin outwardly, satisfies us still by the assurance of a certain generosity at the roots. In swamps, where there is only here and there an evergreen tree amid the quaking moss and cranberry beds, the bareness does not suggest poverty. The single spruce, which I had hardly noticed in gardens, attracts me in such places, and now first I understand why men try to make them grow about their houses. But though there may be very perfect specimens in front-yard plots, their beauty is for the most part ineffectual there, for there is no such assurance of kindred wealth beneath and around them, to make them show to advantage. As we have said, Nature is a greater and more perfect art, the art of God; though, referred to herself, she is genius; and there is a similarity between her operations and man's art even in the details and trifles. When the overhanging pine drops into the water, by the sun and water, and the wind rubbing it against the shore, its boughs are worn into fantastic shapes, and white and smooth, as if turned in a lathe. Man's art has wisely imitated those forms into which all matter is most inclined to run, as foliage and fruit. A hammock swung in a grove assumes the exact form of a canoe, broader or narrower, and higher or lower at the ends, as more or fewer persons are in it, and it rolls in the air with the motion of the body, like a canoe in the water. Our art leaves its shavings and its dust about; her art exhibits itself even in the shavings and the dust which we make. She has perfected herself by an eternity of practice. The world is well kept; no rubbish accumulates; the morning air is clear even at this day, and no dust has settled on the grass. Behold how the evening now steals over the fields, the shadows of the trees creeping farther and farther into the meadow, and ere long the stars will come to bathe in these retired waters. Her undertakings are secure and never fail. If I were awakened from a deep sleep, I should know which side of the meridian the sun might be by the aspect of nature, and by the chirp of the crickets, and yet no painter can paint this difference. The landscape contains a thousand dials which indicate the natural divisions of time, the shadows of a thousand styles point to the hour.

> "Not only o'er the dial's face
>   This silent phantom day by day,
>   With slow, unseen, unceasing pace
>   Steals moments, months, and years away;
>   From hoary rock and aged tree,
>   From proud Palmyra's mouldering walls,
>   From Teneriffe, towering o'er the sea,
>   From every blade of grass it falls."

It is almost the only game which the trees play at, this tit-for-tat, now this side in the sun, now that, the drama of the day. In deep ravines under the eastern sides of cliffs, Night forwardly plants her foot even at noonday, and as Day retreats she steps into his trenches, skulking from tree to tree, from fence to fence, until at last she sits in her citadel and draws out her forces into the plain. It may be that the forenoon is brighter than the afternoon, not only because of the greater transparency of its atmosphere, but because we naturally look most into the west, as forward into the day, and so in the forenoon see the sunny side of things, but in the afternoon the shadow of every tree.

The afternoon is now far advanced, and a fresh and leisurely wind is blowing over the river, making long reaches of bright ripples. The river has done its stint, and appears not to flow, but lie at its length reflecting the light, and the haze over the woods is like the inaudible panting, or rather the gentle perspiration of resting nature, rising from a myriad of pores into the attenuated atmosphere.

On the thirty-first day of March, one hundred and forty-two years before this, probably about this time in the afternoon, there were hurriedly paddling down this part of the river, between the pine woods which then fringed these banks, two white women and a boy, who had left an island at the mouth of the Contoocook before daybreak. They were slightly clad for the season, in the English fashion, and handled their paddles unskillfully, but with nervous energy and determination,

and at the bottom of their canoe lay the still bleeding
scalps of ten of the aborigines. They were Hannah
Dustan, and her nurse, Mary Neff, both of Haverhill,
eighteen miles from the mouth of this river, and an
English boy, named Samuel Lennardson, escaping from
captivity among the Indians. On the 15th of March
previous, Hannah Dustan had been compelled to rise
from childbed, and half dressed, with one foot bare, accompanied by her nurse, commence an uncertain march,
in still inclement weather, through the snow and the
wilderness. She had seen her seven elder children flee
with their father, but knew not of their fate. She had
seen her infant's brains dashed out against an apple
tree, and had left her own and her neighbors' dwellings
in ashes. When she reached the wigwam of her captor,
situated on an island in the Merrimack, more than
twenty miles above where we now are, she had been
told that she and her nurse were soon to be taken to a
distant Indian settlement, and there made to run the
gauntlet naked. The family of this Indian consisted of
two men, three women, and seven children, besides an
English boy, whom she found a prisoner among them.
Having determined to attempt her escape, she instructed
the boy to inquire of one of the men, how he should
dispatch an enemy in the quickest manner, and take his
scalp. " Strike 'em there," said he, placing his finger
on his temple, and he also showed him how to take off
the scalp. On the morning of the 31st she arose before
daybreak, and awoke her nurse and the boy, and taking
the Indians' tomahawks, they killed them all in their
sleep, excepting one favorite boy, and one squaw who

fled wounded with him to the woods. The English boy struck the Indian who had given him the information, on the temple, as he had been directed. They then collected all the provision they could find, and took their master's tomahawk and gun, and scuttling all the canoes but one, commenced their flight to Haverhill, distant about sixty miles by the river. But after having proceeded a short distance, fearing that her story would not be believed if she should escape to tell it, they returned to the silent wigwam, and taking off the scalps of the dead, put them into a bag as proofs of what they had done, and then, retracing their steps to the shore in the twilight, recommenced their voyage.

Early this morning this deed was performed, and now, perchance, these tired women and this boy, their clothes stained with blood, and their minds racked with alternate resolution and fear, are making a hasty meal of parched corn and moose-meat, while their canoe glides under these pine roots whose stumps are still standing on the bank. They are thinking of the dead whom they have left behind on that solitary isle far up the stream, and of the relentless living warriors who are in pursuit. Every withered leaf which the winter has left seems to know their story, and in its rustling to repeat it and betray them. An Indian lurks behind every rock and pine, and their nerves cannot bear the tapping of a woodpecker. Or they forget their own dangers and their deeds in conjecturing the fate of their kindred, and whether, if they escape the Indians, they shall find the former still alive. They do not stop to cook their meals upon the bank, nor land, except to

carry their canoe about the falls. The stolen birch forgets its master and does them good service, and the
swollen current bears them swiftly along with little
need of the paddle, except to steer and keep them
warm by exercise. For ice is floating in the river; the
spring is opening; the muskrat and the beaver are
driven out of their holes by the flood; deer gaze at
them from the bank; a few faint-singing forest birds,
perchance, fly across the river to the northernmost
shore; the fishhawk sails and screams overhead, and
geese fly over with a startling clangor; but they do not
observe these things, or they speedily forget them.
They do not smile or chat all day. Sometimes they
pass an Indian grave surrounded by its paling on the
bank, or the frame of a wigwam, with a few coals left
behind, or the withered stalks still rustling in the Indian's solitary corn-field on the interval. The birch
stripped of its bark, or the charred stump where a
tree has been burned down to be made into a canoe,
— these are the only traces of man, a fabulous wild
man to us. On either side, the primeval forest stretches
away uninterrupted to Canada, or to the " South Sea;"
to the white man a drear and howling wilderness, but
to the Indian a home, adapted to his nature, and cheerful as the smile of the Great Spirit.

While we loiter here this autumn evening, looking
for a spot retired enough, where we shall quietly rest
to-night, they thus, in that chilly March evening, one
hundred and forty-two years before us, with wind and
current favoring, have already glided out of sight, not
to camp, as we shall, at night, but while two sleep,

one will manage the canoe, and the swift stream bear
them onward to the settlements, it may be, even to old
John Lovewell's house on Salmon Brook to-night.

According to the historian, they escaped as by a
miracle all roving bands of Indians, and reached their
homes in safety, with their trophies, for which the
General Court paid them fifty pounds. The family of
Hannah Dustan all assembled alive once more, except
the infant whose brains were dashed out against the
apple tree, and there have been many who in later
time have lived to say that they have eaten of the fruit
of that apple tree.

This seems a long while ago, and yet it happened
since Milton wrote his Paradise Lost. But its antiquity
is not the less great for that, for we do not regulate
our historical time by the English standard, nor did
the English by the Roman, nor the Roman by the
Greek. "We must look a long way back," says Raleigh, "to find the Romans giving laws to nations, and
their consuls bringing kings and princes bound in
chains to Rome in triumph ; to see men go to Greece
for wisdom, or Ophir for gold ; when now nothing remains but a poor paper remembrance of their former
condition." And yet, in one sense, not so far back as
to find the Penacooks and Pawtuckets using bows and
arrows and hatchets of stone, on the banks of the
Merrimack. From this September afternoon, and from
between these now cultivated shores, those times seemed
more remote than the dark ages. On beholding an old
picture of Concord, as it appeared but seventy-five

years ago, with a fair open prospect and a light on
trees and river, as if it were broad noon, I find that
I had not thought the sun shone in those days, or
that men lived in broad daylight then. Still less do
we imagine the sun shining on hill and valley during
Philip's war, on the war-path of Church or Philip,
or later of Lovewell or Paugus, with serene summer
weather, but they must have lived and fought in a dim
twilight or night.

The age of the world is great enough for our imaginations, even according to the Mosaic account, without
borrowing any years from the geologist. From Adam
and Eve at one leap sheer down to the deluge, and then
through the ancient monarchies, through Babylon and
Thebes, Brahma and Abraham, to Greece and the Argonauts ; whence we might start again with Orpheus, and
the Trojan war, the Pyramids and the Olympic games,
and Homer and Athens, for our stages ; and after a
breathing space at the building of Rome, continue our
journey down through Odin and Christ to — America.
It is a wearisome while. And yet the lives of but sixty
old women, such as live under the hill, say of a century
each, strung together, are sufficient to reach over the
whole ground. Taking hold of hands they would span
the interval from Eve to my own mother. A respectable tea-party merely, — whose gossip would be Universal History. The fourth old woman from myself
suckled Columbus, — the ninth was nurse to the Norman Conqueror, — the nineteenth was the Virgin Mary,
— the twenty-fourth the Cumæan Sibyl, — the thirtieth
was at the Trojan war and Helen her name, — the

thirty-eighth was Queen Semiramis, — the sixtieth was
Eve, the mother of mankind. So much for the

> "Old woman that lives under the hill,
>   And if she's not gone she lives there still."

It will not take a very great-granddaughter of hers to
be in at the death of Time.

We can never safely exceed the actual facts in our
narratives. Of pure invention, such as some suppose,
there is no instance. To write a true work of fiction
even is only to take leisure and liberty to describe
some things more exactly as they are. A true account
of the actual is the rarest poetry, for common sense
always takes a hasty and superficial view. Though I
am not much acquainted with the works of Goethe, I
should say that it was one of his chief excellences as a
writer, that he was satisfied with giving an exact description of things as they appeared to him, and their
effect upon him. Most travelers have not self-respect
enough to do this simply, and make objects and events
stand around them as the centre, but still imagine
more favorable positions and relations than the actual
ones, and so we get no valuable report from them at
all. In his "Italian Travels" Goethe jogs along at a
snail's pace, but always mindful that the earth is beneath and the heavens are above him. His Italy is not
merely the fatherland of lazzaroni and virtuosi, and
scene of splendid ruins, but a solid turf-clad soil, daily
shined on by the sun, and nightly by the moon. Even
the few showers are faithfully recorded. He speaks as
an unconcerned spectator, whose object is faithfully to

describe what he sees, and that, for the most part, in the order in which he sees it. Even his reflections do not interfere with his descriptions. In one place he speaks of himself as giving so glowing and truthful a description of an old tower to the peasants who had gathered around him, that they who had been born and brought up in the neighborhood must needs look over their shoulders, " that," to use his own words, " they might behold with their eyes, what I had praised to their ears," — " and I had added nothing, not even the ivy which for centuries had decorated the walls." It would thus be possible for inferior minds to produce invaluable books, if this very moderation were not the evidence of superiority ; for the wise are not so much wiser than others as respecters of their own wisdom. Some, poor in spirit, record plaintively only what has happened to them ; but others how they have happened to the universe, and the judgment which they have awarded to circumstances. Above all, he possessed a hearty good-will to all men, and never wrote a cross or even careless word. On one occasion the post-boy sniveling, " Signor, perdonate, questa è la mia patria," he confesses that " to me poor northerner came something tear-like into the eyes."

Goethe's whole education and life were those of the artist. He lacks the unconsciousness of the poet. In his autobiography he describes accurately the life of the author of Wilhelm Meister. For as there is in that book, mingled with a rare and serene wisdom, a certain pettiness or exaggeration of trifles, wisdom applied to produce a constrained and partial and merely well-bred

man, — a magnifying of the theatre till life itself is
turned into a stage, for which it is our duty to study
our parts well, and conduct with propriety and precision, — so in the autobiography, the fault of his
education is, so to speak, its merely artistic completeness. Nature is hindered, though she prevails at last in
making an unusually catholic impression on the boy.
It is the life of a city boy, whose toys are pictures and
works of art, whose wonders are the theatre and kingly
processions and crownings. As the youth studied minutely the order and the degrees in the imperial procession, and suffered none of its effect to be lost on him, so
the man aimed to secure a rank in society which would
satisfy his notion of fitness and respectability. He
was defrauded of much which the savage boy enjoys.
Indeed, he himself has occasion to say in this very
autobiography, when at last he escapes into the woods
without the gates: " Thus much is certain, that only
the undefinable, wide-expanding feelings of youth and
of uncultivated nations are adapted to the sublime,
which, whenever it may be excited in us through exter-
nal objects, since it is either formless, or else moulded
into forms which are incomprehensible, must surround
us with a grandeur which we find above our reach."
He further says of himself: " I had lived among painters from my childhood, and had accustomed myself
to look at objects, as they did, with reference to art."
And this was his practice to the last. He was even too
well-bred to be thoroughly bred. He says that he had
had no intercourse with the lowest class of his towns-
boys. The child should have the advantage of igno-

rance as well as of knowledge, and is fortunate if he gets his share of neglect and exposure.

"The laws of Nature break the rules of Art."

The Man of Genius may at the same time be, indeed is commonly, an Artist, but the two are not to be confounded. The Man of Genius, referred to mankind, is an originator, an inspired or demonic man, who produces a perfect work in obedience to laws yet unexplored. The artist is he who detects and applies the law from observation of the works of Genius, whether of man or nature. The Artisan is he who merely applies the rules which others have detected. There has been no man of pure Genius, as there has been none wholly destitute of Genius.

Poetry is the mysticism of mankind.

The expressions of the poet cannot be analyzed; his sentence is one word, whose syllables are words. There are indeed no *words* quite worthy to be set to his music. But what matter if we do not hear the words always, if we hear the music?

Much verse fails of being poetry because it was not written exactly at the right crisis, though it may have been inconceivably near to it. It is only by a miracle that poetry is written at all. It is not recoverable thought, but a hue caught from a vaster receding thought.

A poem is one undivided, unimpeded expression fallen ripe into literature, and it is undividedly and unimpededly received by those for whom it was matured.

If you can speak what you will never hear, if you can write what you will never read, you have done rare things.

> The work we choose should be our own
> God lets alone.

The unconsciousness of man is the consciousness of God.

Deep are the foundations of sincerity. Even stone walls have their foundation below the frost.

What is produced by a free stroke charms us, like the forms of lichens and leaves. There is a certain perfection in accident which we never consciously attain. Draw a blunt quill filled with ink over a sheet of paper, and fold the paper before the ink is dry, transversely to this line, and a delicately shaded and regular figure will be produced, in some respects more pleasing than an elaborate drawing.

The talent of composition is very dangerous, — the striking out the heart of life at a blow, as the Indian takes off a scalp. I feel as if my life had grown more outward when I can express it.

On his journey from Brenner to Verona, Goethe writes: " The Tees flows now more gently, and makes in many places broad sands. On the land, near to the water, upon the hillsides, everything is so closely planted one to another, that you think they must choke one another, — vineyards, maize, mulberry-trees, apples, pears, quinces, and nuts. The dwarf elder throws itself vigorously over the walls. Ivy grows with strong stems up the rocks, and spreads itself wide over them,

the lizard glides through the intervals, and everything
that wanders to and fro reminds one of the loveliest
pictures of art. The women's tufts of hair bound up,
the men's bare breasts and light jackets, the excellent
oxen which they drive home from market, the little
asses with their loads, — everything forms a living animated Heinrich Roos. And now that it is evening, in
the mild air a few clouds rest upon the mountains, in
the heavens more stand still than move, and immediately after sunset the chirping of crickets begins to
grow more loud; then one feels for once at home in
the world, and not as concealed or in exile. I am contented as though I had been born and brought up here,
and were now returning from a Greenland or whaling
voyage. Even the dust of my Fatherland, which is
often whirled about the wagon, and which for so long
a time I had not seen, is greeted. The clock-and-bell
jingling of the crickets is altogether lovely, penetrating,
and agreeable. It sounds bravely when roguish boys
whistle in emulation of a field of such songstresses.
One fancies that they really enhance one another.
Also the evening is perfectly mild as the day.

"If one who dwelt in the south, and came hither
from the south, should hear of my rapture hereupon,
he would deem me very childish. Alas! what I here
express I have long known while I suffered under an
unpropitious heaven, and now may I joyful feel this
joy as an exception, which we should enjoy everforth
as an eternal necessity of our nature."

Thus we "sayled by thought and pleasaunce," as

Chaucer says, and all things seemed with us to flow;
the shore itself and the distant cliffs were dissolved by
the undiluted air. The hardest material seemed to obey
the same law with the most fluid, and so indeed in
the long run it does. Trees were but rivers of sap and
woody fibre, flowing from the atmosphere, and emptying into the earth by their trunks, as their roots flowed
upward to the surface. And in the heavens there were
rivers of stars, and milky ways, already beginning to
gleam and ripple over our heads. There were rivers
of rock on the surface of the earth, and rivers of ore
in its bowels, and our thoughts flowed and circulated,
and this portion of time was but the current hour. Let
us wander where we will, the universe is built round
about us, and we are central still. If we look into the
heavens they are concave, and if we were to look into
a gulf as bottomless, it would be concave also. The sky
is curved downward to the earth in the horizon, because
we stand on the plain. I draw down its skirts. The
stars so low there seem loath to depart, but by a cir-
cuitous path to be remembering me, and returning on
their steps.

We had already passed by broad daylight the scene
of our encampment at Coos Falls, and at length we
pitched our camp on the west bank, in the northern
part of Merrimack, nearly opposite to the large island
on which we had spent the noon in our way up the river.

There we went to bed that summer evening, on a
sloping shelf in the bank, a couple of rods from our
boat, which was drawn up on the sand, and just behind
a thin fringe of oaks which bordered the river; with-

out having disturbed any inhabitants but the spiders in the grass, which came out by the light of our lamp, and crawled over our buffaloes. When we looked out from under the tent, the trees were seen dimly through the mist, and a cool dew hung upon the grass, which seemed to rejoice in the night, and with the damp air we inhaled a solid fragrance. Having eaten our supper of hot cocoa and bread and watermelon, we soon grew weary of conversing, and writing in our journals, and putting out the lantern which hung from the tentpole, fell asleep.

Unfortunately, many things have been omitted which should have been recorded in our journal ; for though we made it a rule to set down all our experiences therein, yet such a resolution is very hard to keep, for the important experience rarely allows us to remember such obligations, and so indifferent things get recorded, while that is frequently neglected. It is not easy to write in a journal what interests us at any time, because to write it is not what interests us.

Whenever we awoke in the night, still eking out our dreams with half-awakened thoughts, it was not till after an interval, when the wind breathed harder than usual, flapping the curtains of the tent, and causing its cords to vibrate, that we remembered that we lay on the bank of the Merrimack, and not in our chamber at home. With our heads so low in the grass, we heard the river whirling and sucking, and lapsing downward, kissing the shore as it went, sometimes rippling louder than usual, and again its mighty current making only a slight limpid, trickling sound, as if our water-pail had sprung a leak, and the water were flowing into the

grass by our side. The wind, rustling the oaks and
hazels, impressed us like a wakeful and inconsiderate
person up at midnight, moving about, and putting things
to rights, occasionally stirring up whole drawers full of
leaves at a puff. There seemed to be a great haste and
preparation throughout Nature, as for a distinguished
visitor ; all her aisles had to be swept in the night by
a thousand handmaidens, and a thousand pots to be
boiled for the next day's feasting, — such a whispering
bustle, as if ten thousand fairies made their fingers fly,
silently sewing at the new carpet with which the earth
was to be clothed, and the new drapery which was to
adorn the trees. And then the wind would lull and die
away, and we like it fell asleep again.

FRIDAY

The Boteman strayt
Held on his course with stayed stedfastnesse,
Ne ever shroncke, ne ever sought to bayt
His tryed armes for toylesome wearinesse;
But with his oares did sweepe the watry wildernesse.
                                                SPENSER.
Summer's robe grows
Dusky, and like an oft-dyed garment shows. — DONNE.

As we lay awake long before daybreak, listening to
the rippling of the river and the rustling of the leaves,
in suspense whether the wind blew up or down the
stream, was favorable or unfavorable to our voyage, we
already suspected that there was a change in the weather,
from a freshness as of autumn in these sounds. The
wind in the woods sounded like an incessant waterfall
dashing and roaring amid rocks, and we even felt encouraged by the unusual activity of the element. He
who hears the rippling of rivers in these degenerate
days will not utterly despair. That night was the turn-
ing-point in the season. We had gone to bed in sum
mer, and we awoke in autumn ; for summer passes into
autumn in some unimaginable point of time, like the
turning of a leaf.

We found our boat in the dawn just as we had left
it, and as if waiting for us, there on the shore, in autumn, all cool and dripping with dew, and our tracks
still fresh in the wet sand around it, the fairies all gone
or concealed. Before five o'clock we pushed it into the

fog, and, leaping in, at one shove were out of sight of
the shores, and began to sweep downward with the
rushing river, keeping a sharp lookout for rocks. We
could see only the yellow gurgling water, and a solid
bank of fog on every side, forming a small yard around
us. We soon passed the mouth of the Souhegan, and
the village of Merrimack, and as the mist gradually
rolled away, and we were relieved from the trouble of
watching for rocks, we saw by the flitting clouds, by the
first russet tinge on the hills, by the rushing river, the
cottages on shore, and the shore itself, so coolly fresh
and shining with dew, and later in the day, by the hue
of the grape-vine, the goldfinch on the willow, the
flickers flying in flocks, and when we passed near
enough to the shore, as we fancied, by the faces of men,
that the fall had commenced. The cottages looked
more snug and comfortable, and their inhabitants were
seen only for a moment, and then went quietly in and
shut the door, retreating inward to the haunts of summer.

> "And now the cold autumnal dews are seen
>   To cobweb ev'ry green;
> And by the low-shorn rowens doth appear
>   The fast-declining year."

We heard the sigh of the first autumnal wind, and
even the water had acquired a grayer hue. The su-
mach, grape, and maple were already changed, and the
milkweed had turned to a deep, rich yellow. In all
woods the leaves were fast ripening for their fall ; for
their full veins and lively gloss mark the ripe leaf and
not the sered one of the poets; and we knew that the

maples, stripped of their leaves among the earliest,
would soon stand like a wreath of smoke along the edge
of the meadow. Already the cattle were heard to low
wildly in the pastures and along the highways, restlessly
running to and fro, as if in apprehension of the withering of the grass and of the approach of winter. Our
thoughts, too, began to rustle.

As I pass along the streets of our village of Concord
on the day of our annual Cattle-Show, when it usually
happens that the leaves of the elms and buttonwoods
begin first to strew the ground under the breath of the
October wind, the lively spirits in their sap seem to
mount as high as any plow-boy's let loose that day ;
and they lead my thoughts away to the rustling woods,
where the trees are preparing for their winter campaign.
This autumnal festival, when men are gathered in
crowds in the streets as regularly and by as natural a
law as the leaves cluster and rustle by the wayside, is
naturally associated in my mind with the fall of the
year. The low of cattle in the streets sounds like a
hoarse symphony or running bass to the rustling of the
leaves. The wind goes hurrying down the country,
gleaning every loose straw that is left in the fields,
while every farmer lad too appears to scud before it,—
having donned his best pea-jacket and pepper-and-salt
waistcoat, his unbent trousers, outstanding rigging of
duck or kerseymere or corduroy, and his furry hat
withal, — to country fairs and cattle-shows, to that
Rome among the villages where the treasures of the
year are gathered. All the land over they go leaping
the fences with their tough, idle palms, which have

never learned to hang by their sides, amid the low of
calves and the bleating of sheep, — Amos, Abner, El-
nathan, Elbridge, —

"From steep pine-bearing mountains to the plain."

I love these sons of earth, every mother's son of them,
with their great hearty hearts rushing tumultuously in
herds from spectacle to spectacle, as if fearful lest there
should not be time between sun and sun to see them
all, and the sun does not wait more than in haying-
time.

"Wise Nature's darlings, they live in the world
Perplexing not themselves how it is hurled."

Running hither and thither with appetite for the coarse
pastimes of the day, now with boisterous speed at the
heels of the inspired negro from whose larynx the melo-
dies of all Congo and Guinea Coast have broke loose
into our streets ; now to see the procession of a hundred yoke of oxen, all as august and grave as Osiris, or
the droves of neat cattle and milch cows as unspotted
as Isis or Io. Such as had no love for Nature

"at all,
Came lovers home from this great festival."

They may bring their fattest cattle and richest fruits to
the fair, but they are all eclipsed by the show of men.
These are stirring autumn days, when men sweep by in
crowds, amid the rustle of leaves like migrating finches;
this is the true harvest of the year, when the air is but
the breath of men, and the rustling of leaves is as
the trampling of the crowd. We read nowadays of the
ancient festivals, games, and processions of the Greeks

and Etruscans with a little incredulity, or at least with little sympathy; but how natural and irrepressible in every people is some hearty and palpable greeting of Nature! The Corybantes, the Bacchantes, the rude primitive tragedians with their procession and goat-song, and the whole paraphernalia of the Panathenæa, which appear so antiquated and peculiar, have their parallel now. The husbandman is always a better Greek than the scholar is prepared to appreciate, and the old custom still survives, while antiquarians and scholars grow gray in commemorating it. The farmers crowd to the fair to-day in obedience to the same ancient law, which Solon or Lycurgus did not enact, as naturally as bees swarm and follow their queen.

It is worth the while to see the country's people, how they pour into the town, the sober farmer folk, now all agog, their very shirt and coat collars pointing forward, — collars so broad as if they had put their shirts on wrong end upward, for the fashions always tend to superfluity, — and with an unusual springiness in their gait, jabbering earnestly to one another. The more supple vagabond, too, is sure to appear on the least rumor of such a gathering, and the next day to disappear, and go into his hole like the seventeen-year locust, in an ever-shabby coat, though finer than the farmer's best, yet never dressed; come to see the sport, and have a hand in what is going, — to know "what's the row," if there is any; to be where some men are drunk, some horses race, some cockerels fight; anxious to be shaking props under a table and above all to see the "striped pig." He especially is the creature of the oc-

casion. He empties both his pockets and his character
into the stream, and swims in such a day. He dearly
loves the social slush. There is no reserve of soberness
in him.

I love to see the herd of men feeding heartily on
coarse and succulent pleasures, as cattle on the husks
and stalks of vegetables. Though there are many
crooked and crabbed specimens of humanity among
them, run all to thorn and rind, and crowded out of
shape by adverse circumstances, like the third chestnut
in the bur, so that you wonder to see some heads wear
a whole hat, yet fear not that the race will fail or
waver in them; like the crabs which grow in hedges,
they furnish the stocks of sweet and thrifty fruits still.
Thus is nature recruited from age to age, while the fair
and palatable varieties die out, and have their period.
This is that mankind. How cheap must be the material of which so many men are made!

The wind blew steadily down the stream, so that we
kept our sails set, and lost not a moment of the forenoon by delays, but from early morning until noon
were continually dropping downward. With our hands
on the steering-paddle, which was thrust deep into the
river, or bending to the oar, which indeed we rarely
relinquished, we felt each palpitation in the veins of
our steed, and each impulse of the wings which drew
us above. The current of our thoughts made as sudden
bends as the river, which was continually opening new
prospects to the east or south, but we are aware that
rivers flow most rapidly and shallowest at these points.

The steadfast shores never once turned aside for us, but still trended as they were made; why then should we always turn aside for them?

A man cannot wheedle nor overawe his Genius. It requires to be conciliated by nobler conduct than the world demands or can appreciate. These winged thoughts are like birds, and will not be handled; even hens will not let you touch them like quadrupeds. Nothing was ever so unfamiliar and startling to a man as his own thoughts.

To the rarest genius it is the most expensive to succumb and conform to the ways of the world. Genius is the worst of lumber, if the poet would float upon the breeze of popularity. The bird of paradise is obliged constantly to fly against the wind, lest its gay trappings, pressing close to its body, impede its free movements.

He is the best sailor who can steer within the fewest points of the wind, and extract a motive power out of the greatest obstacles. Most begin to veer and tack as soon as the wind changes from aft, and as within the tropics it does not blow from all points of the compass, there are some harbors which they can never reach.

The poet is no tender slip of fairy stock, who requires peculiar institutions and edicts for his defense, but the toughest son of earth and of Heaven, and by his greater strength and endurance his fainting companions will recognize the God in him. It is the worshipers of beauty, after all, who have done the real pioneer work of the world.

The poet will prevail to be popular in spite of his faults, and in spite of his beauties too. He will hit the nail on the head, and we shall not know the shape of his hammer. He makes us free of his hearth and heart, which is greater than to offer one the freedom of a city.

Great men, unknown to their generation, have their fame among the great who have preceded them, and all true worldly fame subsides from their high estimate beyond the stars.

Orpheus does not hear the strains which issue from his lyre, but only those which are breathed into it; for the original strain precedes the sound, by as much as the echo follows after. The rest is the perquisite of the rocks and trees and beasts.

When I stand in a library where is all the recorded wit of the world, but none of the recording, a mere accumulated, and not truly cumulative treasure; where immortal works stand side by side with anthologies which did not survive their month, and cobweb and mildew have already spread from these to the binding of those; and happily I am reminded of what poetry is, — I perceive that Shakespeare and Milton did not foresee into what company they were to fall. Alas! that so soon the work of a true poet should be swept into such a dust-hole!

The poet will write for his peers alone. He will remember only that he saw truth and beauty from his position, and expect the time when a vision as broad shall overlook the same field as freely.

We are often prompted to speak our thoughts to our neighbors, or the single travelers whom we meet on the road, but poetry is a communication from our home and solitude addressed to all Intelligence. It never whispers in a private ear. Knowing this we may understand those sonnets said to be addressed to particular persons, or " To a Mistress's Eyebrow." Let none feel flattered by them. For poetry write love, and it will be equally true.

No doubt it is an important difference between men of genius or poets, and men not of genius, that the latter are unable to grasp and confront the thought which visits them. But it is because it is too faint for expression, or even conscious impression. What merely quickens or retards the blood in their veins and fills their afternoons with pleasure, they know not whence, conveys a distinct assurance to the finer organization of the poet.

We talk of genius as if it were a mere knack, and the poet could only express what other men conceived. But in comparison with his task, the poet is the least talented of any; the writer of prose has more skill. See what talent the smith has. His material is pliant in his hands. When the poet is most inspired, is stimulated by an *aura* which never even colors the afternoons of common men, then his talent is all gone, and he is no longer a poet. The gods do not grant him any skill more than another. They never put their gifts into his hands, but they encompass and sustain him with their breath.

To say that God has given a man many and great talents frequently means that he has brought his heavens down within reach of his hands.

When the poetic frenzy seizes us, we run and scratch with our pen, intent only on worms, calling our mates around us, like the cock, and delighting in the dust we make, but do not detect where the jewel lies, which, perhaps, we have in the mean time cast to a distance, or quite covered up again.

The poet's body even is not fed like other men's, but he sometimes tastes the genuine nectar and ambrosia of the gods, and lives a divine life. By the healthful and invigorating thrills of inspiration his life is preserved to a serene old age.

Some poems are for holidays only. They are polished and sweet, but it is the sweetness of sugar, and not such as toil gives to sour bread. The breath with which the poet utters his verse must be that by which he lives.

Great prose, of equal elevation, commands our respect more than great verse, since it implies a more permanent and level height, a life more pervaded with the grandeur of the thought. The poet often only makes an irruption, like a Parthian, and is off again, shooting while he retreats; but the prose writer has conquered like a Roman, and settled colonies.

The true poem is not that which the public read. There is always a poem not printed on paper, coincident with the production of this, stereotyped in the poet's life. It is *what he has become through his work.* Not how is the idea expressed in stone, or on canvas or paper, is the question, but how far it has obtained form and expression in the life of the artist. His true work will not stand in any prince's gallery.

> My life has been the poem I would have writ,
> But I could not both live and utter it.

THE POET'S DELAY

In vain I see the morning rise,
  In vain observe the western blaze,
Who idly look to other skies,
  Expecting life by other ways.

Amidst such boundless wealth without,
  I only still am poor within,
The birds have sung their summer out,
  But still my spring does not begin.

Shall I then wait the autumn wind,
  Compelled to seek a milder day,
And leave no curious nest behind,
  No woods still echoing to my lay?

This raw and gusty day, and the creaking of the oaks and pines on shore, reminded us of more northern climes than Greece, and more wintry seas than the Ægean.

The genuine remains of Ossian, or those ancient poems which bear his name, though of less fame and extent, are, in many respects, of the same stamp with the Iliad itself. He asserts the dignity of the bard no less than Homer, and in his era, we hear of no other priest than he. It will not avail to call him a heathen, because he personifies the sun and addresses it; and what if his heroes did "worship the ghosts of their fathers," their thin, airy, and unsubstantial forms? we worship but the ghosts of our fathers in more substantial form. We cannot but respect the vigorous faith of those heathen, who sternly believed somewhat, and are inclined to say to the critics, who are offended by their superstitious rites, Don't interrupt these men's prayers.

As if we knew more about human life and a God, than the heathen and ancients! Does English theology contain the recent discoveries?

Ossian reminds us of the most refined and rudest eras, of Homer, Pindar, Isaiah, and the American Indian. In his poetry, as in Homer's, only the simplest and most enduring features of humanity are seen, such essential parts of a man as Stonehenge exhibits of a temple; we see the circles of stone, and the upright shaft alone. The phenomena of life acquire almost an unreal and gigantic size seen through his mists. Like all older and grander poetry, it is distinguished by the few elements in the lives of its heroes. They stand on the heath, between the stars and the earth, shrunk to the bones and sinews. The earth is a boundless plain for their deeds. They lead such a simple, dry, and everlasting life, as hardly needs depart with the flesh, but is transmitted entire from age to age. There are but few objects to distract their sight, and their life is as unincumbered as the course of the stars they gaze at.

> "The wrathful kings, on cairns apart,
> Look forward from behind their shields,
> And mark the wandering stars,
> That brilliant westward move."

It does not cost much for these heroes to live; they do not want much furniture. They are such forms of men only as can be seen afar through the mist, and have no costume nor dialect, but for language there is the tongue itself, and for costume there are always the skins of beasts and the bark of trees to be had. They live out their years by the vigor of their constitutions. They

survive storms and the spears of their foes, and perform a few heroic deeds, and then

> "Mounds will answer questions of them,
>   For many future years."

Blind and infirm, they spend the remnant of their days
listening to the lays of the bards, and feeling the weapons which laid their enemies low, and when at length
they die, by a convulsion of nature, the bard allows us
a short and misty glance into futurity, yet as clear perchance as their lives had been. When MacRoine was
slain, —

> "His soul departed to his warlike sires,
>   To follow misty forms of boars,
>   In tempestuous islands bleak."

The hero's cairn is erected, and the bard sings a brief
significant strain, which will suffice for epitaph and
biography.

> "The weak will find his bow in the dwelling,
>   The feeble will attempt to bend it."

Compared with this simple, fibrous life, our civilized
history appears the chronicle of debility, of fashion,
and the arts of luxury. But the civilized man misses
no real refinement in the poetry of the rudest era. It
reminds him that civilization does but dress men. It
makes shoes, but it does not toughen the soles of the
feet. It makes cloth of finer texture, but it does not
touch the skin. Inside the civilized man stands the
savage still in the place of honor. We are those blue-
eyed, yellow-haired Saxons, those slender, dark-haired
Normans.

The profession of the bard attracted more respect in those days from the importance attached to fame. It was his province to record the deeds of heroes. When Ossian hears the traditions of inferior bards, he exclaims, —

> "I straightway seize the unfutile tales,
> And send them down in faithful verse."

His philosophy of life is expressed in the opening of the third Duan of Ca-Lodin.

> "Whence have sprung the things that are?
> And whither roll the passing years?
> Where does Time conceal its two heads,
> In dense impenetrable gloom,
> Its surface marked with heroes' deeds alone?
> I view the generations gone;
> The past appears but dim;
> As objects by the moon's faint beams,
> Reflected from a distant lake.
> I see, indeed, the thunderbolts of war,
> But there the unmighty joyless dwell,
> All those who send not down their deeds
> To far, succeeding times."

The ignoble warriors die and are forgotten : —

> "Strangers come to build a tower,
> And throw their ashes overhand;
> Some rusted swords appear in dust,
> One, bending forward, says,
> 'The arms belonged to heroes gone;
> We never heard their praise in song.'"

The grandeur of the similes is another feature which characterizes great poetry. Ossian seems to speak a gigantic and universal language. The images and pictures occupy even much space in the landscape, as if they could be seen only from the sides of mountains, and plains with a wide horizon, or across arms of the sea. The machinery is so massive that it cannot be less than natural. Oivana says to the spirit of her father, "Gray-haired Torkil of Torne," seen in the skies, —

"Thou glidest away like receding ships."

So when the hosts of Fingal and Starne approach to battle, —

"With murmurs loud, like rivers far,
The race of Torne hither moved."

And when compelled to retire, —

"dragging his spear behind,
Cudulin sank in the distant wood,
Like a fire upblazing ere it dies.'

Nor did Fingal want a proper audience when he spoke:

"A thousand orators inclined
To hear the lay of Fingal."

The threats too would have deterred a man. Vengeance and terror were real. Trenmore threatens the young warrior whom he meets on a foreign strand, —

"Thy mother shall find thee pale on the shore,
While lessening on the waves she spies
The sails of him who slew her son."

If Ossian's heroes weep, it is from excess of strength, and not from weakness, a sacrifice or libation of fertile natures, like the perspiration of stone in summer's heat. We hardly know that tears have been shed, and it seems as if weeping were proper only for babes and

heroes. Their joy and their sorrow are made of one
stuff, like rain and snow, the rainbow and the mist.
When Fillan was worsted in fight, and ashamed in the
presence of Fingal, —

> "He strode away forthwith,
> And bent in grief above a stream,
> His cheeks bedewed with tears,
> From time to time the thistles gray
> He lopped with his inverted lance."

Crodar, blind and old, receives Ossian, son of Fingal,
who comes to aid him in war: —

> "'My eyes have failed,' says he, 'Crodar is blind,
> Is thy strength like that of thy fathers?
> Stretch, Ossian, thine arm to the hoary-haired.'
>   I gave my arm to the king.
> The aged hero seized my hand;
> He heaved a heavy sigh;
> Tears flowed incessant down his cheek.
> 'Strong art thou, son of the mighty,
> Though not so dreadful as Morven's prince.
>
>   .   .   .   .
>
> Let my feast be spread in the hall,
> Let every sweet-voiced minstrel sing;
> Great is he who is within my walls,
> Sons of wave-echoing Croma.'"

Even Ossian himself, the hero-bard, pays tribute to the
superior strength of his father Fingal.

> "How beauteous, mighty man, was thy mind,
> Why succeeded Ossian without its strength?"

While we sailed fleetly before the wind, with the
river gurgling under our stern, the thoughts of autumn

coursed as steadily through our minds, and we observed less what was passing on the shore than the
dateless associations and impressions which the season
awakened, anticipating in some measure the progress
of the year.

> I hearing get, who had but ears,
>   And sight, who had but eyes before,
> I moments live, who lived but years,
>   And truth discern, who knew but learning's lore.

Sitting with our faces now up-stream, we studied the
landscape by degrees, as one unrolls a map, — rock,
tree, house, hill, and meadow assuming new and varying positions as wind and water shifted the scene, and
there was variety enough for our entertainment in the
metamorphoses of the simplest objects. Viewed from
this side the scenery appeared new to us.

The most familiar sheet of water, viewed from a
new hilltop, yields a novel and unexpected pleasure.
When we have traveled a few miles, we do not recognize the profiles even of the hills which overlook our
native village, and perhaps no man is quite familiar
with the horizon as seen from the hill nearest to his
house, and can recall its outline distinctly when in the
valley. We do not commonly know, beyond a short
distance, which way the hills range which take in our
houses and farms in their sweep. As if our birth had
at first sundered things, and we had been thrust up
through into nature like a wedge, and not till the
wound heals and the scar disappears do we begin to
discover where we are, and that nature is one and con-
tinuous everywhere. It is an important epoch when a

man who has always lived on the east side of a mountain, and seen it in the west, travels round and sees it in the east. Yet the universe is a sphere whose centre is wherever there is intelligence. The sun is not so central as a man. Upon an isolated hilltop, in an open country, we seem to ourselves to be standing on the boss of an immense shield, the immediate landscape being apparently depressed below the more remote, and rising gradually to the horizon, which is the rim of the shield, — villas, steeples, forests, mountains, one above another, till they are swallowed up in the heavens. The most distant mountains in the horizon appear to rise directly from the shore of that lake in the woods by which we chance to be standing, while from the mountain-top, not only this, but a thousand nearer and larger lakes are equally unobserved.

Seen through this clear atmosphere, the works of the farmer, his plowing and reaping, had a beauty to our eyes which he never saw. How fortunate were we who did not own an acre of these shores, who had not renounced our title to the whole! One who knew how to appropriate the true value of this world would be the poorest man in it. The poor rich man! all he has is what he has bought. What I see is mine. I am a large owner in the Merrimack intervals.

> Men dig and dive but cannot my wealth spend,
>   Who yet no partial store appropriate,
> Who no armed ship into the Indies send,
>   To rob me of my orient estate.

He is the rich man, and enjoys the fruits of riches, who summer and winter forever can find delight in his

own thoughts. Buy a farm! What have I to pay for a
farm which a farmer will take?

When I visit again some haunt of my youth, I am
glad to find that nature wears so well. The landscape
is indeed something real, and solid, and sincere, and I
have not put my foot through it yet. There is a pleasant tract on the bank of the Concord, called Conantum,
which I have in my mind, — the old deserted farmhouse,
the desolate pasture with its bleak cliff, the open wood,
the river-reach, the green meadow in the midst, and
the moss-grown wild-apple orchard, — places where one
may have many thoughts and not decide anything. It
is a scene which I can not only remember, as I might
a vision, but when I will can bodily revisit, and find it
even so, unaccountable, yet unpretending in its pleasant
dreariness. When my thoughts are sensible of change,
I love to see and sit on rocks which I *have* known, and
pry into their moss, and see unchangeableness so established. I not yet gray on rocks forever gray, I no longer
green under the evergreens. There is something even
in the lapse of time by which time recovers itself.

As we have said, it proved a cool as well as breezy
day, and by the time we reached Penichook Brook
we were obliged to sit muffled in our cloaks, while
the wind and current carried us along. We bounded
swiftly over the rippling surface, far by many cultivated
lands and the ends of fences which divided innumerable
farms, with hardly a thought for the various lives which
they separated; now by long rows of alders or groves
of pines or oaks, and now by some homestead where
the women and children stood outside to gaze at us,

till we had swept out of their sight, and beyond the
limit of their longest Saturday ramble. We glided past
the mouth of the Nashua, and not long after, of Salmon
Brook, without more pause than the wind.

> Salmon Brook,
> Penichook,
> Ye sweet waters of my brain,
> When shall I look,
> Or cast the hook,
> In your waves again?

> Silver eels,
> Wooden creels,
> These the baits that still allure,
> And dragon-fly
> That floated by,
> May they still endure?

The shadows chased one another swiftly over wood
and meadow, and their alternation harmonized with our
mood. We could distinguish the clouds which cast each
one, though never so high in the heavens. When a shadow
flits across the landscape of the soul where is the substance? Probably, if we were wise enough, we should
see to what virtue we are indebted for any happier moment we enjoy. No doubt we have earned it at some
time, for the gifts of Heaven are never quite gratui-
tous. The constant abrasion and decay of our lives
makes the soil of our future growth. The wood which
we now mature, when it becomes virgin mould, deter-
mines the character of our second growth, whether that
be oaks or pines. Every man casts a shadow; not his
body only, but his imperfectly mingled spirit. This is

his grief. Let him turn which way he will, it falls opposite to the sun; short at noon, long at eve. Did
you never see it? But, referred to the sun, it is widest
at its base, which is no greater than his own capacity.
The divine light is diffused almost entirely around us,
and by means of the refraction of light, or else by a
certain self-luminousness, or, as some will have it, transparency, if we preserve ourselves untarnished, we are
able to enlighten our shaded side. At any rate, our
darkest grief has that bronze color of the moon eclipsed.
There is no ill which may not be dissipated, like the
dark, if you let in a stronger light upon it. Shadows,
referred to the source of light, are pyramids whose
bases are never greater than those of the substances
which cast them, but light is a spherical congeries of
pyramids, whose very apexes are the sun itself, and
hence the system shines with uninterrupted light. But
if the light we use is but a paltry and narrow taper,
most objects will cast a shadow wider than themselves.

The places where we had stopped or spent the night
in our way up the river had already acquired a slight
historical interest for us; for many upward days' voy-
aging were unraveled in this rapid downward passage.
When one landed to stretch his limbs by walking, he
soon found himself falling behind his companion, and
was obliged to take advantage of the curves, and ford
the brooks and ravines in haste, to recover his ground.
Already the banks and the distant meadows wore a
sober and deepened tinge, for the September air had
shorn them of their summer's pride.

"And what's a life? The flourishing array
Of the proud summer meadow, which to-day
Wears her green plush, and is to-morrow hay."

The air was really the " fine element " which the poets
describe. It had a finer and sharper grain, seen against
the russet pastures and meadows, than before, as if
cleansed of the summer's impurities.

Having passed the New Hampshire line and reached
the Horseshoe Interval in Tyngsborough, where there
is a high and regular second bank, we climbed up this
in haste to get a nearer sight of the autumnal flowers,
asters, goldenrod, and yarrow, and blue-curls (*Tricho-
stema dichotomum*), humble roadside blossoms, and,
lingering still, the harebell and the *Rhexia Virginica*.
The last, growing in patches of lively pink flowers on
the edge of the meadows, had almost too gay an appearance for the rest of the landscape, like a pink ribbon on the bonnet of a Puritan woman. Asters and
goldenrods were the livery which nature wore at present. The latter alone expressed all the ripeness of the
season, and shed their mellow lustre over the fields, as
if the now declining summer's sun had bequeathed its
hues to them. It is the floral solstice a little after midsummer, when the particles of golden light, the sun-
dust, have, as it were, fallen like seeds on the earth,
and produced these blossoms. On every hillside, and
in every valley, stood countless asters, coreopses, tansies,
goldenrods, and the whole race of yellow flowers, like
Brahminical devotees, turning steadily with their luminary from morning till night.

"I see the goldenrod shine bright,
  As sun-showers at the birth of day,
A golden plume of yellow light,
  That robs the Day-god's splendid ray.

"The aster's violet rays divide
  The bank with many stars for me,
And yarrow in blanch tints is dyed,
  As moonlight floats across the sea.

"I see the emerald woods prepare
  To shed their vestiture once more,
And distant elm-trees spot the air
  With yellow pictures softly o'er.

. . . .

"No more the water-lily's pride
  In milk-white circles swims content,
No more the blue-weed's clusters ride
  And mock the heavens' element.

. . . .

"Autumn, thy wreath and mine are blent
  With the same colors, for to me
A richer sky than all is lent,
  While fades my dream-like company.

"Our skies glow purple, but the wind
  Sobs chill through green trees and bright grass,
To-day shines fair, and lurk behind
  The times that into winter pass.

"So fair we seem, so cold we are,
  So fast we hasten to decay,
Yet through our night glows many a star,
  That still shall claim its sunny day."

So sang a Concord poet once.

There is a peculiar interest belonging to the still later flowers, which abide with us the approach of winter. There is something witchlike in the appearance of the witch-hazel, which blossoms late in October and in November, with its irregular and angular spray and petals like furies' hair, or small ribbon streamers. Its blossoming, too, at this irregular period, when other shrubs have lost their leaves, as well as blossoms, looks like witches' craft. Certainly it blooms in no garden of man's. There is a whole fairy-land on the hillside where it grows.

Some have thought that the gales do not at present waft to the voyager the natural and original fragrance of the land, such as the early navigators described, and that the loss of many odoriferous native plants, sweet-scented grasses and medicinal herbs, which formerly sweetened the atmosphere, and rendered it salubrious, — by the grazing of cattle and the rooting of swine, — is the source of many diseases which now prevail ; the earth, say they, having been long subjected to extremely artificial and luxurious modes of cultivation, to gratify the appetite, converted into a stye and hotbed, where men for profit increase the ordinary decay of nature.

According to the record of an old inhabitant of Tyngsborough, now dead, whose farm we were now gliding past, one of the greatest freshets on this river took place in October, 1785, and its height was marked by a nail driven into an apple tree behind his house. One of his descendants has shown this to me, and I judged it to be at least seventeen or eighteen feet above the level of the river at the time. According to Barber, the river rose twenty-one feet above the common high-water mark at Bradford in the year 1818. Before the Lowell and Nashua railroad was built, the engineer made inquiries of the inhabitants along the banks as to how high they had known the river to rise. When he came to this house he was conducted to the apple tree, and as the nail was not then visible, the lady of the house placed her hand on the trunk where she said that she remembered the nail to have been from her childhood. In the meanwhile the old man put his arm inside the tree, which was hollow, and felt the point of the nail sticking through, and it was exactly opposite to her hand. The spot is now plainly marked by a notch in the bark. But as no one else remembered the river to have risen so high as this, the engineer disregarded this statement, and I learn that there has since been a freshet which rose within nine inches of the rails at Biscuit Brook, and such a freshet as that of 1785 would have covered the railroad two feet deep.

The revolutions of nature tell as fine tales, and make as interesting revelations, on this river's banks, as on the Euphrates or the Nile. This apple tree, which stands within a few rods of the river, is called " Elisha's apple tree," from a friendly Indian who was anciently in the service of Jonathan Tyng, and, with one other man, was killed here by his own race in one of the Indian wars, — the particulars of which affair were told us on the spot. He was buried close by, no one knew exactly where, but in the flood of 1785, so great a weight of water standing over the grave caused the earth to settle where it had once been disturbed, and when the

flood went down, a sunken spot, exactly of the form
and size of the grave, revealed its locality ; but this was
now lost again, and no future flood can detect it ;
yet, no doubt, nature will know how to point it out
in due time, if it be necessary, by methods yet more
searching and unexpected. Thus there is not only the
crisis when the spirit ceases to inspire and expand the
body, marked by a fresh mound in the churchyard,
but there is also a crisis when the body ceases to take
up room as such in nature, marked by a fainter de-
pression in the earth.

We sat awhile to rest us here upon the brink of the
western bank, surrounded by the glossy leaves of the
red variety of the mountain laurel, just above the head
of Wicasuck Island, where we could observe some
scows which were loading with clay from the opposite
shore, and also overlook the grounds of the farmer, of
whom I have spoken, who once hospitably entertained
us for a night. He had on his pleasant farm, besides
an abundance of the beach plum, or *Prunus littoralis,*
which grew wild, the Canada plum under cultivation,
fine Porter apples, some peaches and large patches of
musk and water melons, which he cultivated for the
Lowell market. Elisha's apple tree, too, bore a native
fruit, which was prized by the family ; he raised the
blood peach, which, as he showed us with satisfaction,
was more like the oak in the color of its bark and in
the setting of its branches, and was less liable to break
down under the weight of the fruit, or the snow, than
other varieties. It was of slower growth, and its
branches strong and tough. There, also, was his nurs-

cry of native apple trees, thickly set upon the bank, which cost but little care, and which he sold to the neighboring farmers when they were five or six years old. To see a single peach upon its stem makes an impression of paradisaical fertility and luxury. This reminded us even of an old Roman farm, as described by Varro : " Cæsar Vopiscus Ædilicius, when he pleaded before the Censors, said that the grounds of Rosea were the garden (*sumen*, the tidbit) of Italy, in which a pole being left would not be visible the day after, on account of the growth of the herbage." This soil may not have been remarkably fertile, yet at this distance we thought that this anecdote might be told of the Tyngsborough farm.

When we passed Wicasuck Island, there was a pleasure boat containing a youth and a maiden on the island brook, which we were pleased to see, since it proved that there were some hereabouts to whom our excursion would not be wholly strange. Before this, a canal-boatman, of whom we made some inquiries respecting Wicasuck Island, and who told us that it was disputed property, suspected that we had a claim upon it, and though we assured him that all this was news to us, and explained, as well as we could, why we had come to see it, he believed not a word of it, and seriously offered us one hundred dollars for our title. The only other small boats which we met with were used to pick up driftwood. Some of the poorer class along the stream collect, in this way, all the fuel which they require. While one of us landed not far from this island to forage for provisions among the farmhouses whose roofs we saw, — for our supply was now exhausted, — the other, sitting in the boat, which was moored to the shore, was left alone to his reflections.

If there is nothing new on the earth, still the traveler always has a resource in the skies. They are constantly turning a new page to view. The wind sets the types on this blue ground, and the inquiring may always read a new truth there. There are things there written with such fine and subtle tinctures, paler than the juice of limes, that to the diurnal eye they leave no trace, and only the chemistry of night reveals them. Every man's daylight firmament answers in his mind to the brightness of the vision in his starriest hour.

These continents and hemispheres are soon run over, but an always unexplored and infinite region makes off on every side from the mind, further than to sunset, and we can make no highway or beaten track into it, but the grass immediately springs up in the path, for we travel there chiefly with our wings.

Sometimes we see objects as through a thin haze, in their eternal relations, and they stand like Palenque and the Pyramids, and we wonder who set them up, and for what purpose. If we see the reality in things, of what moment is the superficial and apparent longer? What are the earth and all its interests beside the deep surmise which pierces and scatters them? While I sit here listening to the waves which ripple and break on this shore, I am absolved from all obligation to the past, and the council of nations may reconsider its votes. The grating of a pebble annuls them. Still occasionally in my dreams I remember that rippling water.

Oft as I turn me on my pillow o'er
I hear the lapse of waves upon the shore,
Distinct as if it were at broad noonday,
And I were drifting down from Nashua.

With a bending sail we glided rapidly by Tyngsborough and Chelmsford, each holding in one hand
half of a tart country apple pie which we had purchased to celebrate our return, and in the other a
fragment of the newspaper in which it was wrapped,
devouring these with divided relish, and learning the
news which had transpired since we sailed. The river
here opened into a broad and straight reach of great
length, which we bounded merrily over before a smack-
ing breeze, with a devil-may-care look in our faces,
and our boat a white bone in its mouth, and a speed
which greatly astonished some scow boatmen whom
we met. The wind in the horizon rolled like a flood
over valley and plain, and every tree bent to the blast,
and the mountains like school-boys turned their cheeks
to it. They were great and current motions, the flowing sail, the running stream, the waving tree, the roving wind. The north wind stepped readily into the
harness which we had provided, and pulled us along
with good will. Sometimes we sailed as gently and
steadily as the clouds overhead, watching the receding
shores and the motions of our sail; the play of its pulse
so like our own lives, so thin and yet so full of life, so
noiseless when it labored hardest, so noisy and impatient when least effective; now bending to some generous impulse of the breeze, and then fluttering and
flapping with a kind of human suspense. It was the

scale on which the varying temperature of distant
atmospheres was graduated, and it was some attraction for us that the breeze it played with had been
out of doors so long. Thus we sailed, not being able to
fly, but as next best, making a long furrow in the fields
of the Merrimack toward our home, with our wings
spread, but never lifting our heel from the watery
trench ; gracefully plowing homeward with our brisk
and willing team, wind and stream, pulling together,
the former yet a wild steer, yoked to his more sedate
fellow. It was very near flying, as when the duck
rushes through the water with an impulse of her
wings, throwing the spray about her before she can
rise. How we had stuck fast if drawn up but a few
feet on the shore!

When we reached the great bend just above Middlesex, where the river runs east thirty-five miles to the
sea, we at length lost the aid of this propitious wind,
though we contrived to make one long and judicious
tack carry us nearly to the locks of the canal. We
were here locked through at noon by our old friend,
the lover of the higher mathematics, who seemed glad
to see us safe back again through so many locks; but
we did not stop to consider any of his problems, though
we could cheerfully have spent a whole autumn in this
way another time, and never have asked what his religion was. It is so rare to meet with a man outdoors
who cherishes a worthy thought in his mind, which is
independent of the labor of his hands. Behind every
man's busy-ness there should be a level of undisturbed
serenity and industry, as within the reef encircling a

coral isle there is always an expanse of still water, where the depositions are going on which will finally raise it above the surface.

The eye which can appreciate the naked and absolute beauty of a scientific truth is far more rare than that which is attracted by a moral one. Few detect the morality in the former, or the science in the latter. Aristotle defined art to be Λόγος τοῦ ἔργου ἄνευ ὕλης, *The principle of the work without the wood ;* but most men prefer to have some of the wood along with the principle; they demand that the truth be clothed in flesh and blood and the warm colors of life. They prefer the partial statement because it fits and measures them and their commodities best. But science still exists everywhere as the sealer of weights and measures at least.

We have heard much about the poetry of mathematics, but very little of it has yet been sung. The ancients had a juster notion of their poetic value than we. The most distinct and beautiful statement of any truth must take at last the mathematical form. We might so simplify the rules of moral philosophy, as well as of arithmetic, that one formula would express them both. All the moral laws are readily translated into natural philosophy, for often we have only to restore the primitive meaning of the words by which they are expressed, or to attend to their literal instead of their metaphorical sense. They are already *supernatural* philosophy. The whole body of what is now called moral or ethical truth existed in the golden age as abstract science. Or, if we prefer, we may say that the laws of Nature are the purest morality. The Tree of Knowledge is a Tree of Knowledge of good and evil. He is not a true man of science who does not bring some sympathy to his studies, and expect to learn something by behavior as well as by application. It is childish to rest in the discovery of mere coincidences, or of partial and extraneous laws. The study of geometry is a petty and idle exercise of the mind, if it is applied to no larger system than the starry one. Mathematics should be mixed not only with physics but with ethics, *that* is *mixed* mathematics. The fact which interests us most is the life of the naturalist. The purest science is still biographical. Nothing will dignify and elevate science while it is sundered so wholly from the moral life of its devotee, and he professes another religion than it teaches, and worships at a foreign shrine. Anciently the faith of a philosopher was identical with his system, or, in other words, his view of the universe.

My friends mistake when they communicate facts to me with so much pains. Their presence, even their exaggerations and loose statements, are equally good facts for me. I have no respect for facts even except when I would use them, and for the most part I am independent of those which I hear, and can afford to be inaccurate, or, in other words, to substitute more present and pressing facts in their place.

The poet uses the results of science and philosophy, and generalizes their widest deductions.

The process of discovery is very simple. An unwearied and systematic application of known laws to

nature causes the unknown to reveal themselves. Almost any *mode* of observation will be successful at last,
for what is most wanted is method. Only let something
be determined and fixed around which observation may
rally. How many new relations a foot-rule alone will
reveal, and to how many things still this has not been
applied! What wonderful discoveries have been and
may still be made with a plumb-line, a level, a survey-
or's compass, a thermometer, or a barometer! Where
there is an observatory and a telescope, we expect that
any eyes will see new worlds at once. I should say
that the most prominent scientific men of our country,
and perhaps of this age, are either serving the arts and
not pure science, or are performing faithful but quite
subordinate labors in particular departments. They
make no steady and systematic approaches to the central fact. A discovery is made, and at once the attention of all observers is distracted to that, and it draws
many analogous discoveries in its train; as if their
work were not already laid out for them, but they had
been lying on their oars. There is wanting constant
and accurate observation with enough of theory to
direct and discipline it.

But, above all, there is wanting genius. Our books
of science, as they improve in accuracy, are in danger
of losing the freshness and vigor and readiness to appreciate the real laws of Nature, which is a marked
merit in the ofttimes false theories of the ancients. I
am attracted by the slight pride and satisfaction, the
emphatic and even exaggerated style, in which some of
the older naturalists speak of the operations of Na-

ture, though they are better qualified to appreciate than to discriminate the facts. Their assertions are not without value when disproved. If they are not facts, they are suggestions for nature herself to act upon. "The Greeks," says Gesner, "had a common proverb (Λαγὸς καθεῦδον), a sleeping hare, for a dissembler or counterfeit; because the hare sees when she sleeps; for this is an admirable and rare work of Nature, that all the residue of her bodily parts take their rest, but the eye standeth continually sentinel."

Observation is so wide awake, and facts are being so rapidly added to the sum of human experience, that it appears as if the theorizer would always be in arrears, and were doomed forever to arrive at imperfect conclusions; but the power to perceive a law is equally rare in all ages of the world, and depends but little on the number of facts observed. The senses of the savage will furnish him with facts enough to set him up as a philosopher. The ancients can still speak to us with authority, even on the themes of geology and chemistry, though these studies are thought to have had their birth in modern times. Much is said about the progress of science in these centuries. I should say that the useful results of science had accumulated, but that there had been no accumulation of knowledge, strictly speaking, for posterity; for knowledge is to be acquired only by a corresponding experience. How can we *know* what we are *told* merely? Each man can interpret another's experience only by his own. We read that Newton discovered the law of gravitation, but how many who have heard of his famous discovery have recognized the same truth that he did? It may be not one. The revelation which was then made to him has not been superseded by the revelation made to any successor.

> We see the *planet* fall,
> And that is all.

In a review of Sir James Clark Ross's "Antarctic Voyage of Discovery," there is a passage which shows how far a body of men are commonly impressed by an object of sublimity, and which is also a good instance of the step from the sublime to the ridiculous. After describing the discovery of the Antarctic Continent, at first seen a hundred miles distant over fields of ice, — stupendous ranges of mountains from seven and eight to twelve and fourteen thousand feet high, covered with eternal snow and ice, in solitary and inaccessible grandeur, at one time the weather being beautifully clear, and the sun shining on the icy landscape; a continent whose islands only are accessible, and these exhibited " not the smallest trace of vegetation," only in a few places the rocks protruding through their icy covering, to convince the beholder that land formed the nucleus, and that it was not an iceberg, — the practical British reviewer proceeds thus, sticking to his last: " On the 22d of January, afternoon, the Expedition made the latitude of 74° 20′, and by 7ʰ P. M., having ground [ground! where did they get ground?] to believe that they were then in a higher southern latitude than had been attained by that enterprising seaman, the late Captain James Weddel, and therefore higher than all their predecessors, an extra allowance of grog was issued to the crews as a reward for their perseverance."

Let not us sailors of late centuries take upon ourselves any airs on account of our Newtons and our Cuviers; we deserve an extra allowance of grog only.

We endeavored in vain to persuade the wind to blow through the long corridor of the canal, which is here cut straight through the woods, and were obliged to resort to our old expedient of drawing by a cord. When we reached the Concord, we were forced to row once more in good earnest, with neither wind nor current in our favor, but by this time the rawness of the day had disappeared, and we experienced the warmth of a summer afternoon. This change in the weather was favorable to our contemplative mood, and disposed us to dream yet deeper at our oars, while we floated in imagination farther down the stream of time, as we had floated down the stream of the Merrimack, to poets of a milder period than had engaged us in the morning. Chelmsford and Billerica appeared like old English towns, compared with Merrimack and Nashua, and many generations of civil poets might have lived and sung here.

What a contrast between the stern and desolate poetry of Ossian, and that of Chaucer, and even of Shakespeare and Milton, much more of Dryden, and Pope, and Gray! Our summer of English poetry, like the Greek and Latin before it, seems well advanced towards its fall, and laden with the fruit and foliage

of the season, with bright autumnal tints, but soon the
winter will scatter its myriad clustering and shading
leaves, and leave only a few desolate and fibrous
boughs to sustain the snow and rime, and creak in the
blasts of age. We cannot escape the impression that
the Muse has stooped a little in her flight, when we
come to the literature of civilized eras. Now first we
hear of various ages and styles of poetry; it is pastoral,
and lyric, and narrative, and didactic; but the poetry
of runic monuments is of one style, and for every age.
The bard has in a great measure lost the dignity and
sacredness of his office. Formerly he was called a seer,
but now it is thought that one man sees as much as
another. He has no longer the bardic rage, and only
conceives the deed, which he formerly stood ready to
perform. Hosts of warriors earnest for battle could not
mistake nor dispense with the ancient bard. His lays
were heard in the pauses of the fight. There was no
danger of his being overlooked by his contemporaries.
But now the hero and the bard are of different professions. When we come to the pleasant English verse,
the storms have all cleared away, and it will never
thunder and lighten more. The poet has come within
doors, and exchanged the forest and crag for the fireside, the hut of the Gael, and Stonehenge, with its
circles of stones, for the house of the Englishman. No
hero stands at the door prepared to break forth into
song or heroic action, but a homely Englishman, who
cultivates the art of poetry. We see the comfortable
fireside, and hear the crackling fagots, in all the verse.
  Notwithstanding the broad humanity of Chaucer

and the many social and domestic comforts which we
meet with in his verse, we have to narrow our vision
somewhat to consider him, as if he occupied less space
in the landscape, and did not stretch over hill and valley as Ossian does. Yet, seen from the side of posterity, as the father of English poetry, preceded by a long
silence or confusion in history, unenlivened by any
strain of pure melody, we easily come to reverence
him. Passing over the earlier Continental poets, since
we are bound to the pleasant archipelago of English
poetry, Chaucer's is the first name after that misty
weather in which Ossian lived, which can detain us
long. Indeed, though he represents so different a culture and society, he may be regarded as in many respects the Homer of the English poets. Perhaps he is
the youthfulest of them all. We return to him as to
the purest well, the fountain farthest removed from
the highway of desultory life. He is so natural and
cheerful, compared with later poets, that we might almost regard him as a personification of spring. To the
faithful reader his muse has even given an aspect to
his times, and when he is fresh from perusing him,
they seem related to the golden age. It is still the
poetry of youth and life, rather than of thought; and
though the moral vein is obvious and constant, it has
not yet banished the sun and daylight from his verse.
The loftiest strains of the Muse are, for the most part,
sublimely plaintive, and not a carol as free as Nature's.
The content which the sun shines to celebrate from
morning to evening is unsung. The Muse solaces herself, and is not ravished but consoled. There is a ca-

tastrophe implied, and a tragic element in all our verse, and less of the lark and morning dews, than of the nightingale and evening shades. But in Homer and Chaucer there is more of the innocence and serenity of youth than in the more modern and moral poets. The Iliad is not Sabbath but morning reading, and men cling to this old song, because they still have moments of unbaptized and uncommitted life, which give them an appetite for more. To the innocent there are neither cherubim nor angels. At rare intervals we rise above the necessity of virtue into an unchangeable morning light, in which we have only to live right on and breathe the ambrosial air. The Iliad represents no creed nor opinion, and we read it with a rare sense of freedom and irresponsibility, as if we trod on native ground, and were autochthones of the soil.

Chaucer had eminently the habits of a literary man and a scholar. There were never any times so stirring that there were not to be found some sedentary still. He was surrounded by the din of arms. The battles of Hallidon Hill and Neville's Cross, and the still more memorable battles of Cressy and Poictiers, were fought in his youth; but these did not concern our poet much, Wickliffe and his reform much more. He regarded himself always as one privileged to sit and converse with books. He helped to establish the literary class. His character as one of the fathers of the English language would alone make his works important, even those which have little poetical merit. He was as simple as Wordsworth in preferring his homely but vigorous Saxon tongue, when it was neglected by the court, and

had not yet attained to the dignity of a literature, and
rendered a similar service to his country to that which
Dante rendered to Italy. If Greek sufficeth for Greek,
and Arabic for Arabian, and Hebrew for Jew, and
Latin for Latin, then English shall suffice for him, for
any of these will serve to teach truth " right as divers
pathes leaden divers folke the right waye to Rome." In
the Testament of Love he writes, " Let then clerkes
enditen in Latin, for they have the propertie of science,
and the knowinge in that facultie, and lette Frenchmen
in their Frenche also enditen their queinte termes, for it
is kyndely to their mouthes, and let us shewe our fan-
tasies in soche wordes as we lerneden of our dames
tonge."

He will know how to appreciate Chaucer best who
has come down to him the natural way, through the
meagre pastures of Saxon and ante-Chaucerian poetry;
and yet, so human and wise he appears after such diet,
that we are liable to misjudge him still. In the Saxon
poetry extant, in the earliest English, and the contemporary Scottish poetry, there is less to remind the
reader of the rudeness and vigor of youth than of the
feebleness of a declining age. It is for the most part
translation of imitation merely, with only an occasional
and slight tinge of poetry, oftentimes the falsehood and
exaggeration of fable, without its imagination to redeem
it, and we look in vain to find antiquity restored, hu-
manized, and made blithe again by some natural sympathy between it and the present. But Chaucer is fresh
and modern still, and no dust settles on his true passages. It lightens along the line, and we are reminded

that flowers have bloomed, and birds sung, and hearts beaten in England. Before the earnest gaze of the reader, the rust and moss of time gradually drop off, and the original green life is revealed. He was a homely and domestic man, and did breathe quite as modern men do.

There is no wisdom that can take place of humanity, and we find *that* in Chaucer. We can expand at last in his breadth, and we think that we could have been that man's acquaintance. He was worthy to be a citizen of England, while Petrarch and Boccaccio lived in Italy, and Tell and Tamerlane in Switzerland and in Asia, and Bruce in Scotland, and Wickliffe and Gower and Edward the Third and John of Gaunt and the Black Prince were his own countrymen as well as contemporaries; all stout and stirring names. The fame of Roger Bacon came down from the preceding century, and the name of Dante still possessed the influence of a living presence. On the whole, Chaucer impresses us as greater than his reputation, and not a little like Homer and Shakespeare, for he would have held up his head in their company. Among early English poets he is the landlord and host, and has the authority of such. The affectionate mention which succeeding early poets make of him, coupling him with Homer and Virgil, is to be taken into the account in estimating his character and influence. King James and Dunbar of Scotland speak of him with more love and reverence than any modern author of his predecessors of the last century. The same childlike relation is without a parallel now. For the most part we read him without criticism, for he does not plead his own cause, but speaks for his readers, and has that greatness of trust and reliance which compels popularity. He confides in the reader, and speaks privily with him, keeping nothing back. And in return the reader has great confidence in him, that he tells no lies, and reads his story with indulgence, as if it were the circumlocution of a child, but often discovers afterwards that he has spoken with more directness and economy of words than a sage. He is never heartless,

> "For first the thing is thought within the hart,
> Er any word out from the mouth astart."

And so new was all his theme in those days, that he did not have to invent, but only to tell.

We admire Chaucer for his sturdy English wit. The easy height he speaks from in his Prologue to the Canterbury Tales, as if he were equal to any of the company there assembled, is as good as any particular excellence in it. But though it is full of good sense and humanity, it is not transcendent poetry. For picturesque description of persons it is, perhaps, without a parallel in English poetry; yet it is essentially humorous, as the loftiest genius never is. Humor, however broad and genial, takes a narrower view than enthusiasm. To his own finer vein he added all the common wit and wisdom of his time, and everywhere in his works his remarkable knowledge of the world and nice perception of character, his rare common sense and proverbial wisdom, are apparent. His genius does not soar like Milton's, but is genial and familiar. It shows great tenderness and delicacy, but not the heroic sentiment. It is only a greater portion of humanity with all

its weakness. He is not heroic, as Raleigh, nor pious,
as Herbert, nor philosophical, as Shakespeare, but he
is the child of the English muse, that child which is
the father of the man. The charm of his poetry consists often only in an exceeding naturalness, perfect sincerity, with the behavior of a child rather than of a man.

Gentleness and delicacy of character are everywhere
apparent in his verse. The simplest and humblest words
come readily to his lips. No one can read the Prioress's
tale, understanding the spirit in which it was written,
and in which the child sings *O alma redemptoris mater*, or
the account of the departure of Constance with her
child upon the sea, in the Man of Lawe's tale, without
feeling the native innocence and refinement of the author.
Nor can we be mistaken respecting the essential purity
of his character, disregarding the apology of the manners of the age. A simple pathos and feminine gentleness, which Wordsworth only occasionally approaches,
but does not equal, are peculiar to him. We are tempted
to say that his genius was feminine, not masculine. It
was such a feminineness, however, as is rarest to find
in woman, though not the appreciation of it ; perhaps
it is not to be found at all in woman, but is only the
feminine in man.

Such pure and genuine and childlike love of Nature
is hardly to be found in any poet.

Chaucer's remarkably trustful and affectionate character appears in his familiar, yet innocent and reverent
manner of speaking of his God. He comes into his
thought without any false reverence, and with no more
parade than the zephyr to his ear. If Nature is our

mother, then God is our father. There is less love and
simple, practical trust in Shakespeare and Milton.
How rarely in our English tongue do we find expressed
any affection for God! Certainly, there is no sentiment
so rare as the love of God. Herbert almost alone expresses it, " Ah, my dear God ! " Our poet uses similar
words with propriety ; and whenever he sees a beautiful person, or other object, prides himself on the " mais-
try " of his God. He even recommends Dido to be
his bride, —

> "If that God that heaven and yearth made,
> Would have a love for beauty and goodnesse,
> And womanhede, trouth, and semeliness."

But in justification of our praise, we must refer to
his works themselves ; to the prologue to the Canterbury Tales, the account of Gentilesse, the Flower and
the Leaf, the stories of Griselda, Virginia, Ariadne, and
Blanche the Duchesse, and much more of less distinguished merit. There are many poets of more taste,
and better manners, who knew how to leave out their
dullness ; but such negative genius cannot detain us
long ; we shall return to Chaucer still with love. Some
natures which are really rude and ill-developed, have
yet a higher standard of perfection than others which
are refined and well balanced. Even the clown has taste,
whose dictates, though he disregards them, are higher
and purer than those which the artist obeys. If we
have to wander through many dull and prosaic passages
in Chaucer, we have at least the satisfaction of knowing that it is not an artificial dullness, but too easily
matched by many passages in life. We confess that we

feel a disposition commonly to concentrate sweets, and accumulate pleasures ; but the poet may be presumed always to speak as a traveler, who leads us through a varied scenery, from one eminence to another, and it is, perhaps, more pleasing, after all, to meet with a fine thought in its natural setting. Surely fate has enshrined it in these circumstances for some end. Nature strews her nuts and flowers broadcast, and never collects them into heaps. This was the soil it grew in, and this the hour it bloomed in ; if sun, wind, and rain came here to cherish and expand the flower, shall not we come here to pluck it ?

A true poem is distinguished not so much by a felicitous expression, or any thought it suggests, as by the atmosphere which surrounds it. Most have beauty of outline merely, and are striking as the form and bearing of a stranger ; but true verses come toward us indistinctly, as the very breath of all friendliness, and envelop us in their spirit and fragrance. Much of our poetry has the very best manners, but no character. It is only an unusual precision and elasticity of speech, as if its author had taken, not an intoxicating draught, but an electuary. It has the distinct outline of sculpture, and chronicles an early hour. Under the influence of passion all men speak thus distinctly, but wrath is not always divine.

There are two classes of men called poets. The one cultivates life, the other art, — one seeks food for nutriment, the other for flavor ; one satisfies hunger, the other gratifies the palate. There are two kinds of writing, both great and rare, — one that of genius, or the inspired, the other of intellect and taste, in the intervals of inspiration. The former is above criticism, always correct, giving the law to criticism. It vibrates and pulsates with life forever. It is sacred, and to be read with reverence, as the works of nature are studied. There are few instances of a sustained style of this kind ; perhaps every man has spoken words, but the speaker is then careless of the record. Such a style removes us out of personal relations with its author ; we do not take his words on our lips, but his sense into our hearts. It is the stream of inspiration, which bubbles out, now here, now there, now in this man, now in that. It matters not through what ice-crystals it is seen, now a fountain, now the ocean stream running underground. It is in Shakespeare, Alpheus, in Burns, Arethuse ; but ever the same. The other is self-possessed and wise. It is reverent of genius, and greedy of inspiration. It is conscious in the highest and the least degree. It consists with the most perfect command of the faculties. It dwells in a repose as of the desert, and objects are as distinct in it as oases or palms in the horizon of sand. The train of thought moves with subdued and measured step, like a caravan. But the pen is only an instrument in its hand, and not instinct with life, like a longer arm. It leaves a thin varnish or glaze over all its work. The works of Goethe furnish remarkable instances of the latter.

There is no just and serene criticism as yet. Nothing is considered simply as it lies in the lap of eternal beauty, but our thoughts, as well as our bodies, must

be dressed after the latest fashions. Our taste is too
delicate and particular. It says nay to the poet's work,
but never yea to his hope. It invites him to adorn his
deformities, and not to cast them off by expansion, as
the tree its bark. We are a people who live in a bright
light, in houses of pearl and porcelain, and drink only
light wines, whose teeth are easily set on edge by the
least natural sour. If we had been consulted, the backbone of the earth would have been made, not of granite, but of Bristol spar. A modern author would have
died in infancy in a ruder age. But the poet is something more than a scald, " a smoother and polisher of
language; " he is a Cincinnatus in literature, and oc-
cupies no west end of the world. Like the sun, he will
indifferently select his rhymes, and with a liberal taste
weave into his verse the planet and the stubble.

In these old books the stucco has long since crum-
bled away, and we read what was sculptured in the
granite. They are rude and massive in their proportions,
rather than smooth and delicate in their finish. The
workers in stone polish only their chimney ornaments,
but their pyramids are roughly done. There is a soberness in a rough aspect, as of unhewn granite, which
addresses a depth in us, but a polished surface hits only
the ball of the eye. The true finish is the work of time,
and the use to which a thing is put. The elements are
still polishing the pyramids. Art may varnish and gild,
but it can do no more. A work of genius is rough-hewn
from the first, because it anticipates the lapse of time,
and has an ingrained polish, which still appears when
fragments are broken off, an essential quality of its

substance. Its beauty is at the same time its strength, and it breaks with a lustre.

The great poem must have the stamp of greatness as well as its essence. The reader easily goes within the shallowest contemporary poetry, and informs it with all the life and promise of the day, as the pilgrim goes within the temple, and hears the faintest strains of the worshipers; but it will have to speak to posterity, traversing these deserts, through the ruins of its outmost walls, by the grandeur and beauty of its proportions.

But here on the stream of the Concord, where we have all the while been bodily, Nature, who is superior to all styles and ages, is now, with pensive face, composing her poem Autumn, with which no work of man will bear to be compared.

In summer we live out of doors, and have only impulses and feelings, which are all for action, and must wait commonly for the stillness and longer nights of autumn and winter before any thought will subside; we are sensible that behind the rustling leaves, and the stacks of grain, and the bare clusters of the grape, there is the field of a wholly new life, which no man has lived; that even this earth was made for more mysterious and nobler inhabitants than men and women. In the hues of October sunsets, we see the portals to other mansions than those which we occupy, not far off geographically, —

> "There is a place beyond that flaming hill,
>   From whence the stars their thin appearance shed,
> A place beyond all place, where never ill,
>   Nor impure thought was ever harbored."

Sometimes a mortal feels in himself Nature, — not his Father but his Mother stirs within him, and he becomes immortal with her immortality. From time to time she claims kindredship with us, and some globule from her veins steals up into our own.

> I am the autumnal sun,
> With autumn gales my race is run;
> When will the hazel put forth its flowers,
> Or the grape ripen under my bowers?
> When will the harvest or the hunter's moon
> Turn my midnight into mid-noon?
> I am all sere and yellow,
> And to my core mellow.
> The mast is dropping within my woods,
> The winter is lurking within my moods,
> And the rustling of the withered leaf
> Is the constant music of my grief.

To an unskillful rhymer the Muse thus spoke in prose: —

The moon no longer reflects the day, but rises to her absolute rule, and the husbandman and hunter acknowledge her for their mistress. Asters and goldenrods reign along the way, and the life-everlasting withers not. The fields are reaped and shorn of their pride, but an inward verdure still crowns them. The thistle scatters its down on the pool, and yellow leaves clothe the vine, and naught disturbs the serious life of men. But behind the sheaves, and under the sod, there lurks a ripe fruit, which the reapers have not gathered, the true harvest of the year, which it bears forever, annually watering and maturing it, and man never severs the stalk which bears this palatable fruit.

Men nowhere, east or west, live yet a *natural* life, round which the vine clings, and which the elm willingly shadows. Man would desecrate it by his touch, and so the beauty of the world remains veiled to him. He needs not only to be spiritualized, but *naturalized*, on the soil of earth. Who shall conceive what kind of roof the heavens might extend over him, what seasons minister to him, and what employment dignify his life! Only the convalescent raise the veil of nature. An immortality in his life would confer immortality on his abode. The winds should be his breath, the seasons his moods, and he should impart of his serenity to Nature herself. But such as we know him he is ephemeral like the scenery which surrounds him, and does not aspire to an enduring existence. When we come down into the distant village, visible from the mountain-top, the nobler inhabitants with whom we peopled it have departed, and left only vermin in its desolate streets. It is the imagination of poets which puts those brave speeches into the mouths of their heroes. They may feign that Cato's last words were

> "The earth, the air and seas I know, and all
> The joys and horrors of their peace and wars;
> And now will view the Gods' state and the stars,"

but such are not the thoughts nor the destiny of common men. What is this heaven which they expect, if it is no better than they expect? Are they prepared for a better than they can now imagine? Where is the heaven of him who dies on a stage, in a theatre? Here or nowhere is our heaven.

> "Although we see celestial bodies move
> Above the earth, the earth we till and love."

We can conceive of nothing more fair than something which we have experienced. "The remembrance of youth is a sigh." We linger in manhood to tell the dreams of our childhood, and they are half forgotten ere we have learned the language. We have need to be earth-born as well as heaven-born, γηγενεῖς, as was said of the Titans of old, or in a better sense than they. There have been heroes for whom this world seemed expressly prepared, as if creation had at last succeeded; whose daily life was the stuff of which our dreams are made, and whose presence enhanced the beauty and ampleness of Nature herself. Where they walked, —

> "Largior hic campos aether et lumine vestit
> Purpureo: Solemque suum, sua sidera norunt."

"Here a more copious air invests the fields, and clothes with purple light; and they know their own sun and their own stars." We love to hear some men speak, though we hear not what they say; the very air they breathe is rich and perfumed, and the sound of their voices falls on the ear like the rustling of leaves or the crackling of the fire. They stand many deep. They have the heavens for their abettors, as those who have never stood from under them, and they look at the stars with an answering ray. Their eyes are like glow-worms, and their motions graceful and flowing, as if a place were already found for them, like rivers flowing through valleys. The distinctions of morality, of right and wrong, sense and nonsense, are petty, and have lost their significance, beside these pure primeval natures. When I consider the clouds stretched in stupendous masses across the sky, frowning with darkness or glowing with downy light, or gilded with the rays of the setting sun, like the battlements of a city in the heavens, their grandeur appears thrown away on the meanness of my employment; the drapery is altogether too rich for such poor acting. I am hardly worthy to be a suburban dweller outside those walls.

> "Unless above himself he can
> Erect himself, how poor a thing is man!"

With our music we would fain challenge transiently another and finer sort of intercourse than our daily toil permits. The strains come back to us amended in the echo, as when a friend reads our verse. Why have they so painted the fruits, and freighted them with such fragrance as to satisfy a more than animal appetite?

> "I asked the schoolman, his advice was free,
> But scored me out too intricate a way."

These things imply, perchance, that we live on the verge of another and purer realm, from which these odors and sounds are wafted over to us. The borders of our plot are set with flowers, whose seeds were blown from more Elysian fields adjacent. They are the potherbs of the gods. Some fairer fruits and sweeter fragrances wafted over to us betray another realm's vicinity. There, too, does Echo dwell, and there is the abutment of the rainbow's arch.

> A finer race and finer fed
> Feast and revel o'er our head,

And we titmen are only able
To catch the fragments from their table.
Theirs is the fragrance of the fruits,
While we consume the pulp and roots.
What are the moments that we stand
Astonished on the Olympian land!

We need pray for no higher heaven than the pure
senses can furnish, a *purely* sensuous life. Our present
senses are but the rudiments of what they are destined
to become. We are comparatively deaf and dumb and
blind, and without smell or taste or feeling. Every
generation makes the discovery that its divine vigor has
been dissipated, and each sense and faculty misapplied
and debauched. The ears were made, not for such
trivial uses as men are wont to suppose, but to hear
celestial sounds. The eyes were not made for such
groveling uses as they are now put to and worn out by,
but to behold beauty now invisible. May we not *see*
God? Are we to be put off and amused in this life, as
it were with a mere allegory? Is not Nature, rightly
read, that of which she is commonly taken to be the
symbol merely? When the common man looks into
the sky, which he has not so much profaned, he thinks
it less gross than the earth, and with reverence speaks
of " the Heavens," but the seer will in the same sense
speak of " the Earths," and his Father who is in them.
" Did not he that made that which is *within* make that
which is *without* also? " What is it, then, to educate
but to develop these divine germs called the senses?
for individuals and states to deal magnanimously with
the rising generation, leading it not into temptation,

— not teach the eye to squint, nor attune the ear to profanity. But where is the instructed teacher? Where are the *normal* schools?

A Hindoo sage said, "As a dancer, having exhibited herself to the spectator, desists from the dance, so does Nature desist, having manifested herself to soul. Nothing, in my opinion, is more gentle than Nature ; once aware of having been seen, she does not again expose herself to the gaze of soul."

It is easier to discover another such a new world as Columbus did, than to go within one fold of this which we appear to know so well; the land is lost sight of, the compass varies, and mankind mutiny; and still history accumulates like rubbish before the portals of nature. But there is only necessary a moment's sanity and sound senses, to teach us that there is a nature behind the ordinary, in which we have only some vague preëmption right and western reserve as yet. We live on the outskirts of that region. Carved wood, and floating boughs, and sunset skies are all that we know of it. We are not to be imposed on by the longest spell of weather. Let us not, my friends, be wheedled and cheated into good behavior to earn the salt of our eternal porridge, whoever they are that attempt it. Let us wait a little, and not purchase any clearing here, trusting that richer bottoms will soon be put up. It is but thin soil where we stand; I have felt my roots in a richer ere this. I have seen a bunch of violets in a glass vase, tied loosely with a straw, which reminded me of myself.

I am a parcel of vain strivings tied
     By a chance bond together,
   Dangling this way and that, their links
     Were made so loose and wide,
         Methinks,
      For milder weather.

A bunch of violets without their roots,
     And sorrel intermixed,
   Encircled by a wisp of straw
     Once coiled about their shoots,
         The law
      By which I'm fixed.

A nosegay which Time clutched from out
     Those fair Elysian fields,
   With weeds and broken stems, in haste,
     Doth make the rabble rout
         That waste
      The day he yields.

And here I bloom for a short hour unseen,
     Drinking my juices up,
   With no root in the land
     To keep my branches green,
         But stand
      In a bare cup.

Some tender buds were left upon my stem
     In mimicry of life,
   But ah! the children will not know,
     Till time has withered them,
         The woe
      With which they 're rife.

But now I see I was not plucked for naught,
     And after in life's vase
   Of glass set while I might survive,
     But by a kind hand brought
         Alive
      To a strange place.

> That stock thus thinned will soon redeem its hours,
>   And by another year,
>   Such as God knows, with freer air,
>   More fruits and fairer flowers
>   Will bear,
>   While I droop here.

This world has many rings, like Saturn, and we live now on the outmost of them all. None can say deliberately that he inhabits the same sphere, or is contemporary, with the flower which his hands have plucked, and though his feet may seem to crush it, inconceivable spaces and ages separate them, and perchance there is no danger that he will hurt it. What do the botanists know? Our lives should go between the lichen and the bark. The eye may see for the hand, but not for the mind. We are still being born, and have as yet but a dim vision of sea and land, sun, moon, and stars, and shall not see clearly till after nine days at least. That is a pathetic inquiry among travelers and geographers after the site of ancient Troy. It is not near where they think it is. When a thing is decayed and gone, how indistinct must be the place it occupied!

The anecdotes of modern astronomy affect me in the same way as do those faint revelations of the Real which are vouchsafed to men from time to time, or rather from eternity to eternity. When I remember the history of that faint light in our firmament which we call Venus, which ancient men regarded, and which most modern men still regard, as a bright spark attached to a hollow sphere revolving about our earth, but which we have discovered to be *another world*, in itself, — how Coper-

nicus, reasoning long and patiently about the matter,
predicted confidently concerning it, before yet the telescope had been invented, that if ever men came to see
it more clearly than they did then, they would discover
that it had phases like our moon, and that within a
century after his death the telescope was invented, and
that prediction verified, by Galileo, — I am not without
hope that we may, even here and now, obtain some accurate information concerning that OTHER WORLD which
the instinct of mankind has so long predicted. Indeed,
all that we call science, as well as all that we call poetry,
is a particle of such information, accurate as far as it
goes, though it be but to the confines of the truth. If we
can reason so accurately, and with such wonderful con-
firmation of our reasoning, respecting so-called material
objects and events infinitely removed beyond the range
of our natural vision, so that the mind hesitates to
trust its calculations even when they are confirmed by
observation, why may not our speculations penetrate
as far into the immaterial starry system, of which the
former is but the outward and visible type? Surely,
we are provided with senses as well fitted to penetrate
the spaces of the real, the substantial, the eternal, as
these outward are to penetrate the material universe.
Veias, Menu, Zoroaster, Socrates, Christ, Shakespeare,
Swedenborg, — these are some of our astronomers.

There are perturbations in our orbits produced by
the influences of outlying spheres, and no astronomer
has ever yet calculated the elements of that undis-
covered world which produces them. I perceive in the
common train of my thoughts a natural and uninter-

rupted sequence, each implying the next, or, if interruption occurs, it is occasioned by a new object being presented to my *senses*. But a steep, and sudden, and by these means unaccountable transition is that from a comparatively narrow and partial, what is called common-sense view of things, to an infinitely expanded and liberating one, from seeing things as men describe them, to seeing them as men cannot describe them. This implies a sense which is not common, but rare in the wisest man's experience ; which is sensible or sentient of more than common.

In what inclosures does the astronomer loiter! His skies are shoal, and imagination, like a thirsty traveler, pants to be through their desert. The roving mind impatiently bursts the fetters of astronomical orbits, like cobwebs in a corner of its universe, and launches itself to where distance fails to follow, and law, such as science has discovered, grows weak and weary. The mind knows a distance and a space of which all those sums combined do not make a unit of measure, — the interval between that which *appears* and that which *is*. I know that there are many stars, I know that they are far enough off, bright enough, steady enough in their orbits, — but what are they all worth ? They are more waste land in the West, — star territory, — to be made slave States, perchance, if we colonize them. I have interest but for six feet of star, and that interest is transient. Then farewell to all ye bodies, such as I have known ye.

Every man, if he is wise, will stand on such bottom

as will sustain him, and if one gravitates downward more strongly than another, he will not venture on those meads where the latter walks securely, but rather leave the cranberries which grow there unraked by himself. Perchance, some spring, a higher freshet will float them within his reach, though they may be watery and frost-bitten by that time. Such shriveled berries I have seen in many a poor man's garret, ay, in many a church-bin and state-coffer, and with a little water and heat they swell again to their original size and fairness, and added sugar enough, stead mankind for sauce to this world's dish.

What is called common sense is excellent in its department, and as invaluable as the virtue of conformity in the army and navy, — for there must be subordination, — but uncommon sense, that sense which is common only to the wisest, is as much more excellent as it is more rare. Some aspire to excellence in the subordinate department, and may God speed them. What Fuller says of masters of colleges is universally applicable, that "a little alloy of dullness in a master of a college makes him fitter to manage secular affairs."

> "He that wants faith, and apprehends a grief
>   Because he wants it, hath a true belief;
>   And he that grieves because his grief 's so small,
>   Has a true grief, and the best Faith of all."

Or be encouraged by this other poet's strain:—

> "By them went Fido, marshal of the field:
>   Weak was his mother when she gave him day;
>   And he at first a sick and weakly child,
>   As e'er with tears welcomed the sunny ray;

Yet when more years afford more growth and might,
A champion stout he was, and puissant knight,
As ever came in field, or shone in armor bright.

"Mountains he flings in seas with mighty hand;
Stops and turns back the sun's impetuous course;
Nature breaks Nature's laws at his command;
No force of Hell or Heaven withstands his force;
Events to come yet many ages hence,
He present makes, by wondrous prescience;
Proving the senses blind by being blind to sense."

"Yesterday, at dawn," says Hafiz, "God delivered me from all worldly affliction; and amidst the gloom of night presented me with the water of immortality."

In the life of Sadi by Dowlat Shah occurs this sentence: "The eagle of the immaterial soul of Shaikh Sadi shook from his plumage the dust of his body."

Thus thoughtfully we were rowing homeward to find some autumnal work to do, and help on the revolution of the seasons. Perhaps Nature would condescend to make use of us even without our knowledge, as when we help to scatter her seeds in our walks, and carry burs and cockles on our clothes from field to field.

All things are current found
On earthly ground,
Spirits and elements
Have their descents.

Night and day, year on year,
High and low, far and near,
These are our own aspects,
These are our own regrets.

Ye gods of the shore,
Who abide evermore,
I see your far headland,
Stretching on either hand;

I hear the sweet evening sounds
From your undecaying grounds;
Cheat me no more with time,
Take me to your clime.

As it grew later in the afternoon, and we rowed leisurely up the gentle stream, shut in between fragrant
and blooming banks, where we had first pitched our
tent, and drew nearer to the fields where our lives
had passed, we seemed to detect the hues of our native sky in the southwest horizon. The sun was just
setting behind the edge of a wooded hill, so rich a sunset as would never have ended but for some reason
unknown to men, and to be marked with brighter colors than ordinary in the scroll of time. Though the
shadows of the hills were beginning to steal over the
stream, the whole river valley undulated with mild
light, purer and more memorable than the noon. For
so day bids farewell even to solitary vales uninhabited by man. Two herons (*Ardea herodias*), with their
long and slender limbs relieved against the sky, were
seen traveling high over our heads, — their lofty and
silent flight, as they were wending their way at evening, surely not to alight in any marsh on the earth's
surface, but, perchance, on the other side of our atmosphere, a symbol for the ages to study, whether
impressed upon the sky or sculptured amid the hieroglyphics of Egypt. Bound to some northern meadow,

they held on their stately, stationary flight, like the storks in the picture, and disappeared at length behind the clouds. Dense flocks of blackbirds were winging their way along the river's course, as if on a short evening pilgrimage to some shrine of theirs, or to celebrate so fair a sunset.

> "Therefore, as doth the pilgrim, whom the night
> Hastes darkly to imprison on his way,
> Think on thy home, my soul, and think aright
> Of what's yet left thee of life's wasting day:
> Thy sun posts westward, passed is thy morn,
> And twice it is not given thee to be born."

The sun-setting presumed all men at leisure, and in a contemplative mood; but the farmer's boy only whistled the more thoughtfully as he drove his cows home from pasture, and the teamster refrained from cracking his whip, and guided his team with a subdued voice. The last vestiges of daylight at length disappeared, and as we rowed silently along with our backs toward home through the darkness, only a few stars being visible, we had little to say, but sat absorbed in thought, or in silence listened to the monotonous sound of our oars, a sort of rudimental music, suitable for the ear of Night and the acoustics of her dimly lighted halls;

> "Pulsae referunt ad sidera valles,"

and the valleys echoed the sound to the stars.

As we looked up in silence to those distant lights, we were reminded that it was a rare imagination which first taught that the stars are worlds, and had conferred a great benefit on mankind. It is recorded in the

Chronicle of Bernaldez that in Columbus's first voyage the natives " pointed towards the heavens, making signs that they believed that there was all power and holiness." We have reason to be grateful for celestial phenomena, for they chiefly answer to the ideal in man. The stars are distant and unobtrusive, but bright and enduring as our fairest and most memorable experiences. " Let the immortal depth of your soul lead you, but earnestly extend your eyes upwards."

As the truest society approaches always nearer to solitude, so the most excellent speech finally falls into Silence. Silence is audible to all men, at all times, and in all places. She is when we hear inwardly, sound when we hear outwardly. Creation has not displaced her, but is her visible framework and foil. All sounds are her servants, and purveyors, proclaiming not only that their mistress is, but is a rare mistress, and earnestly to be sought after. They are so far akin to Silence that they are but bubbles on her surface, which straightway burst, an evidence of the strength and prolificness of the under-current; a faint utterance of Silence, and then only agreeable to our auditory nerves when they contrast themselves with and relieve the former. In proportion as they do this, and are heighteners and intensifiers of the Silence, they are harmony and purest melody.

Silence is the universal refuge, the sequel to all dull discourses and all foolish acts, a balm to our every chagrin, as welcome after satiety as after disappointment; that background which the painter may not daub, be he master or bungler, and which, however awkward a figure we may have made in the foreground, remains ever our inviolable asylum, where no indignity can assail, no personality disturb us.

The orator puts off his individuality, and is then most eloquent when most silent. He listens while he speaks, and is a hearer along with his audience. Who has not hearkened to her infinite din? She is Truth's speaking-trumpet, the sole oracle, the true Delphi and Dodona, which kings and courtiers would do well to consult, nor will they be balked by an ambiguous answer. For through her all revelations have been made, and just in proportion as men have consulted her oracle within, they have obtained a clear insight, and their age has been marked as an enlightened one. But as often as they have gone gadding abroad to a strange Delphi and her mad priestess, their age has been dark and leaden. Such were garrulous and noisy eras, which no longer yield any sound, but the Grecian or silent and melodious era is ever sounding and resounding in the ears of men.

A good book is the plectrum with which our else silent lyres are struck. We not unfrequently refer the interest which belongs to our own unwritten sequel to the written and comparatively lifeless body of the work. Of all books this sequel is the most indispensable part. It should be the author's aim to say once and emphatically, "He said," ἔφη. This is the most the bookmaker can attain to. If he make his volume a mole whereon the waves of Silence may break, it is well.

It were vain for me to endeavor to interpret the Silence. She cannot be done into English. For six thousand years men have translated her with what fidelity belonged to each, and still she is little better than a sealed book. A man may run on confidently for a time, thinking he has her under his thumb, and shall one day exhaust her, but he too must at last be silent, and men remark only how brave a beginning he made; for when he at length dives into her, so vast is the disproportion of the told to the untold that the former will seem but the bubble on the surface where he disappeared. Nevertheless, we will go on, like those Chinese cliff swallows, feathering our nests with the froth which may one day be bread of life to such as dwell by the seashore.

We had made about fifty miles this day with sail and oar, and now, far in the evening, our boat was grating against the bulrushes of its native port, and its keel recognized the Concord mud, where some semblance of its outline was still preserved in the flattened flags which had scarce yet erected themselves since our departure; and we leaped gladly on shore, drawing it up and fastening it to the wild apple tree, whose stem still bore the mark which its chain had worn in the chafing of the spring freshets.

TABLE OF POETICAL QUOTATIONS

TABLE OF POETICAL QUOTATIONS

USED IN

"A WEEK ON THE CONCORD AND MERRIMACK RIVERS"

93. *Jam laeto turgent in palmite gemmae.* — VIRGIL.
93. *Strata jacent passim sua quaeque sub arbore poma.* — VIRGIL.
95. As from the clouds appears the full moon. — HOMER.
95. While it was dawn, and sacred day was advancing. — HOMER.
95. They, thinking great things, upon the neutral ground of war. — HOMER.
96. Went down the Idæan mountains to far Olympus. — HOMER.
96. For there are very many. — HOMER.
96. Then rose up to them sweet-worded Nestor, the shrill orator of the Pylians. — HOMER.
97. Homer is gone; and where is Jove? and where.
99. You grov'ling worldlings, you whose wisdom trades.
100. Merchants, arise. — FRANCIS QUARLES.
100. To Athens gowned he goes, and from that school. — FRANCIS QUARLES.
101. What I have learned is mine; I've had my thought.
102. — ask for that which is our whole life's light.
102. Let us set so just. — WILLIAM HABINGTON.
103. Olympian bards who sung. — EMERSON.
104. — lips of cunning fell. — EMERSON.
104. That 't is not in the power of kings to raise. — SAMUEL DANIEL.
104. And that the utmost powers of English rhyme. — SAMUEL DANIEL.
105. And who, in time, knows whither we may vent. — SAMUEL DANIEL.
106. How many thousands never heard the name. — SAMUEL DANIEL.
113. — *campoque recepta.* — OVID.
115. Make bandog thy scout watch to bark at a thief.
121. I thynke for to touche also. — JOHN GOWER.
121. The hye sheryfe of Notynghame. — ROBIN HOOD BALLADS.
121. His shoote it was but loosely shott. — ROBIN HOOD BALLADS.

121. Gazed on the Heavens for what he missed on Earth. — WILLIAM BROWNE.
121. All courageous knichtis.
123. He and his valiant soldiers did range the woods full wide. — OLD BALLAD OF LOVEWELL'S FIGHT.
124. Of all our valiant English, there were but thirty-four. — OLD BALLAD OF LOVEWELL'S FIGHT.
124. And braving many dangers and hardships in the way. — OLD BALLAD OF LOVEWELL'S FIGHT.
125. A man he was of comely form.
126. For as we are informed, so thick and fast they fell. — OLD BALLAD OF LOVEWELL'S FIGHT.
129. Yet I doubt not through the ages one increasing purpose runs. — TENNYSON.
132. Men find that action is another thing — SAMUEL DANIEL.
134. And round about good morrows fly. — CHARLES COTTON.
134. The early pilgrim blythe he hailed. — ROBIN HOOD BALLADS.
136. Now turn again, turn again, said the pindér. — OLD BALLAD.
137. Virtues as rivers pass.
163. Thro' the shadow of the globe we sweep into the younger day. — TENNYSON.
164. Fragments of the lofty strain. — GRAY.
174. They carried these foresters into fair Nottingham. — ROBIN HOOD BALLADS.
175. Gentle river, gentle river. — SPANISH BALLAD IN PERCY: "Rio verde, rio verde."
176. Then did the crimson streams that flowed.
181. When the drum beat at dead of night. — CAMPBELL.
186. Before each van. — MILTON.
188. On either side the river lie. — TENNYSON.
198. Heaven itself shall slide.
199. Flatter the mountain-tops with sovereign eye. — SHAKESPEARE.
199. Anon permit the basest clouds to ride.

199. How may a worm that crawls along the dust. — Giles
Fletcher.
202. And now the taller sons, whom Titan warms. — Giles
Fletcher.
214. In a pleasant glade. — Spenser.
219. Amongst the pumy stones, which seemed to plain. —
Spenser.
219. His reverend locks. — Bishop Percy.
230. Of Syrian peace, immortal leisure. — Emerson.
236. Too quick resolves do resolution wrong.
238. Nor has he ceased his charming song, for still that lyre. —
Simonides.
240. The young and tender stalk.
240–244. Translations from Anacreon.
249. Man is man's foe and destiny. — Charles Cotton.
258. He knew of our haste. — Pindar.
259. — springing up from the bottom. — Pindar.
259. The island sprang from the watery. — Pindar.
264. Rome living was the world's sole ornament. — Spenser.
266. — bees that fly.
283. He that hath love and judgment too.
283. Why love among the virtues is not known. — Dr. Donne
288. And love as well the shepherd can.
291. When manhood shall be matched so.
293. There be mo sterres in the skie than a pair. — Chaucer.
314. Silver sands and pebbles sing.
315. Who dreamt devoutlier than most use to pray. — Dr.
Donne.
316. And, more to lulle him in his slumber soft. — Spenser.
317. He trode the unplanted forest floor, whereon. — Emerson.
327–332. Lines from Persius.
335. Sweet day, so cool, so calm, so bright. — George Herbert.
337. To journey for his marriage. — Chaucer.
338. — The swaying soft. — W. E. Channing.
340. Not only o'er the dial's face. — J. Montgomery.

347. Old woman that lives under the hill. — NURSERY BALLAD.

350. The laws of Nature break the rules of Art. — FRANCIS QUARLES.

356. The Boteman strayt. — SPENSER.

356. Summer's robe grows. — DR. DONNE.

357. And now the cold autumnal dews are seen.

359. From steep pine-bearing mountains to the plain. — MARLOWE.

359. Wise Nature's darlings, they live in the world. — MARLOWE.

359. — at all, Came lovers home from this great festival. — MARLOWE.

367–371. Lines from Ossian.

377. And what's a life? The flourishing array. — FRANCIS QUARLES.

378. I see the goldenrod shine bright. — W. E. CHANNING.

397. For first the thing is thought within the hart. — CHAUCER.

399. If that God that heaven and yearth made. — CHAUCER.

403. There is a place beyond that flaming hill. — SIR WILLIAM DAVENANT.

405. The earth, the air, and seas I know, and all.

406. Although we see celestial bodies move.

406. *Largior hic campos aether et lumine vestit.* — VIRGIL.

407. Unless above himself he can. — SAMUEL DANIEL.

407. I asked the schoolman, his advice was free. — FRANCIS QUARLES.

414. He that wants faith, and apprehends a grief. — FRANCIS QUARLES.

414. By them went Fido, marshal of the field. — PHINEAS FLETCHER.

417. Therefore, as doth the pilgrim, whom the night. — GILES FLETCHER.

417. *Pulsae referunt ad sidera valles.* — VIRGIL.

INDEX

SENTRY EDITIONS

1. A Week on the Concord and Merrimack Rivers
   by Henry David Thoreau
2. A Diary from Dixie *by Mary Boykin Chesnut,*
   edited by Ben Ames Williams
3. The Education of Henry Adams: An Autobiography
4. J.B. *by Archibald MacLeish*
5. John C. Calhoun *by Margaret L. Coit*
6. The Maritime History of Massachusetts: 1783–1860
   by Samuel Eliot Morison
7. My Antonia *by Willa Cather*
8. Patterns of Culture *by Ruth Benedict*
9. Sam Clemens of Hannibal *by Dixon Wecter*
10. The Great Crash, 1929 *by John Kenneth Galbraith*
11. The Year of Decision: 1846 *by Bernard DeVoto*
12. Young Man with a Horn *by Dorothy Baker*
13. Mein Kampf *by Adolf Hitler*
14. The Vital Center *by Arthur M. Schlesinger, Jr.*
15. The Course of Empire *by Bernard DeVoto*
16. O Pioneers! *by Willa Cather*
17. The Armada *by Garrett Mattingly*
18. American Capitalism *by John Kenneth Galbraith*
19. The Emancipation of Massachusetts *by Brooks Adams*
20. Beyond the Hundredth Meridian *by Wallace Stegner*
21. Paul Revere and the World He Lived In *by Esther Forbes*
22. Chosen Country *by John Dos Passos*
23. The Tragic Era *by Claude G. Bowers*
24. Parkinson's Law *by C. Northcote Parkinson*
25. Across the Wide Missouri *by Bernard DeVoto*
26. Manhattan Transfer *by John Dos Passos*
27. A Cartoon History of Architecture *by Osbert Lancaster*
28. The Song of the Lark *by Willa Cather*
29. A Mirror for Witches *by Esther Forbes*
30. The Collected Poems of Archibald MacLeish
31. The Journals of Lewis and Clark, *edited by Bernard DeVoto*
32. Builders of the Bay Colony *by Samuel Eliot Morison*
33. Mont-Saint-Michel and Chartres *by Henry Adams*
34. Laughing Boy *by Oliver La Farge*
35. Wild America *by Roger Tory Peterson and James Fisher*
36. Paths to the Present *by Arthur M. Schlesinger*
37. U.S.A. *by John Dos Passos*
38. Economic Development *by John Kenneth Galbraith*
39. The Crisis of the Old Order *by Arthur M. Schlesinger, Jr.*

SE 9

(continued on next page)